T5-CAO-019

The Force of the FEMININE

Women, Men and the Church

MARGARET ANN FRANKLIN

ALLEN & UNWIN
Sydney London Boston

First published in 1986
Allen & Unwin Australia Pty Ltd
8 Napier Street, North Sydney, NSW 2060, Australia

Allen & Unwin New Zealand Limited
60 Cambridge Terrace, Wellington, New Zealand

George Allen & Unwin (Publishers) Ltd
Park Lane, Hemel Hempstead, Herts HP2 4TE, England

Allen & Unwin Inc.
8 Winchester Place, Winchester, Mass 01890, USA

National Library of Australia
Cataloguing-in-publication entry:

The Force of the feminine.

Includes index.
ISBN 0 86861 930 2.
ISBN 0 86861 914 0 (pbk.).

1. Women in Christianity.   2.   Women's rights.
I. Franklin, Margaret Ann.
261.8'344

Library of Congress Catalog Card Number:
85-073513

Typeset in 9/11 Century Schoolbook by
Singapore National Printers (Pte) Ltd
Printed in Hong Kong

Contents

		Page
	INTRODUCTION	vii
	CONTRIBUTORS	xx
1	WOMAN AND THE CHURCH: Her story *Eileen Jones*	1
2	THE ROLE OF THE CHURCH IN THE EDUCATION OF GIRLS AND WOMEN *Eileen M. Byrne*	10
3	SEXISM AND FUNDAMENTALISM *Barbara Thiering*	28
4	THE ORDINATION OF WOMEN: On whose side is the Bible? *Kevin Giles*	38
5	THE ORDINATION OF WOMEN: The position of the Catholic Church *Leo Hay*	49
6	THE ORDINATION OF WOMEN: A psychological interpretation of the objections *Maggie Kirkman and Norma Grieve*	55

Page

7   INSTITUTIONAL SEXISM AND THE ANGLICAN
    CHURCH   68
    Margaret Ann Franklin

8   MINISTERS' WIVES: Continuity and change
    in relation to their husbands' work   81
    Kenneth Dempsey

9   A CLERGY WIFE'S STORY   100
    Marlene Cohen

10 GOD AND PRONOUNS   113
    Richard Franklin

11 AFFIRMATIVE ACTION IN THE UNITING
    CHURCH 1977–83   120
    Marie Tulip

12 A QUIXOTIC APPROACH: The women's
    movement and the Church in Australia   141
    Veronica Brady

13 THE FEMINISATION OF STRUCTURES IN
    RELIGIOUS ORDERS   149
    Anne McLay

14 IMPLICATIONS OF THE FEMININE
    AND MASCULINE IN PASTORAL MINISTRY   164
    Edward Morgan

15 CHRISTIAN CONVERSION AND THE
    FEMININE   175
    Tony Kelly

    NOTES   187
    INDEX   204

Introduction

There is a stirring today, felt in nearly every denomination in Christendom, which concerns the place of the 'feminine' in Christianity. This involves much more than improving the low status of women in the Church and changing patriarchal structures. It involves accepting the 'feminine' in God and loving our contrasexual selves and calls for a theology which revives the ancient tradition of associating the Holy Spirit with God's femininity.[1] Issues involving the 'feminine' mix together in complex ways, and arouse passionate debate. This book is a contribution to many, though not all of them. To untangle some of the threads we begin by examining the present position of women.

The Force of the Feminine has a message for all Christians, but since the contributors, with one exception, are all Australians, and since they come from the Uniting, Anglican and Catholic churches, we shall start by sketching the role of the Women's Movement and the Australian Council of Churches in improving the status of women in these churches, and then discuss the other issues, concentrating on the greatest current focus of discussion, namely whether women should be ordained as priests or ministers.

In Australia, Christian women seem to have been among the first to have been affected by the Women's Movement, which spread through the Western world in the late sixties and early seventies.[2] This is probably due to the fact that the Church provided opportunities for female bonding in a society where women, for historical and geographical reasons, tended to be isolated from each other.[3] In 1968 a group of Christian feminists established an interdenominational group called Christian Women Concerned. It studied the role of

vii

women in the Church and its male-oriented vocabulary; it also discussed issues such as poverty, racism and peace.[4] In 1973 it published its small but influential journal *Magdalene* and began to establish a national network of women devoted to changing the Church. For many women, attending their first meeting was an experience of growth for it provided them with an atmosphere in which they could voice and share their concern about the rigid patriarchal attitudes they found entrenched in the Church. One woman wrote about how her life was changed after attending a meeting of local women in May 1969:

> I listened to a young Roman Catholic woman, an Anglican and a Quaker, speaking of those things which most disturbed, affected, interested and challenged us in our personal, national and emotional lives. And nothing has ever been quite the same since . . . Wounded and scared by what it cost to be a woman in Sydney in 1969 I sat in that audience of 70 and listened, rejoiced and hoped. Maybe I wasn't a fool, a misfit, a nothing! . . . Here, my own thinking, so often ridiculed, was being expressed by these three, and being appreciated and applauded by the seventy. A spark lit the pile of gathered tinder in my soul that day—and 'Magdalene' kindled it into flame and has kept it burning ever since.[5]

Christian Women Concerned seems to have inspired the Australian Council of Churches branch in New South Wales to establish in 1973 the Commission on the Status of Women in the Church under the presidency of Marie Tulip.[6] Two hundred submissions were received by the commission. These represented eleven denominations: Anglican, Baptist, Roman Catholic, Christian Scientist, Church of Christ, Congregational, Eastern Orthodox, Latter Day Saints, Methodist, Presbyterian, Salvation Army and the Society of Friends (Quakers). After examining the submissions the commission concluded that not only was there an enormous imbalance in the number of men and women serving on decision-making bodies, but, when funds were allocated, constitutions changed or theology discussed, women were largely absent.[7] Alarmed by similar results from surveys in other Christian countries, the World Council of Churches began a project called 'Study on the Community of Men and Women in the Church'. It invited groups around the world to discuss issues such as identity, church teaching and theological education, worship and ministry. Groups were asked to report in August 1980. Australian

Christians were quick to respond to this invitation and in New South Wales, for example, an interdenominational group of men and women met regularly.[8]

In September 1978 the Australian Council of Churches Status of Women Commission set up four task forces. These studied sexist language and the production of non-sexist literature, theological colleges, sexuality and feminist theology. Two years later the commission also sponsored a 'Living Female Conference'. While some progress was made the results of these efforts were not particularly encouraging and a member of the Status of Women Commission of the Australian Council of Churches reported:

> It is not an exaggeration here in Australia to speak of the Church's rigidities in the area of sexism. Men hold effective power in almost every area of the church's life—administration, theological education, local churches, and also in writing theology, hymn book compilation, evangelism campaigns and so on. God is indubitably male, as are most of 'his' priests and ministers, and the dominant culture of the church is a patriarchial culture.[9]

As Australia is still very much a patriarchial society a new national Commission on the Status of Women was recently established by the Australian Council of Churches. Task forces consisting of women from Sydney, Melbourne and Canberra have been set to examine four areas. These are:
1 domestic violence—its relationship to war, patriarchy and theological issues;
2 the economy—taxation and women, and the increasing numbers of women in poverty;
3 bioethics—the moral, theological, physical and social aspects as they impinge on the family, lifestyle and sexuality;
4 language—attitudes to inclusive language in churches and production of a liturgical resource book.[10]

In 1978 Australian women learned that a significant number of women had been ordained in New Zealand, Sweden, the United States and Canada. This inspired a group of theologically trained women to meet in Adelaide in April of that year to try to find 'forms of ministry that are valid at this time'.[11] Other groups began, and in October 1983 some Sydney women started the Movement for the Ordination of Women. This movement, which is ecumenical and which has both male and female members, became a national movement in 1985 and thanks to its energetic spokesperson, Patricia Brennan, has been given a considerable amount of media coverage.

Of the three churches to which our contributors belong, the Uniting Church is in all respects the most advanced. It finds no theological objections to female ordination, and has many women ministers. Moreover, in 1977, well before the Commonwealth government introduced the first voluntary affirmative action program in 1984, the Uniting Church was one of the first institutions in Australia to introduce affirmative action for women. Its program required congregations to review the membership of all their decision-making bodies and to make sure, where possible, of a membership of about a third women. The Uniting Church accepted that if women were to be fully integrated into the total ministry of the Church, it was not enough just to remove legal barriers and discriminatory procedures; rather, positive steps had to be taken to overcome the habits and stereotypes of centuries.

If we turn to Anglicanism, we find that within the worldwide Anglican community there are already women priests. In 1968 there was a consensus of opinion at the Lambeth Conference that there are no fundamental theological objections to the ordination of women. In 1971 the Bishop of Hong Kong ordained two women as priests. Later, churches in the USA, Canada, New Zealand and Kenya also did so. But neither the Church of England nor the rest of the churches in Asia, Australia, the Pacific or South America have done so. The reasons offered are various, and not always easily reconciled. Those who heavily emphasise the Protestant dimension of the Anglican tradition appeal to New Testament texts and to the notion of the God-given authority of the male over the female. Those who are more concerned with the Catholic emphasis in the tradition would agree more with the Catholic Church's viewpoint which we present below.

In Australia as long ago as 1977 the Commission of Doctrine of the (Australian) General Synod concluded that there were no theological objections which constituted a barrier to the ordination of women to the priesthood. Accordingly a proposal to permit such ordination was introduced. Complicated manoeuvrings prevented it being implemented until in 1985 a decision of the Church's supreme body of constitutional and legal matters, the Appellate Tribunal, opened the way. It declared that there was no constitutional or theological principle preventing women being ordained as deacons, priests or bishops. The Anglican General Synod which was held in August 1985 refused to pass a bill which would have acknowledged this situation and given each diocese the choice to ordain women if they so wished.[12] However the decision of the Appellate Tribunal remains in effect, and it seems open to any diocese to act on it without requiring the approval of General Synod. At the same General Synod a bill was passed to permit the ordination of women as deacons (rather than deaconesses). Since the diaconate has been the traditional stepping stone to the priesthood the crucial time for the Anglican Church may come in perhaps a few years when bishops must decide whether to ordain women deacons to the priesthood.

Finally, the Roman Catholic Church, or at least the present Pope, is rigidly opposed to the ordination of women. In 1976 (which was, incidentally, a year after the Decade of Women began) the Vatican Sacred Congregation for the Doctrine of the Faith published a 'Declaration on the question of the Admission of Women to the Ministerial Priesthood'. In the introduction it was stated that 'the Church in fidelity to the example of the Lord, does not consider herself authorised to admit women to priestly ordination'. In the rest of the Declaration 'the Church's constant tradition' is defended by pointing out that Christ, despite his nonconformist attitude to women, never invited any women 'to become part of the Twelve', and that the apostles faithfully followed his practice. It is claimed that there is no evidence to show that Jesus' and the apostles' attitude towards women was determined by social and cultural conditions. Further, it would be impossible for women to be priests because the priest represents Christ at the Mass and only males bear a natural resemblance to him; Christ is the Church's bridegroom and only a male can represent Christ, the Bridegroom.

However, the matter is not quite so clear. There is considerable discussion among theologians (as represented by Leo Hay's chapter in this book), and in particular many Catholic sisters believe that ultimately the ordination of women must be permitted. Apart from this central, contentious issue, the place of women in the life of the Australian Church was an item on the agenda of the meeting of Catholic bishops and major superiors in May 1982. It was decided to launch a national project, and grassroots groups have been established all over Australia. Their primary task is to raise the consciousness of women of all denominations on Christian feminist issues. Representatives from diocesan regional groups will form State core groups and their reports will be used when the Church comes in 1988 to formulate policy for the next twenty years. Cynics have suggested that the men who began this movement are hoping to direct women's thinking along lines that do not threaten male authority on feminist issues.

Behind this intense discussion of feminine ordination which is the central current focus, there are other, and in the end deeper, issues. What *is* the role of the priest or minister in the congregation, and how is it to be understood in the light of the New Testament notion of the 'priesthood of all believers'? What should it mean to have authority in a church whose founder said 'the leaders among you must be your servants' (Matt. 23:11)? What are the appropriate structures for exercising whatever authority and priestly ministry there should be in the Church? How does the notion of authority apply *outside* the Church also—for example in the relationship of husband and wife?

Behind these are deeper questions still. If accustomed practices, which Christians value in their spiritual journey, are challenged by a new viewpoint, then how can we tell whether they are mere historical patterns, which comfort us because we are used to them but which should give way to more appropriate ones, or whether they embody the wisdom of a tradition with which we are not entitled to tamper? As specific examples, how should we think about God? Is God in any sense masculine, or more like a man than a woman? If so, in what sense? If not, then should we continue always to speak of 'Him'? And what else might we say—would it be any more helpful to speak of 'Her'? How far can or should we change the traditional language of the Christian liturgies in such ways? And besides our thinking about God, what of our thinking about ourselves and our own self-understanding? Are the roles of male and female, as delineated in the Bible or church tradition, given immutably? Or are they rather examples of what was appropriate for their time and place, and so should be replaced by patterns appropriate for ours? And what would such patterns be? In particular, should we be seeking a deeper acceptance of our contrasexual selves—that is, of the element of the feminine in every man and of the masculine in every woman? Or should we regard such suggestions with suspicion, as departing from traditional Christian standards?

The writers in this book turn constantly to the theme of the spiritual androgyny of people. Whether discussing the creation of humankind in Genesis, or Jesus' respect for women, or the fact that women as well as men held office in the early Church, they constantly seek to show human beings as not male or female *exclusively*, but as children of God with male and female, masculine and feminine, characteristics, with one set predominant. Edward Morgan's recommendation of the Jungian notion of contrasexuality is perhaps the most explicit of these efforts. Christian feminists know that, just as in our physical bodies we show a mingling of male and female, so the two poles of human being are mingled in every person. It is significant that one of the movements in feminism was a consideration of the notion of androgyny. Androgyny, according to Carolyn Heilbrun, suggests 'a full range of experience open to individuals who may, as women, be aggressive, as men, tender; it suggests a spectrum upon which human beings choose their places without regard to propriety or custom'.[13] The freedom of possibilities this suggests is breathtaking.

The whole direction of Christian feminism is not just to ensure that women have the status in the Church that they see as rightly theirs, but to explore the subtle and complicated business of femininity and masculinity and to bring about a union of the best parts of these in each person; to heal and not to divide; to make whole and not to put asunder. The division into two mutually antagonistic poles of being, masculine and feminine, Christian feminists see as one of the results of the Fall, perhaps the chief result. They believe that Christ came to rebuild the bridges between every part of our divided nature, that this particular division is bridgeable and indeed has to be bridged if we are to be whole human beings, and that it is continuing the work of redemption to try to do so.

When we Christians try to settle these questions we are driven to the issue: by what criteria should we decide them? Do we appeal simply to the words of the Bible? To the authority of two millennia of tradition embodied in the Church? To the working of the Holy Spirit today in the Church (and if so, how is such working to be recognised)? to our God-given powers of reasoning about such matters? And if to more than one of these, then how are they to be related? For all Christians, these are *theological* questions. This means, in the first place, that they cannot be settled simply by appealing to the sorts of considerations by which the community decides whether women should be admitted to the stock exchange. Non-Christians may well see theology as a smokescreen for the avoidance of the obvious and the protection of vested interests. But if Christians are to be Christian, they are in some sense under authority. They must try to relate all their thinking to what they take the will of God to be for themselves and the Church; and their attempts to discern that will must be guided by the whole outlook presented in the Bible and preserved in the Christian tradition. Yet agreement on this point may not solve

problems. For Christians, certain sorts of argument are central which
to outsiders may seem irrelevant, but about the outcome of those
arguments Christians can remain deeply divided.

In the first place, the conception of what is authoritative can differ.
Protestants appeal above all to the Bible. Roman Catholics, Orthodox
and Anglo-Catholics in the Anglican church would insist that the
tradition of the Church is also of fundamental authority. Second, even
agreement on that to which we should appeal may not yield agreement in the result. Protestants differ deeply in their interpretation of
the Bible, and about such things as how far their interpretation of it
should be influenced by historical knowledge of the situation in which
it was written. Those who appeal to the authority of tradition, in turn
also differ deeply about how that authority is manifested in history
and how it is to be recognised. And in each case there are views which
vary from the naivest conviction that the matter is perfectly clear, to
the subtlest evaluation of conflicting considerations.

Finally, though all Christians would agree that the problems are
not to be settled by mere appeal to secular considerations, this
agreement can mask fundamental differences about the role of
secular knowledge *within theology itself*. On the one hand, there are
those who see Christianity as forever needing to maintain itself
against the distortions of non-Christian viewpoints, and hence view
theology as a perpetual fight to preserve the truth against error
seeping in from outside. For such people, typically 'the world lieth in
the evil one' (I John 5:19). On the other hand, there are those who
believe that, with the redemption of the world by Christ and his
promise to send the Holy Spirit to believers (John 16:12–13), it is
already true that in some sense 'the kingdoms of this world have
become the kingdom of our Lord and Christ' (Rev. 11:15). Hence for
them all secular knowledge is indeed to be tested in the light of the
deepest Christian principles, but then, if compatible with them, to be
willingly accepted. Such Christians *expect* the viewpoints manifested
in the New Testament and early Church to be progressively amplified
in the light of greater truth wherever it may be found. And between
these two positions there are many intermediate ones. Hence the
relevance of those considerations to which non-Christians would
naturally appeal, is itself a deep issue among Christians.

In all these appeals to authority, and the search for the correct
criterion by which to judge, a central problem is that the Bible is not
an easy document to interpret. Consisting as it does of a large number
of books written down over a great period of time, virtually everyone

would agree that it is not always easy to reconcile what is said in one place with what is said in another. The accepted principle among theologians is that individual passages are to be interpreted in the light of the total picture which the Bible presents; though at the same time the total picture is essentially the sum of the individual passages. Thus our reflection moves to and fro between the whole and the part, in a way which is sometimes called the 'hermeneutic circle'. This is found in all sound biblical interpretation or exegesis. But the result is that whereas some will take a particular text as perfectly clear (and therefore as limiting the overall picture which can properly be held as consistent with it), others will have another view of the overall picture (perhaps based on taking some other text or texts as particularly significant), and will therefore argue that the first text should be read in the light of that picture.

Such difficulties suggest to some people that the Bible is to be interpreted by an authority, namely the Church, rather than left to the individual reasoning of theologians. Others, however, reply that the very same problem breaks out afresh in relation to any proposed authority. For the Christian tradition has varied greatly from age to age (and nowhere more than in its treatment of the 'feminine'). Hence must we not interpret its pronouncements also in the same way—understanding a particular statement in the light of the general picture, while at the same time discerning this from the total collection of pronouncements? And a similar circle operates again in deciding how far the growth of new knowledge should be allowed to impinge on the biblical tradition. Some will take the Bible (or the Bible as interpreted by tradition) to be that by which all else can be judged, so that what seems to be inconsistent with it may be confidently set aside. Others will say that the whole vast expansion of human knowledge is a gift of the Holy Spirit which gives us a wider overall picture, in the light of which the treasured Christian tradition may be more deeply understood.

The overall picture, which these essays support in various ways, is that Jesus lived, and the Church came into existence, in a male-dominated or patriarchal society, where the status of women was by our standards intolerably low. A striking feature of his ministry was his amazingly free attitude towards women, whereby he continually dealt with them simply as human beings. Afterwards, as the early Church explosively expanded under the pressure of its passionate convictions, modern scholarship increasingly suggests that there was neither a rigidly formalised ministry as we know it today, nor any emphasis on male dominance; but rather that women were used in whatever way their gifts and talents would indicate. Later, however, as the contagious enthusiasm gave way to more organised structures, and specially when Christianity eventually became the official religion of the Roman Empire, general patriarchal attitudes reasserted themselves. The documents of the New Testament were reinterpreted (with sincerity and even with inevitability) as leading up to what was then the present position; for the interpreters were uniformly male, and they could read the documents only from their own perspective. Moreover, the later rise of asceticism, and the fact that the greatest spiritual achievements of the age came from those leading a celibate life, gradually induced an increasing fear of, and hostility towards, sex, which threatened in time to obliterate Jesus' superbly open attitude towards women. The eventual extreme views, whereby women were seen as inherently a source of temptation and evil, would today officially be repudiated by everyone; but it is not nearly so clear that their traces do not still linger.

Given this overall picture, the subordinate position of women in the Church today seems quite unsurprising but also totally unacceptable. We are, in this view, at a stage in the development of the Christian tradition where fidelity to Jesus' great emphasis on the liberation of the human spirit, and the need to translate this liberation into practical action in our life and in the structures of society, show that restrictions on the role of women in the Church must go. We should try to avoid bitterness at the attitudes of past generations, but we cannot make the comfort of familiar patterns an excuse for resting in them.

If that were all, the pressing of the claims of the 'feminine' might be seen merely as the redressing of an injustice. But while no doubt injustice is in any case to be redressed, this position leads to an understanding of human, as well as feminine, liberation in a much deeper sense. For the questions now arise of understanding both God and our own nature more deeply. Again it turns out, on scholarly investigation, that the apparently masculine picture of God which the Bible superficially presents, is, within the Bible itself, balanced by other feminine strands. And as well as our picture of God, a whole new dimension opens up about whether we humans have been encouraged or forced to become too masculine (if we are men) or feminine (if we are women), and whether we ought not both to become more conscious of the supressed aspects of our natures. The ultimate goal would be to restore the 'feminine' in our image of God and to convert Christians to the 'feminine', so that men may love the 'feminine' in themselves and women rejoice in the 'masculine' aspects of their characters. On this view, the present structures and assumptions in the organisation of the Church not merely do injustice to half the human race, but mask a movement of self-understanding and liberation to which the Holy Spirit is calling us in this generation.

To achieve such a general picture, and to begin to become aware of its implications, is only part of the story. For, as the 'hermeneutic circle' indicates, a vision of the whole must be checked by whether it is consistent with the parts, just as the parts must be understood in the light of the whole. The contributors to this book take up detailed aspects of the discussion in various ways, according to their expertise and their own personal experience.

Eileen Jones sketches the historical perspective, and brings out the role of the male-dominated or patriarchal ideology in that history. Eileen Byrne discusses the role of the Church in the education of girls and women. Barbara Thiering examines the link between sexism and the particular Protestant positions known as fundamentalism and conservative Evangelicalism. Leo Hay considers some, though not all, of the arguments used in the Catholic Church to reject the possibility of feminine ordination. Kevin Giles considers the New Testament position, including both the texts which may be taken to prohibit female ordination, and also those which speak of the much misunderstood 'headship' of the male. Maggie Kirkman and Norma Grieve present a psychological interpretation of objections to the ordination of women.

My own chapter is concerned with less technical issues. I offer an example of how patriarchal attitudes may in practice restrict even the opportunities of service which are officially open to women. Similarly Kenneth Dempsey could well have called his chapter 'Institutional sexism and clergy wives', as he outlines some of the implication of his sociological work among the wives of clergy. Then Marlene Cohen poignantly and humorously tells us from her own experience how her career in the Church ended when she married a clergyman whom she had converted to Christianity.

A small aspect of the deepest issues about the nature of God and ourselves is raised by Richard Franklin, who discusses the problem of trying to talk about God in non-sexist ways. Marie Tulip's chapter is concerned with developments in the Uniting Church, which are impressive by comparison with most other denominations. They already show that the 'feminisation' of church structures will benefit the Church in many subtle and unexpected ways. Veronica Brady again considers longer-term issues, beginning with a plea that women should neither withdraw from these issues because of the enormous current pressures that may be placed on them, nor adapt by becoming 'honorary males' if they do gain some power. The Church has much to offer from its own traditions about how power can be expressed and exercised in more 'feminine' ways, but first it must learn to see its own tradition afresh. The point is illustrated in a different context by Anne McLay, who discusses penetratingly the past, present and future of Catholic women's congregations. Here women have a chance to play a genuine part in ordering their own affairs, and she suggests how the 'feminisation' of these structures might occur: the need for a new, and more holistic model of knowledge, which takes into account 'those non-rational abilities which Western society has tended to ignore and dismiss as irrational'; and also a new model of association and the carrying out of business, using consensus rather than the majority vote.

The next chapter, by our only non-Australian contributor, is included because valuable experience can be gained from the North American experience, where women have been involved in pastoral care for many years. Edward Morgan outlines the view, based largely on Jung, that there is an element of the opposite sex in each of us. He applies this, not only to pastoral counselling, but also to an understanding of the creation narrative in Genesis. Similar themes, expressing perhaps the deepest level of the changes to which we may be called, are found finally in Tony Kelly's discussion of the need for 'conversion to the feminine'. He sees this as a process occurring on at least four interrelated levels, which he calls the religious, the intellectual, the moral and the psychological; and he traces something of what such a conversion might mean for all of us.

This book therefore is not a systematic treatment, but is more like a series of sketches of a landscape produced by different artists from different perspectives. Yet we hope it conveys a sense of the importance, the complexity, the vastness and above all the exciting challenge of this new territory which the Holy Spirit is calling us to explore.

Some of the chapters in *The Force of the Feminine* are based on material that has already been published. A version of Kevin Giles' contribution appeared in *St Mark's Review* in June 1979, entitled 'A Biblical Case For The Ordination of Women'. Leo Hay's chapter was originally written for a conference on baptism, eucharist and ministry, organised by the Australian Council of Churches; an edited version was published in *In Unity* in June 1984. Edward Morgan's 'Implications of the Masculine in Pastoral Ministry' first appeared in the American publication *Journal of Pastoral Care*. Maggie Kirkman and Norma Grieve's chapter is an edited version of a paper called 'Women, Power and Ordination: A psychological interpretation of objections to the ordination of women to the priesthood'. It was published in *Women's Studies International Forum* by Pergamon Press in 1984. The authors wish to thank Father Roger Sharr who provided information on scriptural and theological issues pertinent to the ordination of women. Barbara Thiering based her chapter on a paper she wrote for Toleration called 'The Church and Christian Fundamentalists'. Marie Tulip's contribution is a condensation of her book, *Woman in a Man's Church: Changes in the Status of Women in the Uniting Church in Australia 1977–1984*. It was published by the Australian Council of Churches Commission on the Status of Women. We do want to thank all the organisations and publications concerned for permission to republish. We also want to thank Richard Franklin for helping with the introduction, Venetia Nelson for providing editorial assistance and Liz Thompson for secretarial help. Eleanor Brasch acted as our honorary literary agent and we would like to thank her for all she did.

Margaret Ann Franklin
August 1985

Postscript

Things are moving fast in the Anglican communion. On the one hand, the Archbishop of Sydney, the Right Reverend Donald Robinson, employing a rarely used provision has vetoed his diocese's acceptance of women deacons. On the other hand, the Church of England is drafting rules to present to its synod to provide for the ordination of women to the priesthood.

Contributors

Veronica Brady is a Loreto sister who has published several theological books. From 1973–76 she was a member of the Western Australian Appeals Tribunal for the Department of Social Security. She is now a director of the board of the Australian Broadcasting Commission. She also holds the position of Senior Lecturer in English at the University of Western Australia.

Eileen Byrne, who is Anglican, is Professor of Education Policy Studies at the University of Queensland. She trained in linguistics, specialising in medieval and modern French. She has published a book on the education and training of girls for the Commission for the European Community. She has also written a more general book on women and education.

Marlene Cohen is an Anglican lay preacher. Her lecture entitled 'Agenda for a Biblical Church' has been influential. Her aim is to eradicate institutional sexism in the church by educating her own local congregation about ministry gifts as outlined in the New Testament (for men as well as women). The topic of her Master of Theology thesis, which is to be submitted to Sydney University, is 'Educating the Laity in Theological Concepts'.

Kenneth Dempsey trained as a Methodist minister. He is now Senior Lecturer in Sociology at Latrobe University and is a member of the Uniting Church. He has published a book and numerous articles on the sociology of religion in Australian society.

Margaret Ann Franklin is Anglican, a sociologist and a freelance writer. She has written a book and various articles on race relations in Australia and on Aboriginal health. Her research interests now include the role of women in the church in Australia and the status of women in China. In 1985 she led an Australian women's delegation to China and made contact with Christian women there. She tutors in the Department of Continuing Education at the University of New England on womens' issues.

Richard Franklin is Professor of Philosophy at the University of New England. He began his professional life as a barrister and has published in philosophical and legal journals. He has written a book on freewill, and has nearly finished another called *Knowledge and Understanding*. He is an Anglican lay reader.

Kevin Giles is rector of St Matthews Anglican Church, Kensington, in the Diocese of Adelaide. He has lecturered on and written various articles and two books about women's ministry. His latest book, *Created Woman,* was published by Acorn Press. He lectures part-time in New Testament studies at the Adelaide College of Divinity at Flinders University.

Norma Grieve is a Senior Lecturer in the Department of Psychology at the University of Melbourne. She has co-edited *Australian Women: Feminist Perspectives* and has research interests in sex differences in mathematics. She also teaches in an interdisciplinary women's studies course.

Leo Hay is a member of the Franciscan Order and has long been involved in the ecumencial movement. He lectures in systematic theology at the National Pastoral Institute and the Yarra Theological Union, both in Melbourne.

Eileen Jones is a member of the Bridgetine Order. She is a psychologist and has been researching how people remember. Her chapter is based on a lecture she gave at a lunch-time seminar at the University of New England.

Tony Kelly is a member of the Redemptionist Order. He is perhaps best known for his writings in *National Outlook*. His essay 'Restoring the Feminine in Our Image of God', which was published in this

journal, won a Religious Press Association Prize. He is president of
the Yarra Theological Union and also of the Melbourne College of
Divinity. He lectures on systemic theology. His latest book, *Seasons of
Hope,* has recently been published by Dove Press.

Maggie Kirkman is a Tutor in Psychology at the University of
Melbourne. She is working towards a PhD on the effect of growing up
with an intellectually disabled sibling.

Anne McLay is a Mercy sister and member of the order's administrative team in Brisbane. She is also a historian and has written a
biography of Bishop Quinn, Brisbane's first bishop. The Mercy sisters
enjoy being involved with community groups that ask alternative
questions.

Edward Morgan has written about pastoral care and also has first
hand experience in the field. He was rector of St Luke's Episcopal
Church, Alexandria, for 21 years. He now specialises in field education and also teaches pastoral theology. He is particularly concerned
that students should understand the implications of the masculine
and feminine in pastoral ministry. He is Professor of Field Education
at the Protestant Episcopal Theological Seminary in Virginia, USA.

Marie Tulip has been a member of the Commission on the Status of
Women of the Australian Council of Churches since 1974. She has
written articles on feminist theology and spirituality and is a member
of the editorial group of *Magdale.* She is a member of the National
Women's Consultative Council. She teaches English as a Second
Language at Sydney Technical College. Her chapter is a condensation
of her book, *Woman in a Man's Church,* published by the Commission
on the Status of Women of the Australian Council of Churches.

Barbara Thiering is an Anglican theologian. She has written and
edited books on women in the Australian church and has published
numerous essays and articles on this topic. She has lectured and
spoken widely on contemporary theology and biblical studies and on
the status of Australian women. Her chapter is based on a monograph
she wrote called 'The Church and the Christian Fundamentalists',
published by Toleration.

1

Woman and the Church
Her story

EILEEN JONES

The concept of church has been variously defined, but in this chapter I
will be discussing church both as the community of Christian
believers and as the established Catholic Church. The position of
women in the Church is at present the subject of much attention. Not
only is this topic being discussed in theological journals and elsewhere
in ways which place it in the broader context of the women's
movement, but those bastions of masculinity in church organisational
structure, the seminaries, are now both accepting women students
and offering courses which actually explore the status of women,
and particularly women in ministry. Because of the limits of time and
my own life history much of what I say will refer to the experiences of
Catholic women. Those readers who have first-hand experience of
other denominations, as well as those who have made the status of
women their special study, will be able to extrapolate from the
material I present, to other denominations and situations.

There is a heritage common to all Christians: the historical roots of
Christianity in Judaean culture and the influence of early Greek
philosophers on our thought and language. For that reason I shall
spend a little time examining the woman myth in both the Greek and
Judaean traditions and then move on to the ideas of women and
womanhood embodied in the thought of Aristotle. The ideas of these
ancient Greeks and the language in which they are expressed have
exercised a pervasive influence on our perception of the nature of
woman and of male/female roles. Fifteen years ago this chapter could
as easily have been entitled 'the invisible women and the Church'. An
examination of our historical and philosophical roots, cursory though
it may be, will help to explain why women have been largely unseen

1

and unheard in the Church until now. Having dealt with the 'why' of the situation we will be in a better position to discuss the 'how' of necessary change.

The woman myth in very early Greek literature presents her as a source of evil and danger. According to Hesiod (eighth century BC) men were the original earth dwellers and enjoyed an existence free from toil and disease until the first woman, Pandora, arrived bringing with her all kinds of harm. In Hesiod's view, Pandora (and therefore all womankind) is not only the purveyor of evil, but is evil personified, being created that way by Zeus. However, Hesiod's woman had a limited use: as a sex-object, breeder and housekeeper she was an object to be acquired along with a dwelling and oxen, but never a person to be trusted. Here we have a very early record of the functionalist view of women which is typical of patriarchal cultures and which survives still. In the Homeric epics both Helen and Clytemnaestra are shown as open to seduction and prone to treachery. They are presented not as women intrinsically evil but evil through intrinsic weakness. This theme is akin to that in the Judaean myth recorded in Genesis. The woman, Eve, is the purveyor of evil. She falls herself and drags the man, Adam, with her. As punishment she is henceforth to be under Adam's domination. Integrity and strength are therefore to be seen as special prerogatives of the male.

The assumption of male superiority can also be found in the writings of Aristotle. His theory of sexual reproduction suggests the identification of masculinity with clarity, form, power and perfection; and femininity with formlessness, passivity and imperfection. According to Aristotle, a female is formed as a result of a deviation in nature, but a necessary deviation to ensure survival of the species. She is therefore to be regarded as a deformity—an infertile male. It is the male who supplies the form or soul of the offspring; the female merely supplies the inferior matter or body. Maleness is seen to exist because of an inherent ability, femaleness because of an inherent inability. Modern biologists, of course, have stood Aristotle on his head. They tell us that all embryos are first female, and that maleness is added during the course of gestation. Aristotle tells us that as 'the Form is better and more divine than the Matter, it is better also that the superior one should be separate from the inferior one. That is why whenever possible, and so far as is possible, the male is separate from the female'.[1]

The relationship between these myths and ideas, and women's experience of reality, both in the Church and in the wider society, is not hard to trace. Ancient mythology and philosophy both present woman as inferior. The Aristotelian, hierarchical, patriarchal, functionalist view of the world in which the lesser exists to serve the greater is reflected in this quote from Thomas Aquinas cited by Tony Kelly:

> Woman is something deficient and accidental. For the active power of the male intends to produce a perfect likeness of itself in the male sex. If however, a female is conceived, that is due to a lack of strength in the active power or to wrongly disposed matter or to some external influence like that of a humid wind from the South.[2]

This hierarchical model is very much in line with twentieth-century experience of reality, whether in the struggles of the peoples in Third World countries, the reality of our fiercely competitive industrial and commercial life, our educational institutions or our experience of established church structures. Western linguistic expression defines humanity as male and defines woman as relative to man, not as an autonomous person. This situation presents us with a multidimensional problem; most of these dimensions can only be mentioned here. The philosophical problem, of the masculinity= perfection/femininity=imperfection picture has already been outlined. It is generally accepted that the search for truth is the object of intellectual enquiry. However, the philosophical bias emanating from Aristotle's world view which has been so widely and unquestioningly accepted by the West has meant that our explorations of reality have been one-sided. Until very recently history has been explored, interpreted and written by men, about man, for men.

Psychologically, men and women have been trapped in sexual stereotypes and in our own day the mass media have generally served to reinforce those stereotypes. Throughout most of the history of humankind education and even basic literacy have been the prerogative of elites, and by and large of male elites only. Consequently the creativity of most people, and especially of women, has been stunted, distorted or disowned. The Greek philosophical bias which has pervaded the Christian tradition in the West has meant not only that women are perceived as inferior to men, but that aspects of femininity could not be attributed to the Deity. This theological problem is at present being explored. As Tony Kelly points out, our understanding of reality affects the way we affirm God; and the way we think about God affects the way we think about reality.[3] Thus our forebears have

set up a vicious circle of masculinity which needs to be broken. There
are two creation myths in Genesis, one in each of the first two
chapters. The second myth tells us of a female made from Adam's rib
to be his helpmate—again an hierarchical view of the sexes and a
functionalist view of women. The myth recorded in chapter 1 makes
no such distinction. In Genesis 1:27 we read: 'God created man in the
image of himself, in the image of God he created him; male and female
he created them', and there's no prize for guessing which of these two
myths has been most emphasised in the Western Christian churches.
Tony Kelly also comments: 'If the male-female polarity is in the image
of God (Gen. 1:27) then there must be something transcendentally
feminine about God—a consolation, and I suspect, quite a revelation
to most men'.[4]

Linked to the theological problem of demolishing the male stereotypes which have limited and determined our perception and articula-
tion of the concept of God is a problem of morality and justice: that of
equal rights for men and women in the Church. While Christians
generally have given lip-service to the intrinsic value of personhood,
in practice women have been both perceived and treated as inferiors
by the established Church. In the Judaean, Greek and Roman
cultures which prevailed at the time Christianity was founded,
women tended to be categorised as wives, concubines or prostitutes.
While there were minor variations from one culture to another, a
wife's place was in the home where she was expected to provide heirs
but to be seen only occasionally and rarely heard. Women in the
Judaean tradition played no part in public life and even temple
architecture was designed to ensure that women kept their place. The
priestly office was reserved for males only. Males expected to marry a
virgin and wives were honoured in the home. However, Jewish
theocracy imposed severe punishments on women who transgressed
the accepted code of sexual morality, and the law provided that an
adulteress should be stoned.

Christ's encounter with the self-righteous Jews who brought to him
a 'women taken in adultery' for condemnation challenged their double
standards. The result of his challenge is well known: the woman's
accusers slipped away, 'beginning with the eldest' (Jn 8:3–4). Christ's
attitude to women constituted a threat to the establishment, for he
consorted with sinners, lepers, tax collectors and beggars and treated
'public sinners', that is, prostitutes, with respect and courtesy, as
persons, not as second-class citizens. We find at various places in the
New Testament, mention of the women who ministered to him, and at

the last women were prominent on Calvary. The fact that mention is made in the New Testament of the ministry of women is perhaps an indication that this was a novel situation worthy of comment. Luke provides parallel incidents which feature a woman in one and a man in the other, as with the parables of the lost sheep and the lost coin. Gospel writers selected and arranged their material to make a point and Luke appears to be indicating that women and men are of equal importance in salvation history.

In the first stages of Christianity women continued to be prominent. Thus Prisca, Junia and Phoebe are mentioned by Paul (Rom. 16) but by the second century we find that this initial status of women has been eroded and that Tertullian rails against women who dared to 'teach, to participate in theological disputes, to exorcise, to promise healings and to baptise'.[5] It is interesting evidence that they were in fact doing so. Once Christianity moved from being a fringe element to integration into the establishment, woman was defined according to the Aristotelian model, by her reproductive function and household duties. Woman's place was in the home, of which the husband was the head and where she was expected to take a passive, submissive role. These were, and in part still are, the expectations placed on women, both religious and lay, by ecclesiastical authorities. In other words, what feminist writers call patriarchal ideology gradually prevailed over the equal status found in the early Church and implied by Jesus' ministry. Evidence of the prevalence of this attitude among Catholics during the early years of this century is provided in the records of the 1904 Catholic Congress. Patrick and Deirdre O'Farrell[6] in their short bulletin on the status of Catholic women in Australia, tell us that at the 1904 Catholic Congress, all papers prepared by women, and there were several, had to be read by a man. 'Women were permitted to listen to, but not to utter their own words'. A major strand in clerical attitudes to women's rights at that time was that 'they might be permissible in theory, but they were undesirable in practice'. A formal resolution of the whole congress reads: 'That woman's special sphere of duty and dignity and security is the home, to be guarded against pagan ideas, principles and practices'.

Social, political and industrial change, which has occurred in the last three centuries, has forced a modification of women's inferior status both within and outside the Church. Demands for equality and liberty for all men resulted in political change which attempted to abolish authoritarian rule and replace it with some form of democracy and enfranchisement of the masses. Industrial and technological development meant that women were increasingly employed outside the home, and basic literacy became a necessity if workers were to manage efficiently the increasingly sophisticated technology. These changes could not be ignored by the Church, even though the consequences of some of them have been fiercely resisted and others given lip-service only.

Perhaps the most visible sign of the status, or lack of it, for women in the Australian church, has been the exclusion of women not only from ordained ministry but even from theological colleges until the last few years. Pope Pius X (Pope 1904–1913) was liberal for his time and encouraged women to acquire higher education, but drew the line at women studying theology, or pursuing politics. Some Australian Catholic laymen are on record as sharing the reactionary view of the clergy that women should not exercise political power. Not only public life but church politics were once proscribed for women. The O'Farrells tell of a meeting called in 1862 at Ipswich, which was to be held in the church building after Mass to settle disputes about church internal affairs. It was decided that women and children had no business at the meeting. This desire to exclude women from involvement in public affairs of any kind is partly explained by the contemporary attitudes to Mary as model. She was interpreted as a static, conservative force in which submissiveness was lauded. This interpretation of the woman who showed active concern for others at the Cana marriage, and had the moral fibre to stand by Christ on Calvary is unrealistic, to say the least, and it was reflected in an exalted idea of femininity which was also unrealistic.

In the political climate of the time many viewed the demands for female equality as an anti-religious assault on society. In fact the franchise for women was supported by some male Catholics, not because they acknowledged woman's intrinsic worth, but as a means of increasing the anti-socialist vote. In spite of the rather radical working-class origins of Australian Catholicism, by the turn of this century it was beginning to acquire most of the trappings of middle-class respectability. Moreover in the climate of bitter sectarianism which prevailed in Australian society during the early years of this century, Catholics and Protestants saw themselves as arch rivals. Neither faction was prepared to be outnumbered unnecessarily at the polls, so all churches actively encouraged women to enrol once they recognised that extension of the franchise to women was inevitable. Similarly Australian churchmen encouraged the education of 'female children' so that they could better fulfil the functionalist roles

assigned to them by the unwritten patriarchal norms of the mascu-
line-oriented culture.

During the last 75 years the social fabric of our culture has
undergone persistent change, and within the Catholic Church this
change has been accelerated by Vatican II. Two world wars separated
by the depression of the thirties, the increased availability of both
elementary and higher education, the universal franchise, rapid
improvements in the means of transport and communication have all
contributed to a shift in the power base and resulted in a more
egalitarian society. In the nineteenth century the power base was
land or wealth derived from land, and/or trade and commerce. In
today's society information is power, and thanks to the electronic
media information is no longer dependent on print literacy. These
changes have of necessity had an impact on the Church, for women as
well as men are much better educated and more articulate than they
were in the early years of Australia's history. Historically, theology
and church law have been exclusive male provinces but there are now
a small but growing number of women theologians and scripture
scholars, in the Catholic and other churches, while women regularly
contribute to theological and church publications. Vatican II has been
a catalyst in speeding up the changed self-perception and church-
perception of women. It makes numerous statements on the value of
personhood and the need for Christians to become actively involved in
bringing about a more just and humane society. This passage from
'The Church Today' is pertinent to our discussion and typical of the
tenor of the documents of Vatican II generally:

> Since all men possess a rational soul and are created in
> God's likeness . . . the basic equality of all must receive
> increasingly greater recognition.
>   . . . with respect to the fundamental rights of the person,
> every type of discrimination, whether social or cultural,
> whether based on sex, race, colour, social condition,
> language, or religion, is to be overcome and eradicated as
> contrary to God's intent. For in truth it must still be
> regretted that fundamental personal rights are not yet
> being universally honoured. Such is the case of a woman
> who is denied the right and freedom to choose a husband,
> to embrace a state of life, or to acquire an education or
> cultural benefits equal to those recognised for men.
>   . . . Above all the education of youth from every social
> background has to be undertaken, so that there can be
> produced not only men and women of refined talents, but

> those greatsouled persons who are so desperately required
> by our times . . . We can justly consider that the future of
> humanity lies in the hands of those who are strong enough
> to provide coming generations with reasons for living and
> hoping.[7]

The women's movement is instrumental in realising this hope. It calls woman to define herself as a human person, equal in capacity, in aspiration and in sinfulness with men. Modern women, increasingly aware of their potential, see themselves as autonomous, and are increasingly becoming involved in public life in both ecclesiastical and secular spheres. Within the contemporary Catholic Church, women are serving as members of pastoral teams; they are directors of religious education, and prepare adults as well as children for reception of the sacraments. They act as extraordinary ministers of the Eucharist and bring the Sacrament to the aged and bedridden. They are involved in hospital and campus chaplaincies; they preach retreats and act as spiritual directors—even to males. As well they work with Marriage Encounter groups and teenage organisations. They are even occasionally invited to preach to a church congregation, and a very small number lecture in seminaries. Others seek to change the political and social structures which cause and perpetuate poverty and alienation.

In spite of these changes, the image projected by church structures is still one of a masculine, clerical and hierarchical system. The structures of the Catholic Church are perceived by some as inhibiting rather than promoting full human and spiritual freedom: a power structure that rewards conformity. It is not surprising then, that some women who wish to minister hesitate to move into this structure, and others leave what they consider a depersonalising system destructive of the Christian spirit of ministry. Other women, and also some men, are disappointed that the Catholic Church is not proceeding to the ordination of women in the foreseeable future. These people see the inclusion of women in the ordained ministry as a means of acknowledging in fact the worth of woman, and of humanising church structures.

Humphrey O'Leary has formulated a schema which reflects how the Church has dealt with change in law over the centuries. His five stages are that new discipline is i not mentioned; ii rejected; iii allowed as exception; iv encouraged; and v imposed.[8] He gives several examples to support his schema, one of which is the Catholic shift from non-participation to involvement in the ecumenical movement. Others are admission of married men to ordination, and eucharistic intercommunion which are examples of a Stage iii situation. He then suggests that the issue of admission of women to the ministerial priesthood could be construed as a Stage ii situation. It is inconsistent for the Church in her official documents to call for equal opportunities for all persons whether male or female, and in her practice to perpetuate exclusively masculine ministerial and administrative structures. Such a stance is at variance with Paul's famous passage from Gal. 3:28: 'All are baptised in Christ, you have been clothed yourselves in Christ, and there are no more distinctions between Jew and Greek, slave and free, male and female, but all of you are one in Christ Jesus'.

I have mentioned the institutionalised structures of church and society which impede necessary and worthwhile change. I see a danger of the Women's Movement succumbing to the same pitfalls, for increasing professionalism and institutionalism is the hallmark of modern society. However an examination of early church practice would help develop a greater awareness and realisation of the contributions that members of a disadvantaged group can make to the welfare of the individuals who constitute it.[9] In this respect local social networks are invaluable. There is evidence already that both men and women are beginning to realise that the hierarchical and functionalist approach to relationships between human persons is natural in the same way that moral suffering, degradation and death are 'natural' to us.[10] The Christian woman can no longer acquiesce in or accept these evils. There is a need for a spirituality that recognises the feminine and shows how women can be brought into the full liberty of the children of God. This integration demands a thorough spiritual transformation and an education of both men and women into a new set of values, attitudes, aims and relationships.

All have within themselves masculine and feminine elements. The masculine in each of us has to eschew the pursuit of power which is divorced from love, rooted in violence, lust and deceit and expressed in arrogance. The feminine in us must refuse to acquiesce in violence and injustice and the acquisition of false power. It must learn to cooperate with the creative force of the Spirit in order to slough off subservience. The spirit of the Lord is given to proclaim liberty, to bring new sight to the blind and to set the downtrodden free (Luke 4:18). In short, we need people who are at one and the same time theologically perceptive, seriously concerned for human welfare and alert to the psychological and sociological dimensions of their work and its effects upon its recipients.[11]

2

The role of the Church in the education of girls and women

EILEEN M. BYRNE

If we tried
To sink the past beneath our feet
Be sure the future would not stand.
Elizabeth Barrett Browning *Aurora Leigh*

We cannot understand the role of the Church in education unless we set our thinking in the context of the historical and social origins of the policies which have their roots in past theology and ideologies. The provision, curriculum and style of education has always been determined by the perceptions of those controlling the education system of the social roles for which they are preparing boys and girls respectively. Because therefore the control of schooling has been mainly in the hands of the established Church for over eighteen of our twenty centuries, it follows that the attitudes of the leadership of the Church towards the education of girls at all, and towards the type of schooling considered suitable, has been a major determinant of their access to and quality of education. Women's invisibility in church affairs reflects an historic undertreatment of their role in Christianity. In the 1981 Sheffield Report of the World Council of Churches on the role of women and men in the Church, a woman consultant from Germany reminded us that 'Church history begins when a few women set out to pay their last respects to their dead friend, Jesus . . . This story as told by Matthew is generally known as the Easter Story, but never as the beginning of Church history . . .'.[1]

But what in fact do we mean by the Church? Its leadership defines the Church as the handing down of a core of beliefs, doctrines, dogmas and spiritual experiences, stitched into tradition by the apostolic succession to give us decisive guidance. But in so far as we say with conviction in the Communion service 'We are the body of Christ', we may also see the Church as all of the Christians who commit themselves to active participation in one of the branches of the Church: women and men alike. In this chapter we look at policy and developments in the light of both interpretations, that is, the influence of the established leadership in each age, and the role of individual churchwomen and men in opening up education to women.

It is clearly impossible to cover the whole history and ideology in one brief overview, and the account which follows is to be regarded as an *illustrative* analysis using landmarks in the development or decline of Church influence, rather than a full ecumenical account. Yet although the very different histories of the different branches of Christianity deserve more scholarly and complete justice, there are nevertheless some principal themes and trends which emerge which have transfer value. With rare exceptions, we can substantiate a general conclusion that the leadership of the established Church has hindered the equal access of girls to schooling and education in three ways until very recently: by denying access to systematic schooling at all for nearly a thousand years; by constructing and imposing an inferior and non-vocational education aimed at keeping women subordinate, domestic and socially defined in relation to male kinfolk; and by limiting girls to a less advanced education than their brothers.

Nor will readers find here an Australian account, since much of the necessary research remains still to be done which will enlighten the history of the education of women in this country. The limited published Australian sources documenting the Church—State battles have concentrated on the provision and funding of Catholic systemic schooling, rather than on qualitative issues within the theme of church influences. Yet the history of this country lies within the history of England and Europe, and the history of the Church stands sui generis. Today's church attitudes are born in yesterday's policies.

It is proposed to look at church influence in four main phases: early Christianity, medieval education, Renaissance and Reformation influences and the post-industrial period. Within these ages, three issues arise. What were prevailing church attitudes to women's role for which education should prepare them? What access did girls have to schooling or higher education? Did they have the *same* provision and content as their brothers?

Early Christianity

Christianity has its roots in the Jewish religion, and it is interesting to note that, by 65 AD, the Jews had established universal elementary education from the age of seven, operative in towns and provinces. However, boys and girls were seen as having different vocations. The threefold duty of a Jewish father was to 'instruct his *sons* in the Law, bring them into wedlock and teach them a handicraft'.[2] One must remember that the New Testament, and particularly the Epistles, need to be interpreted against the prevailing practices of the time, and of the age in which their (former Jewish) writers composed them.

Donaldson, an Anglican Edwardian scholar of repute, records the prevailing view of the turn of this century that Paul's stringent views on women's subordination were formed by his perception of the character of the women of his native Tarsus (prim and modest and shrouded in appearance but allegedly licentious and corrupt behind their veils).[3] Donaldson reminds us that women in late Roman times were socially unfettered, dining in the company of men unveiled, studying literature and philosophy, helping their husbands to govern provinces and defending their own law cases where necessary. 'Accordingly at the very first stage, women take a prominent part in the spread of Christianity'. In the first enthusiasm they were allowed to do whatever they seemed most fitted for because 'the idea that regulated the forms of organisation was that each member should contribute to the Church, in an orderly way, any gift that God had given him'.[4] Hence we meet with prophetesses, the four daughters of Philip the Evangelist, women who worked with the apostles in spreading the Gospel, and the original deaconesses.

But any expectation that this early equality in the sight of God (from direct evangelism to martyrdom) would lead to equality in education or training for the same roles, vanished by the third century when the cult of virginity began to replace the respectability of widowhood. Deaconesses were limited to functions of doorkeeping at services and preparing women for baptism; they were however prohibited from teaching. Those sects in which women declared the right to preach or prophesy were labelled as heretical. St Augustine of Canterbury, who landed in Britain in 596, proclaimed the doctrine of indissoluble marriage and the total submission of wives and daughters to what he saw as the God-appointed male heads of their households. By the time St Augustine of Canterbury became influential, Tertullian, third-century Carthaginian theologian, had firmly established the anti-marriage ascetic cult for celibacy as a nobler aim than marriage for childbearing. His instruction to women to be silent and to remain in the home, and his designation of children as 'burdens which are to most of us unsuitable, as being perilous to faith', made any serious consideration of children and their education perceivedly irrelevant.[5] Fourth-century St Jerome further elevated celibacy as a spiritual ambition by his example as a hermit. Augustine's influence on early educational thought was seminal, but in *De Magistro* he speaks only of schoolmasters and of boys. It is difficult to interpret his treatises on challenging concepts of truth and vision, from his writing on Divine Illumination to his extension of vision and understanding to mathematical theory, as other than intended for male comprehension (*De Trinitate*). Other early Christian writers such as Clement of Alexandria designated women as temptresses, causing them to be instructed to exercise only 'spinning and weaving and superintending of cooking if necessary' and to be entirely covered. Thus women's role was redefined as both domestic and dependent.

At this stage, of course, neither sex had access to schooling as such, but the expectation that men would become church leaders, would travel, would carry on the oral traditions and written scholarship of the new beliefs, meant that at least a minority of boys received formal teaching. After the Dark Ages, under the influence of Alcuin of York, Charlemagne ordered the establishment of cathedral schools in France in the ninth century, at a time when the Pope also enjoined all bishops in 826 to establish teachers and to inspect the emergent schools in their dioceses. In England, records exist of the decline of the religious nature of the few nunneries in pre-medieval times and their opening to the daughters of the rich laity where they could learn reading, writing, and some rhetoric as well as church embroidery and other crafts. Eadburga, for example, a former English abbess, wrote Latin and taught girls 'in the poetical tradition'.[6] Somewhat earlier in 635, Oswald of Northumbria had invited Aidan from Iona to establish schools in the region, and these monastery centres of learning certainly produced future (male) clerics for some time before the more systematic provision of town grammar schools in the Middle Ages. All this is notwithstanding the *Cura Pastoralis* of Pope Gregory I which commanded his bishops to call together 'the people of *every condition and sex* and plainly teach them who rarely hear the Word of God' (my emphasis).

Leach argued that song schools attached to the early cathedral schools (for example, Canterbury and York) were established as early as the ninth century, and that although most schools would be monastic, secular schools to teach Latin would have been established as soon as churches were built.[7] Lawson found no evidence of song schools before the twelfth century, but in either event, the provision was still wholly male.[8] In the first place, the Licentia Docendi (licence to teach) was held only by bishops from the ninth to the sixteenth century, and they accordingly controlled how many boys would be taught to read Latin (fewer to write it), and excluded girls. The purpose of song schools was to teach the plainchant and Latin needed for the liturgy, and hence was also limited to boys by definition.

Medieval education

The twelfth-century reorganisation of cathedrals on a collegial basis not only developed them as centres of learning, but represents the first origins of systemic schooling. The development of ecclesiastical and canon law, and the rediscovery of Roman civil law also created a demand for higher education in the burgeoning medieval universities like Paris, Ravenna, Bologna, Oxford and Cambridge. The Third Lateran Council of 1129 (some authorities say 1179) instructed cathedral authorities to give clerics and 'other poor scholars' *free* instruction in reading, and the Fourth Lateran Council in 1215 extended this instruction to all churches. But the schools set up as a result were for the younger priests, deacons and vicars choral, clerks and choristers, who were naturally male. Hence when in due course secular education in these non-monastic schools was opened up to a few children from the upper classes, it was to sons only and not to daughters.

This exclusion was more serious than simply exclusion from preparation for roles in the Church. Already some secular knowledge was becoming necessary to back up the growing merchant and trade system. The traditional seven Liberal Arts which were established as the 'core curriculum' were to dominate education until post-Reformation reconstruction. The elementary *trivium* of grammar, rhetoric and logic, and the *quadrivium* of geometry, astronomy, arithmetic and music were not available to girls, with very rare exceptions. It is less easy to understand this when one remembers that it was a woman, Aspasia, who in fact taught Pericles and Socrates logic and rhetoric in Athens, and that in feudal England and France, women had to run their husbands' estates, albeit through estates managers, while their husbands were away fighting the Crusades. The rationale for extending education to upper-class sons only was to extend the country's male power base. The strong influence of theologians like Aquinas, who argued that women were 'defective and misbegotten', subsequently provided a further reinforcement of church policy that access to grammar school, cathedral, choir and chantry schools, was inappropriate for girls and women.

Lawson however holds that the contribution of nuns to medieval education has been much underestimated, and that while it cannot be statistically assessed any more accurately than that of monks, 'relatively it was probably greater, and may indeed have been their chief social justification'. Eileen Power, still one of the most respected authorities on medieval English nunneries, suggested that a majority of them boarded children from the upper classes, typically about twenty or so girls and a few small boys at a time. Unlike the boys' almonry and choir or chantry schools which employed schoolmasters after the Lateran Council edicts, the teaching in the nunnery schools was covered by the nuns themselves. It was not likely that the nuns refrained from teaching the Word of God along with the English, French, needlework and herbal knowledge, reading and (rarely) Latin which was considered an appropriate female curriculum. Although there is of course some evidence of nun scribes by the fourteenth century, and indeed illuminators of manuscripts would have been trained in nunneries from Whitby Abbey onwards, the 'normal' female curriculum would not have included writing (because women did not become church clerics), long after writing became standard for boys in town grammar schools. Out of a population of three million in England in 1500, Power estimated that perhaps 1,000 girls had received some form of convent education.[9] It is perhaps a singular irony that the growth of boys-only chorister schools in the fourteenth century had been as a result of the rising cult of the worship of the Virgin Mary.[10]

Women were similarly excluded from the great movement of medieval universities, for predictable reasons, since the universities sprang out of the development of Scholasticism after Aquinas, the rediscovery of Aristotle in the thirteenth century, and of Quintilian in 1416, as well as the ricochets of the debates on the Great Schism. The widening of university powers beyond the teaching of theology and philosophy to law and medicine (Salerno examined potential doctors from 1231, Bologna taught secular letter writing as an art in the thirteenth century, and Paris became political after the decline of Scholasticism in the fifteenth century), still meant that medieval educators constructed the university faculties around preparation for occupations which had been controlled, by Church and State alike, as only accessible to men. It is often overlooked that medieval education was mainly *vocational* (Latin was a vocational skill!) and that the concept of liberal education for its own sake was a much later arrival.

The development of a new merchant class and of an embryonic middle class contributed to the laicisation of schooling as the guilds grew in status and power. And here we note the first stage at which, at least in theory, girls are regarded as having the same rights as boys to basic education. In 1406 the Statute of Apprentices declared that a child of *either sex* could be sent to learn Latin at any school, even villeins, a right which the Church had hitherto strictly limited to boys of the upper class or to intending clerics. Over the next three centuries, town schools were founded by guilds, by mayor and corporation, by the landed gentry for the poor of the town (among the earliest, Wotton-under-Edge was endowed by a Lady Barclay). In a most scholarly work, Fletcher traces how many of these early endowments were founded for children—not boys—and should have been open to girls, but how for four centuries until the Schools Inquiry Commission and its aftermath in 1868 and beyond, the endowments were increasingly and corruptly diverted to provide only for the sons of the merchant and middle classes, or the indigenous yeomanry. Endowments which referred to the 'children of the poor' were not aimed at the kind of poverty which was characteristic of the labouring classes in the nineteenth century, but at the poorer relations of the upper classes and the lower squirearchy and upper tradesmen.[11] On the one hand, therefore, we find that increased lay control theoretically widened girls' *potential* access; on the other, that the concept of 'automatic male priority' merely shifted from the Church to the financial and political power structure. Caution should be observed in interpreting these generalisations, to the extent that the position of girls in the upper, merchant and yeoman classes varied considerably and they merit separate study. For example, Sir Thomas More, a churchman of stature, encouraged his daughter Margaret to study seriously, and her Latin reply to Quintilian and her translation of Eusebius from the Greek to Latin, were praised by Cardinal Pope. Lady Jane Grey read Plato in the original at fourteen, as well as French, Italian, Latin, Hebrew and Arabic.

Renaissance to industrialisation

In England, the period up to the nineteenth century is mainly marked by two trends: on the one hand, a steady decline in the quality of education in the grammar and dame schools; on the other, the rise of dissent and evangelism creating a new demand for literacy. In France, however, three movements became established which were highly significant in the development of educational theory, but which continued the exclusion of girls.

The founding of the Jesuit order by St Ignatius Loyola in 1534 gave a further reinforcement to the automatic male priority which had been established through church schooling, and hence in the ladder to power in both Church and State. Loyola being a former soldier, the Jesuit movement was organised on a military basis and focused on teaching the catechism to boys, grammar to male scholars and philosophy and theology to male students in universities. Thus both the classical and theological core of studies in the *Ratio Studiorum* which dominated schools from 1559 till its revision in 1832, and the nineteenth-century additions of history, geography, mathematics and science, were denied to the Catholic sisters of the 1000-strong boy enrolments of the Jesuit colleges. By 1610, these numbered over 300, some in the New World. The founding of the Oratory schools by Berulle in 1611 'to reform the life and learning of the French clergy', providing in due course for 36 influential Oratory schools, added more male opportunities. Some see the schools of Port-Royal however as more pervasively influential, if more short-lived. The Abbaye of Port-Royal was founded in 1204 southwest of Paris and 'the original aim of the foundation placed under the supervision of the Cistercians *was the education of girls*'[12] (my emphasis) but in a now familiar pattern, the Renaissance church leaders ignored this. By 1637, St Cyran was able to found the Petites Ecoles of Port-Royal for boys only. The Grandes Ecoles were licensed to teach Latin to boys only, university scholars; but the Petites Ecoles had a Licentia Docendi to teach both boys and girls French as the mother tongue. Nevertheless, the Port-Royal schools diverged from their original foundation to teach secondary education to sons but not daughters, because of their perception that women had no part to play in either the church hierarchy or in professional spheres in society. The third great French movement was the Christian Brothers Community, founded in 1684 and currently described as the largest teaching order in the world. These schools of the Christian Brothers sprang from the work of Jean-Baptiste De La Salle, who incorporated charity schools for boys into the new community from the outset. De La Salle's innovations in the area of teacher training (he established one of the earliest seminaries), and his work with adult students, were again limited to young men— unusually for his time, some boys of genuinely poor families.

Meanwhile, for two centuries in England, Reformation and Dissent
had as profound an impact on educational policy as they were to have
on Church and State politics. One principal influence was the
insistence of Dissenters on their right to educate their children (not
only their sons) in the way of their conscience and according to their
tenets. The new movement, founded as it was on the importance of
direct access to the Scriptures for each person, gave equal weight to
the right and need of their daughters as of their sons, for the level of
education thought suitable to their class.

The Society of Friends developed an educational policy from the
outset in marked contrast to the more rigid Church of England
system, providing an important alternative to the sex-segregated and
vocationally segregated schools set up by other church interests later.
Quakers believed that men and women were equal in the sight of God,
and the Quaker principle of individualism hindered any sex-stereo-
typing from the start. By 1691 there were fifteen Quaker schools in
England which taught science and English as well as Latin *to both
sexes*. Ackworth school, founded in 1779, was described as for both
boys and girls 'not in affluence'. By 1840 most of the Friends' schools
for the middle classes, (67 in England) were mixed at a time when
secondary schooling was not available for middle-class girls elsewhere, and when only church elementary schools were available in
towns and villages in Britain. By the 1860s, girls at the Quaker girls'
school, The Mount, were studying algebra, geometry and trigo-
nometry some years ahead of the availability of this in the schools to
be later founded by Dorothea Beale, Frances Buss and the Girls
Public Day Schools Trust.[13] Boys of course had had access to
mathematics through the *Quadrivium* since the establishment of
medieval education.

But even the Quaker movement became influenced by nineteenth-
century sex-differentiation of social roles. Although women had been
teachers in nunneries in the Middle Ages, and despite knowledge of
many distinguished women scholars over centuries of culture, teacher
training at the Quaker Flounders Institute originally provided
scholarships for male students only. Scholarships were to be open to
women 'only when finances allowed', to enable them to study at the
new university centres.[14] Characteristic of normal Quaker
upbringing, however, was that of Elizabeth Fry, the prison reformer,
whose mother Catherine Gurney took as much trouble to teach her
daughters because of her belief that boys and girls were equal in the
sight of God. Elizabeth learned Latin, French, 'the simple beauties of

mathematics', modern history and geography, natural history and drawing, in addition to the household economy and sewing thought essential for all girls at the time.[15]

Some hundred years earlier, in 1737, Susannah Wesley, mother of John and Charles, described to John in a letter the principles and method she had used to bring them up and teach them, and one notes with interest the eighth principle, that

> [n]o girl be taught to work till she can read very well: and that she be kept to the work with the same application and for the same time that she was held to in reading. This rule also is much to be observed, for the putting children to learn sewing before they can read perfectly is the very reason why so few women can read fit to be heard and never to be well understood.[16]

Such ideas were advanced for their time, and since the letter was written after many requests from John and Charles for Susannah to do so, one may well argue that the views of this remarkable church-woman (she conducted household prayers and preached to the family and servants in her minister husband's absence—to his disapproval) were strongly influential in the characteristic Methodist respect for education for girls as well as boys.

The children of the poor had experienced less sex-differentiation in that they had had little systematic education at all, for either sex. By the eighteenth century, the medieval grammar schools had fallen into disrepair and disrepute. No elementary school system had been created, despite the longstanding post-Lutheran insistence on direct access to the Bible, until Robert Raikes, Hannah More and Mrs Trimmer started the Sunday School movement for general literacy.[17] Only reading was taught, because the prevailing Establishment view was that we are called into a certain rank and station by divine foresight, and writing was not necessary for the lower classes. For the next hundred years, educational policy was to be dogged by the Church's reluctance to open up education beyond what it saw as predestined roles for the poor and for women.

Public morals had declined in the eighteenth-century. The Society for Promoting Christian Knowledge was founded in 1698 from a desire to reform the young to a more pious orthodoxy, and the breakdown of the old Tudor Poor Law system was accompanied by a new social consciousness of class hierarchy. These and other factors led to the charity school movement which led to further laicisation of church control. Charity schools were set up by citizens (Grey Coat

Hospital), by Aldermen (Red Maids, Bristol) and only occasionally by the diocese (Launceston); they were paid for by public subscription and provided an endless stream of well-trained domestic servants and craftsmen. One must remember that even this was a much better future in those days than the children of the poor and penurious could otherwise have expected. The early schools were predominantly for girls, but as the movement spread, provision became heavily weighted to boys, for whom public subscription could more easily be raised. But despite the apparent lay control, the Church of England was not prepared to cede its control of the country's educational policy. The pupils were publicly examined in church, some schools were used to combat 'Popery' and all were monitored to prevent children moving above 'their rank and station'.

Thus even as industrialisation created new social and educational needs, the Church remained an instrument of reinforcement of social roles which were still seen as theologically predestined.

Nineteenth-century education

The history of the opening up of secondary and higher education to women is too complex and detailed to treat here, and interested readers may follow through the different strands of girls' education in the well-documented results of recent research.[18] My purpose here is to highlight the contrast of the role of the Church as such and of individual churchwomen and men. The former has been repressive; to the latter we owe our emancipation.

For working-class girls, the early schools founded by the National Society for Promoting the Education of the Poor (the Anglican society) reiterated the Church doctrine of obedience and conformity.

> The facility of communicating instruction by the system now intended to be brought into general use . . . the entire provision which it takes of their minds, so as to render them pliant and obedient to discipline . . . are powerful instruments both for infusing into their minds good knowledge and forming them to good habits.[19]

Sixty years later, the *Church Quarterly Review* reported that the vast majority of schools in the country were church schools (grant-aided by government) 'founded to carry out Church views. Education as a whole was a Church work, was so treated by the State, was legislated for on that basis . . .'[20] Thus we may expect that the prevailing view of leading churchmen would define very clearly the education thought appropriate for girls and boys respectively; and it did. The working-class girl learned the same as her brother in basic education, but was required to learn in due course the cooking, laundry and household management which have bedevilled elementary and high school education for girls ever since. Girls were held to be wholly responsible for homemaking, and the curriculum imposed on them in both church schools and the School Board schools which followed the 1870 and 1876 acts to provide state education, prepared them for domesticity, but their brothers for the labouring (later, the skilled) trades. The sex segregation of the manual crafts and domestic crafts which remains an attitudinal block to boys preparing for parenting and home responsibility, and to girls from entering skilled trades today, has its direct roots in the enforced elementary curriculum of Victorian England. Even the School Boards were often dominated by diocesan interests, as were the great commissions of inquiry into the schooling needs of the new industrialisation. But the thrust for educating more than a chosen elite has tended to follow major reforms not always of the Church's own choosing. Without Tyndale's English Bible and the Lutheran demand for direct Bible teaching in the vernacular, we would probably still have vestiges of a medieval grammar school system—the curriculum of which lingered long past its usefulness in Victorian England. Similarly, two developments accelerated the removal of girls' education from the stranglehold of church domi-nance: the rise of the commercial middle class who sought more relevant education for their daughters in the latter half of the century, and the devout Church of England women who enlisted their help to demand full and the same secondary education for girls. Archer called them 'a hardheaded, hardworking, religiously minded and commonsense group of middle class women'.[21]

The history of the founding of the first boarding school for middle-class girls, Cheltenham Ladies College, by Dorothea Beale; of the North London Collegiate school for the daughters of the 'other middle class' (trade) by Frances Buss; the great fight with the Endowed Schools Commission to reclaim the endowments misappropriated for boys over the centuries to provide for secondary schools for girls (of which there were none at the turn of the nineteenth century) are now part of mainstream as well as feminist history. What has been little recorded is the religious motivation which drove these women, devout as they were, to fight for girls' education against the prevailing social and theological climate of their time. On Dorothea Beale's death in

1906, the *Guardian* obituary wrote of her as 'a loyal Church-
woman . . . She may take rank not only as a great administrator and
educationist but also, we venture to believe, with the great holy
women of the past'.[22] Dorothea herself, writing of Frances Buss on the
death of the latter in 1897 to Joshua Fitch, spoke of her as one who
was 'unostentatiously religious, lived in the spirit of prayer, and had
the love of God in its twofold sense ever guiding her thought and
action'.[23] In Dorothea's case, she saw the parable of the talents as
directly relevant to girls. 'What is God's work for you, my children? To
put out your own talents to interest, to improve and perfect your own
powers . . . We may not keep God's gifts for ourselves', she told the
college girls just before her death in 1906.

Higher education for girls similarly owed its development to
leading members of the established Church, despite the views of more
than one bishop that woman's place did not lie with mathematics and
Greek. The first efforts to provide university lectures for women
otherwise doomed to become underpaid and under-educated governesses, owed much to Rev. David Lang, Vicar of Holy Trinity
Church, and Rev. Frederick Denison Maurice, who persuaded pro-
fessors of King's College London to give lectures to governesses to
qualify them to teach secondary education in place of the superficial
accomplishments inherited from the previous century's decay.
Queen's College and Bedford College both owe their origin to a
combination of church support and feminist fight. (Two of the first
students were Miss Beale and Miss Buss.) Anne Clough, who founded
the North of England Council for Promoting the Higher Education of
Women in 1867 and was later first principal of the newly founded
Newnham College for women, Cambridge, was profoundly influenced
by her 'truly religious' mother and herself lived in the 'constant
realisation of God's presence'. She will also be remembered for
founding the University Association of Women Teachers in 1882.[24]

Among the many histories now available which cover the fight by
Emily Davies and others to open up the university entrance examina-
tions to girls, and to enable them to study the *same* curriculum (that
is, Greek, which had hitherto been limited to boys) the new scholarly
study by Fletcher is especially valuable in researching in great detail
the patient work of women and men alike, including two schools
inspectors, to renegotiate the misappropriated endowments of some
hundreds of years back for provision of secondary education for girls in
the major towns and cities. Resistance came equally from leading
churchmen and from mayors and merchants who held that to use

funds to educate girls' intellect was to go against the will of God, and to take from boys what was their natural, superior right.[25]

Church opinion was similarly divided on the proper role of women attracted by the call of the cloister to form the sisterhoods which were another main provider of education for girls—often against strong male opposition from bishops and church leaders. Many held that women's place was more properly with marriage and childbearing, and that women had no 'moral right' to dedicate lifelong service to God if the promise involved celibacy and rejection of motherhood. Others saw religious vows as such as leading to 'perversion to Papal ... schismatical and corrupt Communion'.[26] Bishop Tait in particular believed that women's imagination led them to see 'some peculiar sanctity' in the cloistered life which he regarded as more appropriately found for *women* in 'the quiet discharge of domestic duties'.[27] The opposite view was taken by Prebendary Bernard Leslie, who 'had not the slightest doubt that such a life is sanctioned by Holy Scripture as well as the Universal Church' and who soundly criticised episcopal interference with sisterhoods as no more justified than episcopal intervention to prohibit voluntary social work or teaching.[28]

There was of course nothing new about religious orders for women. The Ursuline order (still one of the leading orders to provide schools for girls) was founded in 1537 by Angela da Brescia. The order of the Catholic Sisters of Mercy was founded in 1838 and fourteen communities now provide schools for girls. Of the Anglican sisterhoods, many saw a special need for schools for girls staffed by women. The Community of the Sisters of the Church, for example, numbers among its 5000 or so children in sisters' schools, girls at single-sex schools in Croydon, York, Liverpool, and in Canada and Australia. The Community of the Holy Family (1898) was rare in being led by a Mother Superior (Mother Agnes Mason) who took a Moral Science Tripos at Cambridge as early as 1886 and the Lambeth Dip. Theol. by thesis, enabling her to centre on advanced education for girls in England and abroad. Others, too numerous to cover here, include a wide variety of provision for all classes of girls. Priscilla Seddon, founder of the Society of the Most Holy Trinity (Ascot, 1848) focused on the needs of orphan daughters of soldiers and sailors, and provided industrial schooling for other needy girls. Others (The Community of All Hallows; the Community of St Thomas the Martyr; the Society of the Holy and Undivided Trinity) concentrated on girls of the new middle class— tradesmen and upper servants—in country towns. The Community of St Mary the Virgin at Wantage added to the reputation of its

schools for girls and Oxford hostel for women a distinguished reputation for education and training in church embroidery, printing of
plainchant books and arts at the Wantage school and Community.

It is the more unaccountable that so many sisterhoods founded for
community work of great social need should have met with opposition
from some church leaders who still held that women were unsuited to
roles outside the home, given the immediate past history of three
queens who played a role in church affairs, the prominence of
intellectual women in the Church in the eighteenth century and the
known history of outstanding abbesses in the Middle Ages. Hilda of
Whitby ran a major organisation in her abbey, using political skills
and financial experience to maintain it, teaching skills to staff it,
management skills to control it and intellectual skills in spiritual
leadership of her nuns. Precedents were not lacking in church history.
Yet we began the last century with a prevailing view of women as
saintly influences—on the very young—who should not be absent
from those who needed them whatever their own personal talents.
Writing in the *Christian Observer of 1812* a reviewer of the current (if
decadent) systems of education referred to the inauspicious religious
career of the scholar removed from his mother, 'for to the fair sex are
we in general indebted for whatever piety is instilled into our infant
minds'. This view of women's non-intellectual role persisted
throughout most of the Victorian age, the few churchmen who allied
themselves to the feminist pressure for equal and open education
being regarded as neither typical nor wholly respectable by the
leadership. More characteristic of those who served on the commissions and boards of the time was the writer in the *Church Quarterly
Review* of 1876 who believed that 'female readers can hardly be
expected to read for intellectual self-improvement's sake. A girl with
a true thirst for knowledge is rare . . . Lads on the other hand who
have some intelligence and ambition, especially if put to trades that
only occupy their hands, often do like instructive reading and will
pursue it in after life. They need a full supply of books'.[29]

It would be not surprising if the daughters of Victorian households
had not acquired a taste for intellectual reading. The curriculum
controlled by the head of household for those given some home
education, and by the clergymen who dominated the governing boards
of the schools for daughters of gentlefolk and middle-class merchants
and bankers, had been purged of any subjects of substance except in
those rare Nonconformist homes which we have noted, and left with a
vapid diet of light literature, music, some languages and drawing.

The most serious criticism that the pioneers of an equal and identical curriculum for girls faced from the politicians, clergy and academics who opposed them was that they risked making young women unladylike and unpious. After achieving the access which had been steadily eroded since the medieval and Renaissance growth of schools, women caught in the time of the Anglo-Catholic revival of a pressured industrial society, found that they had been placed on a pedestal of role-playing from which descent not infrequently meant the loss of marriage and therefore of security. Tertullian was alive and well: marriage and no external career, or the freedom of Aspasia but no respectability except for a gifted upper-class few.

Women's progress through the development of educational opportunity has all the hallmarks of the Sisyphus syndrome. Opportunity gained has had to be rewon and retaken after reversal in a cyclical reflection of changing views of Church and State on the appropriate roles for which both are preparing the boys and girls in the homes (girls did not even reach the classroom at certain periods). It is arguable that the leadership of the Church has used its power and control of provision, until very recently, to reinforce automatic male priority for whatever was rationed at the time; school places to learn the Latin that opened up clerical work; grammar-school education for the knowledge necessary for trade, marketing and access to political structures; liberal education which upper-class young men seized as of right, however wealthy, as the key to a dynamic open society. Education is the key lifechance to money, power, influence and reform. Differentiation of education means different outcomes in the power structures of Church and State alike.

The Church and education today

Much has been left out of this brief historical overview. It would be possible, given space, to trace the gradual changes in male and female curricula over the centuries where this has been controlled by church interests. Noticeable differences in educational policy for girls and women between systems and countries which are respectively Catholic, Anglican, Lutheran or other Protestant in their main faith, have been noted in Europe.[30] In countries which are strongly Catholic (Italy, Ireland), both the system and the curriculum are strongly sex-segregated, with a heavy accent in girls' educational programs on their future family roles or on occupational preparation for traditionally 'feminine' labour market sectors. (In Ireland, grammar school education is still mainly provided by the church schools.) In strongly secular countries where church schools are a minority of total provision and with mainly Protestant faith (Denmark, Britain), there is a wider overlap between programs attractive to boys and girls respectively. One phenomenon is however common to most countries. A very high proportion of the single-sex girls' schools which remain are Catholic or Anglican schools.

There are two trends in church education today which are likely to be detrimental to girls' advancement, and to the advancement of women teachers. The first is the increased laicisation of the schools formerly run by Catholic and Anglican sisters. The second is the increasing reorganisation of these and other single-sex schools as coeducational. The laicisation of church girls' schools has resulted in a steady replacement of women principals and female staff by male equivalents, and even the appointment of male heads to girls' schools. There is no recorded case of the appointment of a woman head to a boys' school. This, apart from removing promotion opportunities for women staff, also removes role models of women in leadership from the girls' schools. There is a growing research-based hypothesis that the presence of women in leadership and of women teachers of maths and science, is one of the principal positive influences which encourage girls to take 'non-traditional' options in secondary and higher education. The further move towards coeducation raises more complex issues. Over the last decade, there has been conflicting research evidence about differential achievements of boys and girls respectively in mixed and in single-sex schools. Some of the current theory is based on anecdotal rather than research-based evidence, but scholarly work in the area of the teaching of maths and science in Britain and in the USA suggests that girls perform better in an all-girls environment, but boys better in mixed schools. The issue is one of some complexity, and merits study in its own right, but to the extent that church authorities are among the main providers of single-sex schools in Australia, the policy of reorganisation would justify more serious review than perhaps it has received so far, in the specific context of the impact of coeducation on equal and the same education for girls and boys.

At a time when the ordination of women is being debated more seriously than ever against increasing evidence that there is either no scriptural authority for the ordination of men, or there is authority for both sexes, the messages that our children receive in school about male and female roles can no longer remain irrelevant to the Church.

Moreover, social and technological reconstruction are affecting both the labour market and changing sex roles in the home, creating added societal stresses. It becomes more critical that thinking members of the active Christian community remove stereotypes from past church history as models on which to base current church policies, and look at society as its needs face us today. If God put 51 per cent of the world's brains in female heads, He did not intend us to bury our talents in a narrow field.[31] And it is as important that the boys in our schools receive the message that men and women are equal in the sight of God as that our girls learn to expect to achieve to the height of their talent and not according to a perceivedly predestined and separate role.

As one looks back on the Church's gifts to women, one sees that they equal neither in scale nor quality the gifts which we have given the Church and our own society. We have received second measure over the centuries, in return for martyrdom in early Christianity, and community service throughout the years, stitching together again the fabric of societies torn by wars—often religious wars. The steps to be taken to enable the feminine perspective to be heard in the government of the Christian Church as well as under its marquees and behind the coffee urns, will not be achieved unless the boys as well as the girls in our schools learn from the church leadership that 'there is neither male nor female but we are all one in Christ'. The Church is built on a rock. The children in our schools are our future rock, and we cannot build a future on the sands of past educational discrimination or present indifference. Talents are equally distributed between the sexes, and education remains the key lifechance in achieving the fulfilment of these. Women's role in the Church is to use their God-given talents wherever these may lie, and the role of educators is to develop actual gifts and not assumed 'femininity' according to a male-defined Tertullian perception of female inferiority. Women's role is to lead a strengthened Christian community in an increasingly lost world.

3

Sexism and fundamentalism

BARBARA THIERING

The word 'fundamentalism' has been introduced to the public in recent years by journalists. It was applied first to the Muslim revolution, which revived a traditional sexual code and grounded it in primitive Islamic theology. Then, with the visit to Australia of the American Protestant preacher, the Reverend Jerry Falwell, in 1982, the word was more correctly used for his combination of biblical dogmatism with an absolutist attitude to moral values. A group called 'Toleration—a coalition against fanaticism' sprang into existence in Sydney in reaction to his visit. In 1984 Jerry Falwell led a significant faction in the US presidential election, and has been observed to be moving towards a new kind of American established religion which endangers the separation of Church and State.

Originally, the word 'fundamentalism' was used simply for an attitude to the Bible. There is little doubt in the minds of most historians of Christianity that it is a recent phenomenon, and one which is so at variance with classical Christianity that, if we were back in the days of orthodoxy, it would have to be called a heresy. It came into existence in the late nineteenth century, and from its inception flourished in the southern states of the USA. After the First World War it became characteristic of Sydney Protestantism, as its main weapon in the battle against Roman Catholicism. The effect of fundamentalism was to give to the Bible the same sort of authority, based on infallibility, which the Roman Catholic Church had declared for the Pope in 1870. Both Protestants and Catholics were setting up an intellectual authority against the invasions of scientific rationalism, but fundamentalism stepped right into the camp of science by claiming that the factual statements of the Bible had the same kind of truth as scientific descriptions, took priority over them, and were 'proved' by the methods of science.

One reason why biblical fundamentalism flourished in Sydney was that a form of it had been planted here from the beginning. In 1788 the Wesleyan revival had thoroughly permeated the working classes in England, and it was from their lowest levels that the convict founders came. The first chaplain, the Reverend Richard Johnson, was appointed by the Society for the Propagation of the Gospel. In Manning Clark's words,

> [h]is sponsors entertained great hopes for the success of his work, that he would prove a blessing to lost creatures, and hasten the coming of that day when the wilderness became a fruitful field, when the heathen would put off their savageness, and put on the graces of the spirit. To assist him the Society provided a library of tracts and books . . . In addition to Bibles, Books of Common Prayer, and Psalters, Johnson took with him copies of Osterwald on the necessity for reading the scriptures, Kettlewell's offices for the penitent, copies of exercises against lying, of cautions to profane swearers, of exhortations to chastity, of dissuasions from stealing, together with the most fervent wishes from the board of the Society that the divine blessing might go with him.[1]

The Bible was already a symbol of class struggle, and remained so for a long time wherever there was a deep resentment against the ruling classes. The historical circumstances meant that it was given an extraordinary position here as the sole source of religious authority. The convicts and working-class settlers were going to a place where they had no church, and they lacked a sufficient sense of derivation from the Church in England to be able to claim to carry its essence among themselves, unlike the Pilgrim Fathers in North America. Thus, probably for the first time in its history, Christianity was planted in a country on the basis of the Bible alone, rather than on the Bible and the Church, the two traditional pillars.

Further, the dependence on the Bible was held by people who were largely illiterate, and made little connection between relying on it and reading it. Thus began the tradition of making it a magic talisman, no different from a cross or a set of rosary beads, an unsuitable basis on which to add a belief, started in the early twentieth century, that its contents consisted of rational propositions about the physical world.

In the United States, the emphasis was not so much on the Bible as a symbol or magical object as on the Bible as a depository of Christian beliefs that were said to be fundamental and unshakeable, something against which adherence to religion could be measured. Its history has been traced by Gabriel Hebert in his book *Fundamentalism and the Church of God*. Its formal phase began with the publication by the Testimony Publishing Company of Chicago, Illinois, between 1909 and 1915, of three million booklets free of charge to 'every pastor, evangelist, missionary, theological professor, theological student, Sunday School superintendent, YMCA and YWCA secretary, in the English speaking world, so far as the addresses of all these can be obtained'.[2]

The essentials of belief that were called fundamentals in these booklets were emphatically Protestant; in fact Roman Catholicism was classed with heresies. They included: the doctrine of the Atonement (that Christ died vicariously for sinners); the deity of Christ; the reality of hell and the devil; the virgin birth of Christ; the second advent. The authority for these was the Bible, said to be a revelation direct from God, infallible and inerrant. The treatment of it which was then coming into use as a result of both Darwinism and the new comparative literature from the Ancient Near East was condemned as fallacious if not wicked, because it implied that the Bible was a record of human development in a particular place at a particular time, a point of view which was said could not be held side by side with a belief that it was a direct revelation from God in true form for all time.

Fundamentalism rapidly became a bad word, associated with bigotry and fanaticism, and in 1955 the Reverend John Stott said that he preferred in its place the term 'conservative evangelical'. This label was accepted, and is still proudly worn by a very large section of the Protestant Church in Sydney, especially the Anglicans. John Stott himself was among those considered for the position of Archbishop of Sydney in 1982.

In their original form, as stated in the series of booklets, the selection of 'fundamentals' had no precedent in the previous creeds of the Christian Church. The doctrine of Atonement was of course a central tenet of the Reformation, being one of its weapons against the temporal power of Rome, for it meant that every person could gain salvation directly by identification with Christ's death without the intermediacy of a priest. But its meaning had always included admission into a community, which was entered by means of the symbolic death of baptism. Without a strong emphasis on Church, the idea of atonement simply becomes a piece of magical thinking, making no sense, and this is the form in which these booklets teach it.

A belief in the second coming of Christ was held in the first century AD, when they were using a calendar dated from the creation of the world which was about to reach the year 4000, and under contemporary Pythagorean influence they believed that a great crisis ought to happen in that year. Once the Christian era replaced their calendar, the basis for belief in a second coming was removed, and such expectations moved further and further to the fringes of the Church.

Doctrines such as the virgin birth, hell and the devil, were part of the contemporary popular language of the hellenistic period, and were simply accepted and to some extent refined by the Church; they never taught them in opposition to accepted belief, as supernaturalists now try to do; miracles are no longer a common assumption. Further, there never had been such a doctrine of the Bible—infallible and inerrant—even in the Reformation. It was not the detailed information that it contained, but its power as a means of independence of priests, that made the Protestants hold to it. Luther stood quite cheerfully in judgment upon it, selecting those parts of the New Testament he liked and deriding others. The Apostles' Creed contains no statement about the Bible. The attribution of infallibility to the Bible seems to be a direct reaction to the doctrine of papal infallibility promulgated in 1870. In both cases, the hardening of authority was a response to a loss of actual power.

The label 'evangelical', now associated with fundamentalist belief, has been removed from its original context of meaning. The evangelical revival in eighteenth-century England was a recovery of fervour, aroused by the powerful preaching of men like Wesley and Whitefield. Preaching the gospel gives the word 'evangelical', the gospel being a challenge to personal commitment to the figure of Christ. Its meaning is discussed in the Bible, but could be understood without it, being preserved in a continuing community. The Bible became secondarily connected with the evangelical revival, because it was the working classes in England who were aroused by it and given the strength to stand up against the ruling classes, whose advantage was their education. Schooled in the principles of the Enlightenment, they had reduced religion to a rational formula which is certainly not found in the Bible. But the Bible does contain the gospel, the good news, and so it became the manual of the uneducated in their fight against cold rationalism. Now, however, the word 'evangelical' is used for a process of strict reasoning from an assumption that the Bible is a lawbook containing a set of absolute propositions. Enthusiasm and fervour are on the whole distrusted by the Evangelicals, as shown by their reaction to the charismatic outbreak of the 1970s.

The best-known product of biblical fundamentalism, still very much current as a matter of legal, educational and sociological concern, is the doctrine of creationism, which is opposed to the theory of evolution as an account of the way species came into existence. The so-called 'monkey trial' in the United States in 1926 dramatised issues which are still being fought out in their legislation and have now found their way here, with the growth of fundamentalist schools as part of a new phase of private education. Children are being taught that God created human beings directly in their present form, and all species independently, and that it is a matter not only of science but of personal salvation and moral wholeness that this should be believed.

The answer of academic biblical scholars to this and related questions is derived from both theology and historical records. The accounts of the creation and flood found in Mesopotamia in the second half of the nineteenth-century show beyond doubt that they belong to the category of myth. They are intertwined with the stories of gods, and are a kind of primitive metaphysics: an attempt to talk about the nature of reality in terms drawn from human experience. They picture the way things must have been in the light of the way things are now; for example, since conflict between opposing forces leads to a creative synthesis, they pictured the mother goddess Tiamat fighting against the hero god Marduk and being defeated, with the result that the physical world came into existence. The Old Testament is using the same sort of language to put forward a different philosophical point of view: that the world is unified, entirely under the control of a single god, not the helpless victim of a cosmic dialectic. There is every reason to suppose that Genesis is consciously revising and purifying an existing creation story in the interests of monotheism and the observance of the sabbath. Its concern is with theology and ritual, not with natural science.

Theology has also recognised the place of myth and symbol in theological language. As soon as we use language at all, we are dealing in images and symbols, not with things directly. The religious language of the past used them far more extensively. To say that 'God created' is to use a picture derived from our own experience, not from any evidence in the natural world. We create things, and because of that we say that what is out there must be created. 'Creation' is simply a human category of thought. How can we—dare we—say that the whole of the universe really and actually corresponds to human categories of thought?

By the same process, we say that God, acting like a person, is a super-person, and because the dominant persons are male, he also is male. His 'providence' (also a human category) is symbolised by calling him 'father'. But even in Old Testament times they saw the fallacy of calling God a super-person. After the exile the Jews stressed transcendence, not anthropomorphism. So far off did the Jews place God that they would not even pronounce the Name. The Christians, to preserve this insight, inserted a human-divine person for the sake of those who still needed a picture.

Fundamentalism as moral absolutism

The second phase of fundamentalism began to appear in the 1960s and 1970s, in England and America, and was rapidly taken up in Australia. The excesses of sexual experimentation of the sixties led to increasing interest in and concentration on abnormalities, and the public media were the places where the interest was expressed. The degree of explicitness was becoming hurtful to some, and sensitive observers needed to protest. Their cause was taken up by religious people who had been increasingly driven into a corner on doctrinal and dogmatic questions, but who found with relief that they had something to say on moral questions. The Church does act as a repository of traditional wisdom on human behaviour, and can still claim to be the custodian of moral law.

But then a difficulty arose for Protestants, who as the dominant tradition in England, the United States and Australia found themselves given the new responsibility. Where is their moral law? Once again they suffered from their separation from the Church's magisterium, whose work has been to adapt continually in the light of enshrined principles. Their only alternative authority was the Bible, and to this many of them turned, encouraged by the definition it had already been given, that it was a collection of fundamentals which had absolute authority. Those fundamentals were now seen as moral propositions.

The 'fundamentals' of the Moral Majority, put very simply, are: God's law says that you must live in a family consisting of a husband and wife and their two or three immediate offspring. Monogamy is right, divorce is wrong, abortion is wrong, homosexuality is wrong. A woman's first duty is to be a wife and mother. The man's first duty is to be the provider, and care and emotion are not so important to him. The man is the authority and head, the woman must defer to him. Behaviour depends on sex roles, which divide all human beings into two different categories. Marriage is the only healthy condition for adults; other conditions are either inferior or perverse.

These tenets have only to be stated to show what their origin is: they describe the social customs of Western capitalist countries for about the last 100 years. They may or may not be a good way to live, but there is no evidence whatsoever that they are divine law, or have any absolute validity. It is untrue and quite misleading to say that they are contained in the Bible: they are not. Neither the Old nor the New Testaments knows anything about the nuclear family.

In the Old Testament, pre-exilic Israel lived in tribal groupings which were undergoing a process of urbanisation. The normal way of life was to live in large settlements outside the towns consisting of a patriarchal figure, his several wives and concubines, their numerous children, and large numbers of servants or slaves. Women and slaves had the legal status of animals, as shown in the Ten Commandments: 'You shall not covet your neighbour's wife, or his slave, or his ox, or his ass.' The wife of a slave belonged to her master, not to her husband.

In the New Testament, the main teaching on family life is that the family unit is undesirable. With increased urbanisation family groups were becoming more usual, and the Christian Church led the way in a process of preventing them hardening into a norm. It now appears, from increased knowledge of the contemporary setting, that one of the main reasons why the Church succeeded was that it included an attempt to substitute community for family. Aided by the new interest in the vocation of celibacy that was coming into Judaism from Hellenistic thought, it taught that the highest way of life was one of sexual abstinence, as it released one for a spiritual vocation or life of social dedication. Marriage was a regrettable necessity, and married couples should not be an isolated unit but be closely integrated into the community, so that they did not even have private property but gave all their property into the common stock. Relationships in these communities were to take priority over natural ones, and if necessary be a substitute for them. Jesus is credited with saying: 'If any one comes to me and does not hate his own father and mother and wife and children and brothers and sisters . . . he cannot be my disciple'

(Lk 14:26). He rejected his mother and brothers and sisters and, turning to the friends around him said that they were his mother and family. The members of such spiritual families called each other 'mother', 'father', 'sister' and 'brother'. St Paul said that his own unmarried state was a preferable one, that a married man is divided in his loyalties, but that when a man is married his duty to his wife is to love her. Nothing is said about having to provide for her—both were supported by the community.

The nuclear family code, far from being derived from the Bible, is the product of the growth of the middle class in the nineteenth-century. Patricia Grimshaw[3] has seen this also. She traces the breakdown of the earlier working-class rural family, in which all the members shared equally in production under the patriarchal head, to the change where the father went to work outside the home, as the employee of another man. He earned enough to keep his whole family, so the wife gained greater leisure, and began to elevate the care and education of children to a full-time task. It was a more egalitarian arrangement in many ways, and at first was treated as the model life. But the husband compensated for his own subordination by limiting his wife's chances to be independent of him.

It may be added that the nuclear family code also derives from the growth of cities and suburbs, at a considerable distance from one another because of the use of cars. Women were confined to their houses, one to each house, and were expected to accept the imprisonment as ordained by nature or by God.

It is simply not possible to give a theological sanction to these arrangements: the matter is one for sociologists and psychologists to debate. Another common attitude does, however, come closer to New Testament teaching: that the male in the family is to be the head. Ephesians 5 states this explicitly, basing it on a doctrine of hierarchy in the Church. Sydney Anglicans, for whom the Bible, defined as a set of propositions, is the ultimate authority, use the passage to prevent women being ordained, as the office involves the exercise of authority.

It has always been the task of theology to adapt Christian teachings to the conditions of a new age, in order to educate that age in its own language. From the very beginning there have existed side by side in the Church those who have learned the new language, and those who have not yet applied it. The passage in Ephesians is an example of this. Elsewhere in the New Testament it is apparent that Christians, under the direct guidance of Jesus, had attacked the hierarchical and exclusive Jewish system that lay behind them, one in which priests were superior to laymen, and Gentiles were the lowest of all. Jesus himself, although not an Aaronite priest, had adopted the functions of priests by granting forgiveness of sins ('the Son of Man has authority on earth to forgive sins'). Once it had rejected the privileges of Aaronite priests, the Church was able to break away from Judaism. All unclean persons—slaves, Gentiles and women—were now given full rights. The Lord was to act, not as a superior, but as a servant, as was vividly illustrated by the washing of feet at the Last Supper. Christianity does not stand for hierarchy, but for the equality of all before God. But every now and then in the Church's history there has been a return to hierarchy, with the priesthood or clergy claiming a superior position. Such a distortion has always been followed by a lay revolution. The last great occasion was the Protestant Reformation, which broke the power of Rome. We are at present witnessing a revolt of another significant part of the laity—women. If the spirit of Christ is still in the Church, the reformation of which they are at the centre will lead to major historical consequences. The group of Sydney women who nailed a new Ninety-Five Theses to the door of St Andrew's cathedral in 1983 were not simply being provocative, but recognising the tradition in which they stand.

It is not difficult to foresee a great change in theological language also. To speak of God as male is, as suggested above, a culturally determined symbol. Such crude anthropomorphism is again being challenged, and the result will almost certainly be a purer doctrine of God.

In the meantime, however, the dominant churches in Sydney are sufficiently opposed to the ordination of women to have claimed an exemption under the NSW Anti-Discrimination Act. Section 56 not only allows religious bodies to refuse to ordain women, racially different people, and the physically handicapped, but to refuse to appoint them in any capacity whatever. They will not necessarily use the right, of course, but the exemption is there. A reader of the New Testament might point out that to claim it would be directly contrary to the stand Jesus took against the Jews, when he accepted women, Gentiles, the blind and the lame, the rejects, in other words. We appear to be in the ironical situation where the state is enforcing a Christian law in the place of the churches.

It is, of course, not only biblical fundamentalism that sanctions the rejection of women. Some of the same attitudes are found in churches which rely on tradition rather than the Bible. A concentration on prayer and worship, characteristic of Roman Catholic, Anglo-Catholic and Orthodox churches, tends to emphasise ritual purity and to oppose it to sexuality, with the exclusion of women as the symbols of sex.

It is evident that women are excluded from religious practice for a great variety of reasons, and this means that it is not simply from caprice or habit. It is much more deeply based in the human psyche, and has to do with the link between sex and religion that Freud observed. It seems clear enough that the suppression of one leads to the stimulation of the other. While women are understood, and understand themselves, as primarily objects of sex, they will be found to be an impediment to religion. But the higher forms of religion have gone beyond primitivism or fundamentalism on this matter. Neither women nor men are treated as simply objects of sex to one another. 'In Christ there is neither male nor female' is a statement derived from the central Christian doctrine of reconciliation of opposites, the doctrine on which the Church itself was founded as a community accepting Gentiles on an equal basis with Jews. For Christians, there is enough within our own tradition to be able to point out that current official attitudes are a debasement of the faith. Both fundamentalism and sexism are distortions; it is for our own generation of reformers to point this out.

4

The ordination of women
On whose side is the Bible?

KEVIN GILES

In the continuing discussion among Anglicans in Australia about the ordination of women, biblical teaching has been a key issue. Those opposed to women ministers often insist that Scripture is the basis of their objection. The appeal to the Bible is most frequently made by Anglicans of Protestant Evangelical persuasion (sometimes called Low Church) but it is also raised by those of Anglo-Catholic persuasion (sometimes called High Church). The biblical teaching that is believed to be threatened is, however, not the same for both parties. Protestant Anglicans claim that the apostolic comments about women's subordination is the main concern. The Church should do nothing to overthrow this principle. In particular it should not set women over men in the church by allowing them to teach from the pulpit. Catholic Anglicans, on the other hand, make much of the fact that Jesus chose twelve men as apostles and no women. The apostles, they claim, are the first ministers and set a pattern for all times. For this reason the Church should not allow women to preside at the altar.

At first sight both objections seem to raise insurmountable obstacles to the ordination of women. Few Christians would want to deliberately contradict what is perceived as the clear teaching of the New Testament in matters of faith and conduct. A critical evaluation of these arguments and a fresh consideration of what the Bible actually says about the ministry of women suggests however, that in neither instance is the case as clear-cut as we have been led to believe.

The appeal to Scripture on this issue is more complex than many realise for three main reasons. First, the New Testament says very little, if anything, about ordination as such. The Church of the apostles was a lay institution. Neither men nor women are ever called priests; we find no instance of one person in sole charge of a church, and great freedom and variety was allowed in patterns of ministry. Second, the' Bible does not seem to speak with one voice. Numerous examples can be found of women involved in all kinds of spiritual leadership in the New Testament Church (we will discuss these later) but at the same time we find texts which subordinate women and demand their silence (for example 1 Cor. 14:34; 1 Tim. 2:11–12). Third, the ordination of women raises the thorny problem of the extent to which cultural differences should be taken into account. Women in the apostolic age were, as a general rule, married in their very early teens, normally pregnant or nursing from then on, seldom given formal education and granted few rights in common law. Should we then directly apply statements addressed to women in that context to women living in modern Western society where none of these restrictions exists?

The central issue

In this debate the fundamental issue is in fact not women's ordination but whether or not we Christians are going to continue to insist that because a woman is a woman and for no other reason she must be excluded from leadership in the Church. The present position is that no matter what the training, spiritual gifts or perceived calling of a woman may be she cannot lead in Church solely because she is a woman. Those opposed to the ordination of women hotly affirm their belief in the personal equality of the sexes, but when the situation is analysed it is soon seen that women are not being treated as full human beings. The more prestigious, ego-enhancing, leadership positions are all reserved for men and the jobs men do not want such as missionary work in difficult and dangerous locations, minding children, teaching Scripture in schools, the flowers and the tea are left to women. It is like saying we believe women are equal but they can only be nurses not doctors, articled clerks not lawyers, voters not parliamentarians—as was indeed the case once.

For long centuries the Church simply reflected the attitude of society to women and no one questioned their lowly status. It has been the dramatic change in the position of women in modern Western society that has forced the Church to begin to think afresh. God's work in history has written the agenda for us. Society at large has granted women equality of status and opportunity. The only institution now

left which still raises discrimination against women to the level of
principle is the Church. Does the Bible demand this? I for one think
not.

Jesus

Jesus always granted women equality of consideration.[1] Despite the
fact that in first-century Jewish culture, as a general rule, women
were subordinated to men, we find virtually no trace of this in Jesus'
attitude or teaching. He called women as his disciples, he taught them
and he died for them as well as for men. He did not criticise the
woman of Samaria when she preached about him to her men kinsfolk
(John 4), and after the resurrection he sent two women to proclaim the
news of his victory over the grave to the frightened male disciples
(Matt. 28:10, John 20:17). Men of his day, as today, insisted that
women should keep to women's things, but not Jesus. He commended
Mary for listening to his teaching (usually a male preserve) and
criticised Martha for her preoccupation with domestic chores (Luke
10:38–42). The thought that woman's noblest calling was to bear and
care for children Jesus challenged by stating that hearing and
obeying his word must always come first (Luke 11:27–28). It was the
same for women and men. As far as marriage was concerned Jesus
said not one word which would suggest that he believed husbands had
been set over wives. He saw the ideal pattern in Genesis.[2] Before sin
entered the world man and woman were created as personal equals.
The goal of marriage was not an obedient servile wife but the union of
two persons. Both parties were equally responsible for the success or
failure of this God-initiated bond (Mark 10:6–12).

The one possible exception in Jesus' bestowal of equality upon
women was his choosing of the twelve apostles who were all men. So
much has been made of this by opponents of women's ordination that
one would think it was the central point of Jesus' teaching about the
sexes. Two weighty reasons and numerous incidental ones can be
given as to why Jesus did not include women among the twelve. First,
the twelve apostles symbolised the formation of the new people of God,
the new Israel. As the original twelve patriarchs had been men, men
needed to be chosen as the founding fathers of the new Israel if the
symbolism was to be recognised. Second, the foremost task of the
twelve apostles was *to bear witness* to the life, death and resurrection
of Jesus. In Jewish law a woman's testimony was of no value. As

males alone could be witnesses Jesus had to choose men. We might also remember that the twelve were all Jews but we find no one arguing that all ministers should be converted Jews![3] An isolated fact should, however, not be singled out. What is important is Jesus' general attitude and his specific teaching.

This we suggest shows that Jesus gave no place to the thought that women should be subordinated in the home or society but rather insisted that they should be granted equality of consideration. But as he said nothing directly about the structure of the Church or its ministry it is only by inference that we can draw him in to support equality of opportunity in ministry. Nevertheless I believe this conclusion is the only one that follows naturally from the evidence.

The Acts and Epistles

Direct insight into the ordering and life of the Church is found not in the Gospels but in the Acts and the Epistles. The relevant material on ministry divides itself into three categories: theological or normative statements, descriptive statements and regulative statements. We will consider these in turn.

Theological or normative statements

It is important to remember that it is gifts of ministry not ordination which is of central interest in the New Testament.[4] Leadership was given in the congregation as the Holy Spirit raised up and empowered individuals. In a few cases the laying on of hands is mentioned, but not always, and even then it is only a prayerful recognition of gifts already possessed. The following texts reveal the basic apostolic understanding of Christian ministry.

> Acts 2:17–18 In the last days it shall be, God declares, that I will pour out my Spirit upon all flesh, and your sons and your daughters shall prophesy, and your young men shall see visions and your old men shall dream dreams; yea, and on my menservants and my maidservants in those days I will pour out my Spirit and they shall prophesy.

This prediction by the prophet Joel, Peter understood, was fulfilled when the Holy Spirit was given at Pentecost. The gift of the Spirit meant that men *and* women would be empowered to proclaim the

Word of God. The gift of the Spirit carried with it gifts of ministry for the whole Church.

> 1 Cor. 12:7 To each is given the manifestation of spirit for the common good.

In 1 Corinthians chapters 12 and 14 Paul enunciates his view of ministry. In the congregation the Spirit gives to each member a gift or gifts for the edification of the whole.[5] Some teach, some speak in tongues, some lead in singing, some have gifts of healing, some are administrators and so on. It is impossible to read into Paul's discussion the idea that only men are given these gifts or the more important ones are reserved for men. In order of importance he ranks prophecy as the most important congregational ministry (1 Cor. 14:1–3), and interestingly this is one gift he specifically says women exercised (1 Cor. 11:5). Virtually the same teaching, again devoid of sexual bias, is found in Rom. 12:4–8 and Eph. 4:4–16.

> 1 Peter 4:10–11 As each has received a gift employ it for one another, as good stewards of God's varied grace: whoever speaks, as one who utters oracles of God, whoever renders service, as one who renders it by the strength which God supplies.

Once more the teaching is clear. Ministry flows from the gift or gifts given. It has nothing to do with one's sex.

Descriptive statements

The correctness of our reading of these primary theological statements about ministry is convincingly proved by the fact that the apostolic description of ministry in the early churches fits this picture perfectly.[6] Luke, Paul and John[7] all mention women who prophesied in Christian assemblies (Acts 21:9, 1 Cor. 11:5, Rev. 2:20). This is a very important point, for prophecy is unquestionably a form of preaching[8] and in order of importance it ranks before ordinary teaching.[9] We should not be at all surprised to hear of the spiritual leadership of these women, for in Old Testament days God frequently raised up women prophets, some of them married women, to lead his people.[10] Paul commends his fellow labourers in preaching the Gospel, Mary (Rom. 16:6), Tryphaena, Tryphosa and Persis (Rom. 16:12) and Euodia and Syntyche (Phil. 4:3). Luke warmly describes the exceptional teaching gifts of the married couple Prisca and Aquila who taught Apollos 'the way of God more accurately' (Acts 18:24–28).

Luke, and Paul who also knows this couple, usually name Prisca first which may suggest she had some preeminence in the relationship. In the larger circle of apostles which included such people as Paul, Barnabas, James, Silas etc., Paul mentions Junia (Rom. 16:7). Our modern translations usually give a male name Junias in the text but recent research has shown that no commentator before the twelfth-century accepted the poorer reading which gave her a sex change.[11] Twice Paul speaks of women deacons (Rom. 16:1; 1 Tim. 2:9), and twice he uses the term elder of women (1 Tim. 5:2 Tit. 2:3).

We need not go on. The picture is clear. Any discussion of the ordination of women that does not mention these facts is incomplete and unconvincing.

Regulative statements

Often the apostles were asked to give direction on specific problems that had arisen in a given congregation. In many of these cases it is extremely difficult to know exactly what the problem was because we have so little information to go on. We need not consider all these passages as most of them do not bear upon the topic we are discussing. There are just three that demand consideration. The first allows women to preach in church; the other two would seem to disallow them to do so.

The first passage is 1 Cor. 11:2–16. Apparently the Corinthians had asked Paul about appropriate head coverings in church. The apostle replies that the tradition established is that men when they pray or prophesy should leave their heads uncovered and when women lead in prayer or prophesy they should cover their heads (1 Cor. 11:4–5). We do not know what sort of head covering was used or what it symbolised in that society. Translators often add the word veil but this term does not appear in the Greek. By a strange twist of ecclesiastical exegesis this advice was taken to mean that when women came to church as passive spectators they should wear decorative hats! The main point, the apostolic acceptance of the declarative ministry of women, was completely overlooked.

The Corinthians also asked Paul about other matters to do with their meetings as sometimes, it would seem, they had become dis-orderly. At the end of 1 Cor. 14 Paul comes to deal with these questions. Three times he advises some group to keep silent. If there is no one to interpret, let the tongue speakers 'keep silent in church' (14:28). If a prophet is speaking and another has a revelation 'let the first be silent' (14:30). If the women want to ask questions, presumably of the prophets, 'let them ask their husbands at home'—they should keep silent (14:34–35). Paul is obviously not forbidding women from preaching as he has just allowed that women prophesy in church (1 Cor. 11:5). The prohibition seems to apply solely to asking questions which disrupt the service. These verses are not without their difficulties[12] as we do not know the exact nature of the problem, but an exegesis such as we have given is preferable to one that reads them as a prohibition against women preaching and so sets Paul at odds with himself.

The final passage is the most difficult by far. The problem facing the Church addressed in the epistle we know as 1 Timothy is clear. The Christian community was under seige by treacherous teachers who were leading God's people into error. In Ephesus where Timothy was, this had been initiated by women. They had claimed the right to teach with absolute authority. Speaking on this situation, which is carefully spelt out, Paul says 'I permit no woman to teach, to have dominion over a man' (1 Tim 2:12). The word translated 'dominion' (*authentein*) by the NEB and the RV and 'authority' by the RSV only appears here in the New Testament and refers to the exercise of absolute power. It defines the sort of preaching that is forbidden. Paul forbids these women from preaching as if what they said was the infallible Word of God.[13] This means that we do not have here a general prohibition against women teaching but rather a prohibition against a specific form and manner of teaching which Paul would not allow of men either (see Tit. 1:10–11).

Paul's use of this very strong term shows that he is not speaking about ordinary preaching. As John Stott points out, the Christian preacher has no authority in himself; he is but a lowly 'steward' whose tasks it is to point to Christ and allow his Word to speak.[14] The somewhat morbid preoccupation that traditionalists have with this text because it singles out women is quite misplaced.[15] The condemnation of an authoritarian type of ministry, in this instance exercised by women, fits into the general New Testament condemnation of ministerial leadership which adopts the power model rather than the servant model.[16] Jesus warned against those who wanted 'to lord it over' others as the Gentiles did, saying, 'it shall not be so among you; but whoever would be great among you must be your servant' (Matt. 20:20–26 and par). The apostle Peter commands Christian leaders not to 'domineer' over the flock but with other Christians to clothe themselves with humility (1 Peter 5:1–5).

Diotrephes, 'who likes to put himself first', is rebuked by John (3 John 9), while Paul singles out certain 'insubordinate men', in his letter to Titus, and says of them 'they have no right to teach' (Tit. 1:11).

The subordination of women

Our case should be able to rest at this point, for we have proved that the Spirit did give gifts of ministerial leadership to women in the apostolic Church, but it cannot, for the opponents of women's ordination insist that the principle of subordination in itself is an absolute barrier. We are told that God has permanently and unilaterally subordinated either all women to all men or all wives to their husbands and this means that all women, or at the best all married women, are excluded from positions of leadership in the Church on this basis alone. They must continue with the tea-making, the flowers and minding the children for ever and ever.

What evidence do we have for this far-reaching assertion? It is not supported by the creation stories of Genesis 1 and 2, for before sin entered the world man and woman shared the dominion of the earth (Gen. 1:28) and were 'partners' together in marriage (Gen. 2:18 NEB). The Fall was the time man began to domineer over woman (Gen. 3:16) but no responsible theologian suggests this gives the Christian ideal.[17] Not one word on the lips of Jesus can be found to support it and much of what he said and did is quite opposed to it. John and Luke, who rival Paul for the scope of their contribution to the New Testament, never mention it. The evidence consists of four simple exhortations, three by Paul and one by Peter, that wives should be subordinate, Paul's discussion about marriage in Eph. 5:21ff and a few verses taken in isolation from 1 Cor. 11:2–15. Let us then briefly evaluate this evidence on which so much is built.

The simple exhortations addressed to wives to be subordinate are all clearly set in a cultural context.[18] Women living in a male-dominated society are asked for Christ's sake to be subordinate, as indeed are slaves living in a slave-owning society (Eph. 6:5). The apostles base their plea on practical considerations, not weighty theology. In Colossians 2:18 wives are to be subordinate because 'it is fitting in the Lord', in Titus 2:5 so that 'the word of God may not be discredited' and in 1 Peter 3:1 so that husbands 'who do not obey the word may be won without a word'. The only way to understand these exhortations properly is to see them as particular applications of the general Christian truth that in all personal relationships the believer should count others more worthy than himself (Luke 22:25–26, Rom. 12:10, Gal. 5:13, Eph. 4:2, Phil. 2:3 etc.).[19] The remaining parallel exhortation to wives, which we will now consider, explicitly makes this point.

Ephesians 5:21ff gives Paul's most profound discussion about marriage.[20] The exhortation to be subordinate again arises out of the same cultural setting, but because of the theological nature of this passage it stands apart from the texts we have just discussed. Paul begins his comments about marriage by affirming that the mark of the Spirit-filled Christian is subordination to others (5:21). This presumably includes husbands to wives as well as wives to husbands. Only after this does he ask wives in particular to subordinate themselves to their husbands, 'as to the Lord', for 'the husband is the head of the wife' (5:23). The moment we see the word 'head' we immediately think that Paul is giving to husbands the status of boss, director or decision-maker, but in the Greek language this word (*kephale:* head) does not necessarily bear this meaning.[21] When not used literally of the top part of the body it can have a range of meanings, and the appropriate one must be determined by the context. Here Paul explains that the 'headship' of the husband finds its perfect model in the total self-giving of Christ for his bride the Church (5:25). This self-giving is summed up in the greatest of all Christian words—*agape* (love). The resultant union, the apostle concludes, is not an hierarchical power structure but a one-flesh union (5:31). In this bond decisions are made by seeking to find a common mind. This wonderful picture of marriage cannot be used to limit the role of women; it can only be used to encourage a view of marriage in which mutual respect and mutual service prevail.

The last passage, 1 Cor. 11:2–16 is one of the most difficult pieces of Pauline reasoning to be found. Those who wish to subordinate women quote it because here Paul says that 'man is the head of woman' (11:3). The traditional understanding of the English word 'head' supports this idea, but modern scholarly opinion largely agrees that in this context Paul is using the word *kephale* in one of its most common metaphorical senses, so that it means 'source' such as when we speak in English of the source of a river as its head.[22] God is the head of Christ in the sense that he is the source of Christ's life, and man is the head of woman in the sense that Adam, the first man, was the source of life for Eve the first woman (Gen. 2). This 'headship' of the man, Paul believes, does not exclude women from leading in prayer or proclamation in the congregation (11:5), even if tradition demands that they cover their heads when they do this. To support his case that women should cover their heads when leading in worship Paul draws in several pragmatically based arguments, one of which is that woman was originally made for man (11:8), but the grand climax of the passage is reached when the apostle affirms that now 'in the Lord' both sexes are equally dependent on each other (11:11–12). In other words Paul himself negates his comment made in 11:8.[23]

We see then that all the talk about male 'headship' in the sense of authoritative leadership and decision-making has no theological foundation at all and is in fact quite contrary to Christian ideas of leadership which involve not power but service.[24] For practical reasons it may be wise if women often let men take the lead—it is still a fallen world and the male ego is very tender—but Scripture does not demand it and sometimes the opposite should be encouraged.

Conclusion

Our discussion about the ministry of women has shown not only that women should not be discriminated against in the Church but that the New Testament picture of ministry is very different from present-day practice. In the apostolic Church the ministry of the whole body of Christ is primary. Some people naturally stood out as leaders *par excellence* but no one was excluded on principle from offering leadership. It was the Holy Spirit who gave precedence to certain people: there was no ministerial elite on the basis of ordination. This is even so in the congregations influenced by Judaism where elders were nominated as congregational leaders. These elders are always a large group and their existence did not mean others were excluded from leading in the congregation in one way or another.

We cannot reproduce the New Testament Church. That age and its social forms are gone for ever. But we can work to regain a corporate dimension to Christian ministry which has been lost.[25] Ordination, I believe, must remain. It is now a necessary aspect of church order. But it must be extended. More people should be ordained. The ideal would be to have a team ministry in every parish. Within this team some could be stipendiary ministers, some self-supporting, some old, some young, some well trained theologically, some less so, some men, some women. Although they could all hold the same office their contribution would differ. The emphasis would be on the complementary character of their ministries. Women should be ordained so that they are free to offer the ministry which the body of Christ needs from them as women. Their ordination is only the first step in an exciting journey to a renewed Church. We have nothing to fear. There is nothing in the Bible which suggests that women should not be ordained as deacons or priests.

5

The ordination of women
The position of the Catholic Church

LEO HAY

The official position of the Catholic Church on the ordination of women is quite clear. It stated it in a 'Declaration on the question of the Admission of Women to the Ministerial Priesthood' published by the Vatican Sacred Congregation for the Doctrine of the Faith on 15 October 1976. Its position is expressed in the Introduction: 'the SCDF judges it necessary to recall that the Church, in fidelity to the example of the Lord, does not consider herself authorised to admit women to priestly ordination. The Sacred Congregation deems it opportune at the present juncture to explain this position of the Church.'[1]

In the rest of the declaration, the SCDF seeks confirmation of this position in 'the Church's constant tradition' (apart from 'a few heretical sects' the tradition of the non-ordination of women was so entrenched it was never questioned), the attitude of Christ (who, despite his non-conformist attitude to women, never invited any woman 'to become part of the Twelve'), the practice of the apostles (which was faithful to the attitude of Jesus), the permanent value of the attitude of Jesus and the apostles (it has not been proven that Jesus' and the apostles' attitude was determined by the social and cultural conditions of the time), the ministerial priesthood in the light of Christ (the priest is the sacrament of Christ to the point of being his very image; males alone can bear a natural resemblance to him and therefore alone can be priests) and in the light of the Church (Christ is consistently the Bridegroom, the Church, the Bride; only a male can represent Christ the Bridegroom).

I cannot here enter into these arguments in detail, but I would like to point out that they have not been fully accepted into the consciousness of the Catholic Church as convincing arguments. I would also like to draw attention to a statement by Karl Rahner soon after the publication of the declaration. Rahner declares that 'despite papal approval the Declaration is not a definitive decision; it is in principle reformable and it can be ... erroneous'.[2] And a little later, the theologian 'must bring to such a decree the respect it deserves; nevertheless he has not only the right but also the duty of examining it critically and under certain circumstances of contradicting it. The theologian respects the decree by attempting to appreciate as impartially as possible the reasons it puts forward ... even to the point of regarding it as objectively erroneous in its basic thesis. In the nineteenth and twentieth centuries (to say nothing at all about earlier times) there is a whole series of declarations of the Roman authorities on faith which have meanwhile been shown to be erroneous or at least largely obsolete'.[3] Here I wish simply to point to certain disquieting features of the document—features which, in some instances, seem to put it at variance with some of the directions foreshadowed in the Second Vatican Council (1962–65).

The structure of the document

The very structure of the document threatens good method. 'The Sacred Congregation,' it says in its introduction, 'deems it opportune at the present juncture to explain this position of the Church', this position being, as we know, 'No Women Priests'. Such a method assumes its own stated position as theologically certain without having to establish it on scriptural and theological grounds. Consequently it puts the whole burden of proof on its opponents to demonstrate that the attitude of Jesus and the disciples was conditioned by social and cultural circumstances. The question is not approached as an open one.

This method also runs the danger of selecting only that material which supports its a priori position. According to one commentator, 'the exegesis is selective and is marshalled to support the current teaching of the Magisterium. Such exegesis will convince no one who is not disposed to agree with the Declaration on grounds other than the strength of its exegesis'.[4] Rahner also points to a defect in method in the declaration's deduction from the composition of the College of the Twelve who can or cannot be 'an ordinary, simple leader of the community and president of the eucharistic celebration in a particular congregation of a later period'.[5] The document presents evidence of other tendentious choice of evidence in confirmation of its position.[6]

Apparent failure to consult

Another disquieting aspect of the declaration is its apparent failure to consult with the Church in a matter of such importance as this. There is no public indication that the views of the bishops throughout the world were sought and evaluated. On the level of Scriptural expertise we know that the Pontifical Biblical Commission considered the question of the ordination of women in April 1975 and again in April 1976. We know that the commission voted unanimously (17:0) that the New Testament does not settle in a clear way and once and for all whether women can be ordained priests; and by a 12:5 vote that Christ's plan would not be transgressed by permitting the ordination of women.[7] There is no mention of these findings in the declaration and no indication that the SCDF took the Biblical Commission's report into account.

Nor was there any consultation of the laity. The Second Vatican Council spoke emphatically of the prophetic role of the whole Church. 'The body of the faithful as a whole, anointed as they are by the Holy One, cannot err in matters of belief. Thanks to a supernatural sense of the faith which characterises the People as a whole, it manifests this unerring quality when "from the bishops down to the least member of the laity", it shows universal agreement in matters of faith and morals.'[8]

Now it must be admitted that juridically there was no obligation to consult the faithful of the Church before the declaration was composed and published. But it would have been an opportunity to do this and so verify in practice what is stated theoretically in the Second Vatican Council about 'the supernatural sense of the faith which characterises the People as a whole'. Similarly consultation on a wider scale would have lent more credibility to what the same council affirmed on collegiality and on the importance of charisms in the Church, including that of scriptural and theological expertise.

Lack of ecumenical sensitivity

Another disquieting aspect of the document is what we may perhaps describe as a lack of ecumenical sensitivity. The declaration notes

that 'for some years now various christian communities stemming
from the sixteenth century Reformation or of later origin have been
admitting women to the pastoral office on a par with men'.[9] However
there is no attempt at learning from the experience of such churches.
The Second Vatican Council's *Decree on Ecumenism* says: 'Nor should
we forget that whatever is wrought by the grace of the Holy Spirit in
the hearts of our separated brethren can contribute to our own
edification.'[10] After noting the different practices of the churches
concerning the ordination of women, the Baptism, Eucharist and
Ministry text (BEM) prepared by the World Council of Churches
Faith and Order Commission in 1982 declares that 'those obstacles
must not be regarded as substantive hindrance for further efforts
towards mutual recognition. Openness to each other holds the possibility that the Spirit may well speak to one church through the
insights of another. Ecumenical consideration, therefore, should
encourage, not restrain, the facing of this question'.[11] Earlier, BEM
addresses the question of the basis on which some churches practise
the ordination of women. 'It rests for them on the deeply held
theological conviction that the ordained ministry of the Church lacks
fullness when it is limited to one sex. This theological conviction has
been reinforced by their experience during the years in which they
have included women in their ordained ministries. They have found
that women's gifts are as wide and varied as men's and that their
ministry is as fully blessed by the Holy Spirit as the ministry of men.
None has found reason to reconsider its decision.'[12]

One of the questions that the Faith and Order Commission
addresses to all the churches concerns 'the consequences your church
can draw from this text for its relations and dialogues with other
churches, particularly with the churches which also recognise the text
as an expression of the apostolic faith'.[13] One such consequence for the
Catholic Church might well be for it to become a learner from the
experience of those churches who have ordained women to the
ministry. To approach such experience without prejudice and in
docility to the Spirit might well involve for it 'the possibility that the
Spirit may well speak to one church through the insights of
another'.[14] Such an approach may possibly bear fruit for the dialogue
between the Catholic Church and the Anglican communion. Admission of women to priesthood in the Anglican communion constituted,
in the words of Pope Paul VI, a 'grave' and 'new obstacle and threat'
on the path of reconciliation.[15]

Inconclusiveness of the theological arguments

The declaration, in parts 5 and 6, considers the priesthood in the light of the mystery of Christ and the Church in order to clarify with the aid of 'the analogy of faith' the conclusions reached in the first four parts. The declaration admits that these reflections do not constitute a conclusive argument. They are persuasive only to one who is already convinced by the previous sections of the document. In fact the arguments used from the maleness of Christ and from the bridal symbolism of Christ and the Church create problems and tensions in other areas of theology including christology, the theology of the sacraments and especially of baptism and Eucharist, and the theology of the Church. In particular they do not give sufficient attention to the doctrine of Paul in Gal. 3:28: 'there is neither male nor female, for you are all one in Christ Jesus.'[16]

In a reply to Dr Coggan's notifying him on 9 July 1975 that the Anglican communion found no fundamental objections in principle to the ordination of women, Pope Paul VI wrote:

> Your Grace is of course well aware of the Catholic Church's position on this question. She holds that it is not admissible to ordain women to the priesthood for very fundamental reasons. These reasons include: the example recorded in the sacred scriptures of Christ choosing his apostles only from among men; the constant practice of the Church, which has imitated Christ in choosing only men; and her living teaching authority which has consistently held that the exclusion of women from the priesthood is in accordance with God's plan for his Church.[17]

This reply was written on 30 November 1975. It is significant that the argument from the natural physical resemblance to Christ, which was to be used in the declaration, is missing in this letter.

Conclusion

In concluding I would like to stress that I am not rejecting out of hand the arguments brought forward in the declaration on the admission of women to the priesthood. The space at my disposal is not adequate for properly stating these arguments, much less than for passing judgment on them. All I wish to do is to draw attention to some disquieting features of this declaration. I also wish to emphasise that far from settling the issue of the ordination of women in the Catholic Church, the declaration has, unwittingly perhaps, stimulated it through the controversial nature of its argumentation and by drawing attention to some basic issues involved, such as, in the words of the declaration, 'the nature of the real equality of the baptised which is one of the great affirmations of Christianity'[18] and the 'capital importance' of the role of Christian women today.[19]

I would like to finish with the concluding remarks of Rahner:

> The Roman Declaration says that in this question the Church must remain faithful to Jesus Christ. This is of course true in principle. But what fidelity means in connection with this problem remains an open question. Consequently the discussion must continue. Cautiously, with mutual respect, critical of bad arguments on both sides, critical of irrelevant emotionalism expressly or tacitly influencing both sides, but also with that courage for historical change which is part of the fidelity which the Church owes to its Lord.[20]

The official position of the Catholic Church in the ordination of women is clear. The issue, however, is still a live one in the Church.

6

The ordination of women
A psychological interpretation
of the objections

MAGGIE KIRKMAN and NORMA GRIEVE

The teachings of Christ suggest that the opportunities for women to serve Him are similar to those for men. The practices of the Christian church however, belie this possibility, particularly in the strong objections to the ordination of women to the priesthood.

We shall argue in this chapter that these objections are specific examples of patriarchal attitudes. Patriarchy is a term used loosely to describe the cultural rule which, all other things such as age, caste and class being equal, accords higher value to the activities, and greater power to the person, of those assigned to the male rather than the female gender. We will apply to the ordination debate the thesis of Dorothy Dinnerstein who claims that patriarchy is sustained at its core by irrational and unconscious motives. In particular, we will argue that justifications for the exclusion of women from the priesthood are more or less transparent expressions of attitudes exemplifying Dinnerstein's claim that patriarchy is a social expression of the flight from maternal power.

Many reasons are given to support the antagonism to women priests. One of the most popular is that Jesus chose no women among the apostles,[1] but seeing that He also chose no Gentiles, the argument fails to be convincing. Although there are some dissenting voices,[2] it is generally considered that there are no theological objections to the ordination of women. The General Synod of the Anglican Church in Australia resolved in 1977 that this was the case, and the Roman Catholic Biblical Commission of 1976 stated that there were insufficient biblical grounds to exclude the possibility. A Roman Catholic nun, a doctoral candidate in canon law, wrote confidently:

> Women will eventually move to an equality with men in
> the ministerial life of the Church. Studies in biblical,

theological, historical and canonical disciplines can offer no substantial reasons for this inequality in the present day life of the Church. There is a long tradition in the Church which has been formed on ambiguous theological conceptions of women. These theological perspectives, coupled with the socio-cultural constructs that favoured the subordination of women, have marked women's role in the Church as one of constant inferiority to men. The result has been a practical and juridical depreciation of her gifts and ministry.[3]

Nevertheless, tradition and custom weigh as heavily as theology. The statement of the Biblical Commission was followed by a firm declaration from the Sacred Congregation for the Doctrine of the Faith (1976) to the effect that women should not be ordained because they had never been ordained in the past. This tends to give doctrinal weight to custom, although further examination of women's ordination in the light of Newman's seven Notes led to a conclusion that it would qualify as acceptable doctrinal development.[4]

Other arguments arise from distaste that the person of a woman should represent Christ to the people. This position was adopted in the 1976 Roman declaration:

When Christ's role in the Eucharist is to be expressed sacramentally, there would not be this natural resemblance, which must exist between Christ and his minister, if the role of Christ were not taken by a man: in such a case it would be difficult to see in the minister the image of Christ. For Christ Himself was and remains a man.[5]

One may well ask why the resemblance stops at sex: why not demand of priests that they be short, bearded Jews aged 30 with skills in carpentry? The declaration also deals with the image of Christ as the bridegroom and the Church as the bride as further justification for a male priesthood. It does not use the image to demand an all-female congregation of brides. As Ruether pointed out, the maleness of Jesus was not used in patristic theology as an argument against the ordination of women. It arose in medieval scholastic theology which adopted the Aristotelian view of women as misbegotten males (see chapter 1).[6] Augustine, for example, claimed that women were not made in the image of God (except as an appendage to men) and could not therefore be priests:

The woman together with her husband is the image of God, so that the whole substance may be one image. But

> when she is referred to separately in her quality of a
> helpmate, which regards the woman herself alone, then
> she is not in the image of God. But as regards the man
> alone, he is the image of God as fully and completely as
> when the woman too is joined with him.[7]

Neal[8] discusses the role of symbols as both embodying and reinforcing socially understood meaning. Those in power control the
operative images of God; in a patriarchal society, the images of God
are male. In the West, God (who in theory is beyond sex) is character-
istically symbolised as the father of a family, and any change to this is
perceived as a threat to the integrity of God: 'As the drive for the
ordination of women has proceeded, it has become apparent that what
is involved is the very Doctrine of God. It is not only feminising the
image of the priest, but feminising the image of God. The priest stands
as an image of Christ, who is the image of God.'[9] Terwilliger, in
company with others, sees no need to explain why a feminine God is
any more abhorrent than a masculine one. As Mary Daly puts it so
succinctly: 'Even if "in Christ there is neither male nor female",
everywhere else there damn well is.'[10]

The Anglican layman C.S. Lewis argued that although women can
do all that a priest can do, only a man can represent God. He wrote of
the 'inarticulate distaste, a sense of discomfort' aroused by the mere
thought of women priests, even though 'no one among those who
dislike the proposal is maintaining that women are less capable than
men of piety, zeal, learning and whatever else seems necessary for the
pastoral office'.[11] However, he continued, it is 'not mere prejudice
begotten by tradition' which produces 'the horror, which the idea of
turning all our theological language into the feminine gender arouses
in most Christians'. It is justified by the fact that 'God himself taught
us how to speak of Him'.[12] Blessed by sanctions from a higher
authority supporting male superiority, Lewis is able to be suitably
humble in accepting the honour:

> It is painful, being a man, to have to assert the privilege,
> or the burden, which Christianity lays upon my own sex. I
> am crushingly aware how inadequate most of us are, in
> our actual and historical individualities to fill the place
> prepared for us. But it is an old saying in the army that
> you salute the uniform not the wearer. Only one wearing
> the masculine uniform can ... represent the Lord to the
> Church: for we are all, corporately and individually,
> feminine to Him. We men may often make very bad

priests. That is because we are insufficiently masculine. It
is no cure to call in those who are not masculine at all.[13]

In order to ward off the inevitable question as to why men have
exclusive claims to spiritual androgyny, whereas women who wish to
share male power are asking the world 'to treat human beings as
neuters', Lewis offers a suitably mystical threat:

> With the Church . . . we are dealing with male and female
> not merely as facts of nature but as the live and awful
> shadows of realities utterly beyond our control and largely
> beyond our direct knowledge. Or rather, we are not
> dealing with them but (as we shall soon learn if we
> meddle) they are dealing with us.[14]

C.S. Lewis has been quoted in some detail because he draws
together threads of objection spun by other sources. For example, the
threat to God-given masculinity and femininity if women occupy male
preserves is claimed also by Barth, Bouyer and Terwilliger;[15] and the
mystical increase in or conferring of masculinity (undefined) at
ordination is asserted by Balthasar and Boyer.[16]

Let it not be said, however, that male domination should be
maintained only for the good of men. Those who oppose women priests
do so for the good of women. Bouyer, for example, wishes to safeguard
women from losing their identity (whether or not they want such
protection): 'it is precisely this safeguarding of a necessary complementarity, without which women's claimed equality would be
nothing but the annihilation of her originality and of her own
identity, that motivates exclusive attribution of the priestly ministry
to man: to the male.'[17] 'Femininity' may be 'crushed', he continued, by
'conferring on her a ministry which is not suitable for her.' Women's
unsuitability is related only to tradition, which implies the existence
of 'a fundamental principle', the nature of which Bouyer chooses not to
divulge. He expressed pious hopes that suitable ministries would soon
be discovered for women. According to Bouyer, 'more experienced
psychologists and sociologists' know that the current mistaken view
that equality equals identity provides 'unfavourable conditions' for
true equality. He also supports apartheid because it allows the blacks
to retain their identity, and uses this as an analogy for the male/
female state. The fact that in both cases it is the dominant group
evincing concern for the identity of the oppressed emphasises that the
issue is one of power. These views could be enjoyed as harmless
eccentricities were it not for the fact that men such as Bouyer and
Lewis hold respected positions at the heart of Christian orthodoxy.

Even Karl Barth, a courageous champion of human rights against the Nazis, maintained that the subordination of women was decreed by God.[18] His argument seems to have been based on a misunderstanding of the second (Yahwist) Creation story, which is recognised as a theological attempt to explain contemporary patriarchal society.[19] Such blind spots in otherwise liberal people; the hunt for pragmatic barriers to the ordination of women when theological arguments fail; the fact that so few women have offered themselves for ordination when the opportunity has arisen; and (particularly) the fact that women share the antagonism towards the mere idea of women priests[20] all these combine to suggest that a psychological explanation may be appropriate. Because the limits set upon female activity in the Church are representative of the ubiquitous secular dominance of men, it seems appropriate to suggest an explanation in terms of a universal feature of the experience of the human race.

Female childcare and fear of women

The significant universal experience has been defined by the psychologist Dorothy Dinnerstein as the fact that it is nearly always a woman who provides the infant with the primary initial contact with humanity and with nature.[21]

The detrimental effects of a mother-reared infancy may be focused particularly sharply in the Church because of its central association with matters spiritual and mystical. According to Dinnerstein, female-dominated childcare guarantees certain forms of antagonism (shared by men and women) against women; her summary of the nature of these antagonisms reads like a distillation of the relation of women to the Church, symbolised by the extremes of virgin and whore, experienced both as a servant and as a threat to male virtue:

> These antagonisms include fury at the sheer existence of her autonomous subjectivity; loathing of her fleshly mortality; a deep ingrained conviction that she is intellectually and spiritually defective; fear that she is untrustworthy and malevolent. At the same time they include an assumption that she exists as a natural resource, as an asset to be owned and harnessed, harvested and mined, with no fellow-feeling for her depletion and no responsibility for her conservation or replenishment. Finally, they include a sense of primitive outrage at meeting her in any position of worldly authority.[22]

Dinnerstein is not the first to relate patriarchy and its particular manifestations to the structure and dynamics of early life in the family. Other psycho-analytically oriented theorists share her basic claim, notably its progenitor Freud.[23] However, Dinnerstein locates the crucial formative period not in the oedipal conflict but in the pre-oedipal period. She bases her thesis on aspects of the work of Melanie Klein[24] and on object-relations theory, particularly emphasising the primitive unconscious defence mechanism of 'splitting'.

We will examine Dinnerstein's thesis in the following terms: ambivalent attitudes towards women; women and sexuality; women's collusion in patriarchy; the capriciousness of women and nature; women as quasi-persons; the wholeness of men; and finally, women and power. Each of these will be linked to aspects of objections to the ordination of women.

Ambivalent attitudes to women

Dinnerstein interprets Klein metaphorically. The essential insight she adopts is that the feelings binding the pre-verbal, pre-logical infant to the adult who cares for it are dominated by the infant's boundless need and by the adult's nurturing response to that need. The child remains dependent after he/she becomes aware of that dependence and resents it. The nurturant response can never fully satisfy the rapacious desires of the infant, so the source of good is also a source of bad. To prevent the internalised object of good being overwhelmed by the bad, the infant 'splits' the two into separate internal objects. The bad object then menaces both the good object and the ego. An ambivalent relation to the mother develops when the good and bad objects (previously not recognised as belonging together) are united when the mother comes to be seen as a whole person, and the infant's internal world is imposed on external persons and situations.

The Christian Church might have been designed as a deliberate demonstration of ambivalent attitudes to women. Mary Magdalene the whore and Mary the Virgin Mother of God exemplify this ambivalence; both refer to women in sexual terms, both imply the association of women with the dangers and degradations of the flesh. As Chaucer put it in the prologue to the Wife of Bath's tale:

> For trusteth wel, it is an impossible
> That any clerk wol speke good of wyves,
> But if it be of hooly seintes lyves[25]

Less ambiguously, in the Christian scheme of things, woman has been traditionally assigned to the evil part of the good/evil polarity. She is the Flesh fighting perpetually against Reason to enslave man, as in this typical traditional medieval account:

> for the flesche may be likened to an yuel condicioned [ill-bred] womman, of whiche seith the wise man Salamon: the more men foloweth her wille the more froward [unruly] and schrewed [wicked] is sche. [The example of Sampson follows] . . . Right so whoso foloweth & suffreth the wille of his flesche hit wole byneme [take from] him the strengthe of his resoun & caste him into the thraldom of synne . . . And therfor hit is nedeful to holde the flesche vnder the gouernance of resoun . . .[26]

Even more fundamentally, women is Vice needing to be held in check by Virtue. In one of Veronese's frescoes in the villa at Maser, Treviso, Virtue, a male figure, sits in a relaxed open posture looking up to heaven, holding in one hand the rod of governance, while the other is upraised and holds the reins of a bridle; the bit is in the mouth of a female figure, the Passions or Vices, who stares malevolently downward and whose clenched posture suggests extreme tension. The line from Eve the apple-eater through Solomon (a reminder that the ambivalence is much older than Christianity) to such allegories is unbroken.

Women and sexuality

The relationship of the infant with its mother is intimately physical. Dinnerstein sees in this the source of our ambivalent attitudes to sexuality and our bodies, and particularly to the sexuality of women: the independent sexuality of the female is feared because it recalls the terrifying erotic independence of the baby's mother. 'To soothe the fear we subordinate Eve's lust to Adam's, but this cure only makes the sickness worse; subordinated, Eve's lust is more frightening still.'[27]

In a lively and interesting history of the cult of the Virgin, Marina Warner[28] describes the way in which the cult of Mary is inextricably interwoven with Christian ideas about the dangers of the flesh and their special connection with women. Perhaps it is for this reason that the early Church found sexless women most acceptable; for them the highest accolade was to be honorary men.[29] Seminarians in our own time have been warned: 'Beware the daughters of Eve!'[30] and for many years Roman Catholic priests were forbidden to be alone in a room with a woman. The Australian Church's Plenary Council of 1938 extended this restriction to motor vehicles; Costigan reports that some priests refused to drive alone with their mothers.

In a heterosexual relationship, Dinnerstein perceives the man to be more vulnerable because the woman can bring out the dependent child in him. The two forms of male escape Dinnerstein describes are both recognisable in the Church, particularly in a celibate male priesthood. One escape is to keep heterosexual love superficial, both emotionally and physically; the other is to dissociate the emotional from the physical.

These options are not open to women, who tend to be able to give way to heterosexual physical pleasure only when it is accompanied by sentiment. This is partly because women can deal with the split between bad and good aspects of the first parent by projecting a substantial proportion of the (maternally aroused) good feelings to the second parent and hence to all men. Bad feelings can be projected onto and contained in other women, particularly those women who could occupy positions where others would have direct experience of their power.

However, if man is to live heterosexually, thus directing his passions towards women, his relations with her must embrace at a primitive level both the worshipful and derogatory, the affectionate and the hostile feeling towards the mother. If man divides the tender and the sensual, his lust carries the anger from which the trusting and protective side is insulated. It is illuminating to consider the explanations offered by church officials when a woman journalist was excluded from the ceremony in the Sistine Chapel to mark the meeting of Pope Paul VI and the Archbishop of Canterbury; 'The presence of a woman will sully this holy occasion for the Pope'; 'To you, women are people, but to us they are temptation.'[31]

Women's collusion in patriarchy

It is of particular interest that so many women appear as committed as men to maintaining patriarchal power.

Following de Beauvoir, Dinnerstein observes that women, unlike men, are offered a cultural immunity to the demands and risks of public life. A woman can vicariously enjoy the public triumphs of a man in return for her witness, support, nurturance and recognition. For Dinnerstein this 'socially sanctioned existential cowardice' is yet another expression of the 'morbid core' of our (collusive) sexual arrangements.[32] Female initiative and will are as problematic for women 'as they are for men since human infantile experience of maternal power is associated and confused with an inchoate sense of vulnerability and punishment.

There are two additional features of the development of female sexuality within mother-reared infancy which incline girls toward becoming childish and submissive women. First, the prospect of adult heterosexual maturity requires for a woman the severance from her first female love and offers her a 'solution of sorts' to her maternal ambivalence not applicable to the boy, who maintains the female as the object of love. Dinnerstein suggests that the girl can

> dodge the work of healing the split between bad and good feelings toward the first parent by shifting a substantial portion of the magically good ones onto the second, so that her love for the opposite sex comes to be infused with the infant's grateful passion toward the mother while most of the hostile derogatory attitudes remain attached to their original object.[33]

Women and nature are capricious

It is interesting that not only Dinnerstein but also those who have written specifically on the issue of the priesthood should associate our attitude to nature with our attitude to women.[34] In Western thought, nature and women are perceived (by both sexes) as objects to be used, subjugated and exploited, reflecting the rapacious desires of the infant.[35] At the same time, nature and women are paradoxically cherished as sources of life. Nevertheless, as the forces of nature are seen as capricious, the ways of women are understood in similarly wilful terms. The accusations of dividing the Church directed at women who wish to be ordained[36] carry implications of the malevolent wilfulness of women. The frequently expressed horror at the mere idea of goddesses[37] may be because of the association of women with nature and hence with paganism.

Women as quasi-persons

The association of women with nature arises from the same source as the failure to perceive women as fully sentient, individual beings. The earliest roots of antagonism toward women lie in the period before the infant has any clear idea of where the self ends and the outside world begins, or any way of knowing that the mother is a sentient human being. The mother is 'the centre of non-self'.[38] When she is perceived finally as a person, her person-ness is infused for the child with these earlier qualities, and all women come to be defined as quasi-persons. Augustine's comments on the necessity of women to be united with man in order to be the image of God fit this pattern. The child learns its own 'I'-ness in the face of the mother as 'it'. According to Dinnerstein: ' "I"-ness wholly free of the chaotic carnal atmosphere of infancy, uncontaminated humanness, is reserved for man'.[39] Thus also is the priesthood. Thomas Aquinas refused to accept women as priests on the fundamental grounds that because women did not have the 'eminence of degree' of the male sex, ordination would not even take place. Her 'state of subjection' makes her less fully human than men; 'a misbegotten male' (as Aristotle had claimed). Aquinas' attitude may still be found in the world (not just the church) today. C.S. Lewis's 'inarticulate distaste' succinctly expresses the pre-verbal apprehension of the not-quite-human.

The wholeness of men

In Dinnerstein's view, the wholeness of men and their relative freedom from being objects of ambivalent attitudes stem from the fact that infants become aware of their fathers only after developing rational appreciation of others as independent 'I's. To mother-raised humans, she claims, male authority (and, in the present case, male priestly authority) is bound to look like a reasonable refuge from female power. Men also represent the freedom of the world beyond maternal control, which makes them doubly attractive.

Russell and Dewey provide an explicit cultural expression of this theme. They assert that maternal care cannot prepare the (male) child for insertion into the world. An unspecified paternal influence is necessary to complete socialisation:

> Is a 'bad' father ... not as bad for the child as a 'bad'
> mother? The answer is No. Simply by being a father, he
> represents a phase in the child's development which
> carries him into the world, beyond the reach of the
> mother, good or bad. This is not, of course, a mere matter
> of personalities, but one of archetypes; and at that level a

good mother, like a bad mother, must in the end be 'bad'
for her child in a fashion not true even of the bad father.[40]

These authors go on to argue that to endorse women priests would
constitute a return to the pre-rational thraldom in which our mothers
held us. Male priests exemplify the essential, continuing paternal
influence: 'A "child" (of whatever age), if he is to grow up, he needs a
father to lead him away from the blandishments of the "best" as from
tyranny of the "worst" of mothers.'[41]

Women and power

The pre-logical and therefore mystical power of all women (as
generalisations of the mother) has special significance for the sacred
power of the priesthood. On one level, perhaps the most conscious
level, women can be perceived as polluting the 'clean', spiritual power
of men. Terwilliger, for example, asks with rhetorical horror: 'Is the
Church by permitting female priesthood actually depriving the
church sacramentally?'[42] On another level, ordination may be seen as
conferring even greater power on already powerful women. It is, in
fact, the Catholic denominations (both Anglican and Roman) which
have resisted the ordination of women most strongly. In this tradition,
ordination is a sacrament which conveys grace. For an Evangelical,
ordination simply refers to the public and prayerful nomination of a
person, who is recognised to have gifts of ministry, for a particular
work in the Christian community. Ordination is thus an aspect of
church order and not a sacrament. In the congregational Christian
churches in which the Eucharist is more a memorial of an event than
an event in itself, there has been less objection to seeing it celebrated
by women, presumably both because of the nature of the Eucharist
and the nature of priesthood. Nevertheless, in both cases, ordination
for women has not meant full participation in the ministerial roles or
in ecclesiastical decision-making.[43] Even the streams of churchman-
ship in the Anglican Church reveal these sacramental differences.[44] A
survey of attitudes to the ordination of women conducted for the
Anglican Diocese of Melbourne[45] found that the strongest opposition
to female ordination came from Anglo-Catholics.

In Dinnerstein's terms, this may express the fear of maternal power
which still threatens the adult as it once threatened the infant:

> The woman . . . is the overwhelmingly external will in the
> face of which the child first learns the necessity for

submission, the first being to whose wishes the child may
be forced by punishment to subordinate its own, the first
powerful and loved creature whom the child tries volun-
tarily to please.[46]

A woman in authority represents (to both men and women) a relapse
into submission to the mother; it is much more fearful when that
authority is coupled with the magic of priesthood. C.S. Lewis
expressed his alarmed distaste interrogatively: 'So you really want a
matriarchal world? Do you really like women in authority? When you
seek authority yourself, do you naturally seek it in a woman?'[47]

The mother-reared man still needs women, but in a strictly limited
and controlled way to enable him to feel that he has overcome the
power of the mother. Karl Barth was clear on this matter, incorporating in his statement an element of maternal applause:

Properly speaking, the business of woman, her task and
function, is to actualise the fellowship in which man can
only precede her, stimulating, leading and inspiring. How
could she do this alone, without the precedence of man?
How could she reject or envy his precedence, his task and
function, as the one who stimulates, leads and
inspires? . . . The establishment of an equality with man
might well lead to a state of affairs in which her position is
genuinely and irreparably deplorable because both it and
that of man are left as it were hanging in the void.[48]

The power of the sensual and dominating mother and, by association,
all women (since they potentially embody the omnipotent mother of
our infancy) must be controlled in our adult social arrangements.
Social power, in the hands of women, must be kept trivial. Simone de
Beauvoir was even more clear on this matter than Barth. She sees in
the Virgin Mother a symbolic resolution of the need to contain
maternal power: 'For the first time in human history the mother
kneels before her son; she freely accepts her inferiority. This is the
supreme masculine victory, consummated in the cult of the Virgin—it
is the rehabilitation of woman through the accomplishment of her
defeat.'[49] However, de Beauvoir was wrong on one count; women were
not rehabilitated, because the very conditions that make the Virgin
sublime (that is, asexual maternity) are beyond the powers of women
to fulfil. The love of the Virgin does not erase but presupposes
ambivalence towards real women.

Dinnerstein's solution

Dinnerstein's solution is a radical one, arguably utopian, and unlikely to occur in the near future. She appeals for a change in human childrearing arrangements in order to remove the burdens of ambivalence and fantasies of fearful power from the shoulders solely of women. She argues that although women have no choice in the matter of childbearing, modern culture and technology no longer require the exclusion of men from subsequent infant care. The involvement of men would force us to deal with our ambivalence, instead of associating the bad aspects with women and construing only men as persons. One cannot crush 'the massive orienting passions' of a dependent infancy, but they may be more equitably focused: men may then also be endowed with some of the parental magic. The necessity of integrating the bad and the good (brought about by the absence of female scapegoats) should also lead people to a new maturity, a new sense of self. The fear of infant helplessness is better outgrown than translated into irrational fantasies, beliefs and attitudes.

In the meantime, acknowledging our irrational fears permits some clarification of our attitudes and allows us to rectify them. Some churches have found already that the reality of women in authority has not fulfilled apprehensive predictions. New arguments, often self-serving, will doubtless be generated and require confrontation and analysis, but a reconciliation of men and women, clergy and laity, the human and the natural world is long overdue.

7

Institutional sexism and the Anglican Church

MARGARET ANN FRANKLIN

This chapter focuses on a case study of the gap between theological discussion on the status of women in the Anglican Church in New South Wales and actual practice in a parish in a large country town. It looks at this from a sociological perspective and includes an outline of the institutional structure of the Anglican Church today.

Christianity created a complete change in the position of women in the religious congregation. In the Jewish synagogue women were inactive participants, usually separated from the men by an opaque lattice. In contrast in the early Christian community women were recognised as full members of the congregation, and more than that, as Kevil Giles has shown, were known to have held office in the Church. Eileen Jones showed how what we call patriarchal ideology, on both Jewish and Greek lines, overthrew this Christian newness and imprisoned women once again as lesser beings, subject to men's domination, responsible for evil, and explicitly excluded from office in the Church. Eileen Byrne has shown how such a view is reflected in the educational opportunity offered to girls; Maggie Kirkham and Norma Grieve have offered a psychological explanation.

An ideology is a set of beliefs and values which expresses the interests of a particular group. Typically, as here, we are concerned with an ideology being used by a dominant group to mask social reality and legitimate the activities of those in power. In a patriarchal ideology the dominant group is men, and it is men's interests that are served; the differences that are noticed between men and women operate in one direction: towards women's subjection and exclusion. Such an ideology justifies what we may call institutional sexism. This is the erection into a power system of the perennial misogyny expressed by individuals (for example by C.S. Lewis—see chapter 6) and the accumulated anti-feminism of ancient and Christian thought. Christianity as it developed through the early centuries failed to overturn an attitude to women already ancient and, indeed, came to reinforce this attitude and entrench it in its power structure. The inferiority, subordination and dependence of women vis-a-vis men is reflected in the way the Anglican and other churches are constituted, not only in the exclusion of women from the ministry but, in the case of the Anglican Church, in what it expects of ministers' wives and what place it assigns to women generally—the sphere of the domestic and the ancillary. The Church therefore does not transcend the world, which is its mission, but actually embraces an injustice so old we cannot see its origins; it has thereby deeply, we believe, abandoned the inspired justice of its founder. Fortunately the psychological and sociological explanations now being offered by feminists and others are being absorbed by non-fundamentalist theologians and give some hope that the Church will change.

When Christian men and women internalise the Christian patriarchal ideology, like colonised people they come to believe, despite what Christ taught and practised, that Christian males are always entitled to a higher status than Christian women. The acceptance of such an ideology has locked Christian women and men into gender cages and has deprived the Church of competent female leadership. Furthermore, it has ensured that the most serious concerns of Christians are discussed in a male-oriented vocabulary and in a male context, and are deprived of female experience.

Women's status in the Anglican Church

Like its companion Christian churches, the Anglican Church has always been organised around the differences between males and females rather than the similarities, and the gifts of women have consequently been under-used or ignored. In Australia the Church's organisation and practice have reinforced the all-too-obvious sexism of Australian society, reserving leadership, scholarship and decision-making for men and casting women into serving and caring roles. In a country where parishes are not endowed, as they are in England, Anglican women have always been important fundraisers, but they have rarely had the power of deciding how the money they raise should be spent. Until quite recently women were barred from being on parish councils, vestries or synods. While Anglican women have often been influential they have usually remained in the background, exercising their power covertly through their husbands.[1]

In 1972 the Australian theologian Barbara Thiering recognised the presence of institutional sexism in the Church when she suggested that in Australia the Christian Church, both Catholic and Protestant, was one of the main agencies for reinforcing the low status of women. She complained that the Church had tended to canonise a status quo prevailing in society as a whole, one in which women were severely deprived.[2] Two years later the Australian Council of Churches (NSW) *Enquiry Into The Status of Women in the Church* provided empirical evidence supporting her statement.

Six dioceses of the province of the Anglican Church in New South Wales (then called the Church of England and affiliated with the American Episcopalian Church) sent submissions to the Enquiry. They stated that women could not be admitted to the orders of bishop, priest or deacon. Sydney was the only diocese that permitted women to be elected as parish representatives on the synod of that diocese. There were at the time of the Enquiry three women parish representatives among 600 clerical and lay representatives. The fact that the other dioceses would not allow women to sit on their synods meant that most women were unable to sit on the powerful general or provincial synods as membership was selected from diocesan synods. While Sydney allowed women to sit on its synod it stated that they could not be members of the Church Property Trust or the Glebe Administration Board, nor could they be churchwardens. The Riverina did not want women churchwardens either, but Canberra-Goulburn and Bathurst had no objections.

All dioceses permitted women to serve on parochial councils, and in the diocese of Grafton women made up about 25 per cent of the membership. Perhaps fearing a female takeover, the diocese of the Riverina insisted that women parochial councillors could not exceed one-third of the total membership. While women in the Sydney diocese were permitted to be elected as a Parochial Nominator, a woman's election was declared void if her husband was elected to the same position. Although all dioceses were happy to have their registries staffed by women and welcomed women as organists and choir members, some would not allow women to assist at the service of Holy Communion, nor did they like the idea of women preaching. Both activities were explicitly prohibited by the diocese of Sydney, though it would allow a deaconess to give an address in a church providing she talked only about her work.[3]

In secular society such discrimination is now under challenge. The Women's Movement gained momentum in Australia during the seventies and early eighties. The formation of the Women's Liberation Movement in 1969 and Women's Electoral Lobby in 1972 has forced political discussion of women's issues. Some specific reforms, such as equal pay, paid maternity leave for both married and single women in the Commonwealth Public Service, the appointment of an adviser on women's issues, appeared under the Whitlam Labor government, despite the heavy male domination of the ALP. Equal pay did not bring equal opportunity, however, either in industry or in higher education, and women still tend to lose in the battle for equal status. Anti-discrimination legislation and equal opportunity programs aimed at reducing the continuing inequality have had some kind of success. Two things, however, are clear: women are still suffering discrimination in very many ways, and the Australian community is showing more and more concern about it as the evidence mounts.[4] In the face of such concern the churches have not been able to maintain their traditional attitudes unchallenged.

The Church today

Institutional sexism is not only becoming unacceptable to the Australian community, it is also being questioned by members of the Church. Since the *Enquiry Into The Status of Women* was published the Anglican Church has begun to discriminate less against members who are female. There are now no legal barriers preventing women becoming lay preachers, lay readers, chalice bearers or church wardens. Women can now sit on the prestigious and powerful General and Provincial Synods, though few are elected to these positions. At the 1981 Australian General Synod seven of the representatives were women out of a house of 90 lay members; in the next General Synod held in 1985 there were fifteen women. This pattern of underrepresentation is typical of all decision-making bodies in the Church. The Rt Reverend A.C. Holland, Bishop of Newcastle, wrote recently in a letter: 'On all our diocesan committees we have an open policy and there is no bar to women's membership: but it is true to say that on those official bodies of the Diocese there is no significant female representation.'[5]

The ordination of women is a contentious issue for Anglicans. They have been ordained in Canada, Hong Kong, New Zealand and the

United States, but not in Australia or England. Opponents of ordination, as well as advancing the main theological arguments referred to
in chapter 4, also use an ecumenical one. It is argued that if the
Anglican Church were to ordain women, it would harm relationships
with the Roman Catholic and Orthodox Churches, both of which are
firm in not permitting women to be priests. On the other hand, it can
be pointed out that there are many churches with which the Anglican
Church has close relationships which do ordain women, such as the
Uniting Church, and there is, as we have seen, some discussion on the
question going on in the Catholic Church.

In 1974 the Anglican Church in Australia agreed that there are no
theological objections to the ordination of women as deacons, and at
the 1977 General Synod it took the revolutionary step of declaring by
a considerable majority that the theological objections which have
been raised did not constitute a barrier to the ordination of women to
the priesthood. Despite these pronouncements Anglican women were
not ordained because this involved changing the Church's constitution. In 1981 a provisional bill was presented to alter the constitution
of the Church so that women could be ordained. To become law it had
to be passed by three-quarters of all male-dominated diocesan synods,
including all metropolitan sees. When it became clear that the bill
was not going to get the required majority the Archbishop of Sydney
suggested that the debate on this issue should cease. He wrote: 'What
this means is that the Anglican Church in Australia has joined the
great majority of churches in the Anglican communion in considering
and then rejecting proposals to ordain women.'[6]

If opponents of the ordination of women thought that the issue
would now die because constitutional changes were rejected, they
were wrong. Anglican women are now increasingly entering theological colleges and some are letting it be known that they believe they
are called to the ordained ministry. In October 1983 a group of Sydney
women started the Movement for the Ordination of Women. This
organisation has a considerable number of male members and in 1985
became a national organisation.

Occasionally a woman priest from another part of the Anglican
communion comes to Australia and her presence highlights the
problem of institutional sexism in the Australian Anglican Church.
In September 1983 for example, Melbourne was visited by the
Reverend Joyce Bennett of Hong Kong. She was invited by Archdeacon David Chambers, who is a Christian feminist, to celebrate the
Eucharist in his church, St Stephen's, Richmond. Word of this reached

the Archbishop of Melbourne who told the Archdeacon to celebrate the service himself. Being a man under authority and also believing that women should be ordained, Archdeacon Chambers arranged a concelebration. This is a service at which the consecration of the bread and wine is done jointly by a number of priests. However as James Murray pointed out in an article in the *Australian*[7] on the altered status of women in the Church, the service at St Stephen's was an appearance only of obedience to the archbishop's authority, for the Reverend Joyce Bennett used a separate chalice and paten and gave absolution—a declaration of forgiveness—and a blessing. In the Anglican Church the latter functions cannot be performed by lay people.

The Movement for the Ordination of Women has done a great deal to publicise the debate on this issue. It has organised seminars, lectures and public demonstrations and has embarrassed the Anglican Church by inviting to Australia women who have been ordained in other parts of the Anglican communion. Some clergy have wanted to offer these women priests hospitality; others have preferred to ignore them. In 1985 the question of whether it was legal for an Australian Anglican priest to offer hospitality to an Anglican woman ordained in a foreign country was one of the ones on which the Church's highest legal body, the Appellate Tribunal, was asked for a ruling. It decided that Anglican priests were permitted to offer hospitality to women priests from other countries and could license them to minister in their dioceses. It also declared that the principles of the Church did not prevent women becoming ordained as deacons, priests or bishops. These decisions did not please conservative male members of the male-dominated General Synod. After a heated debate, between those who favoured the ordination of women and those who did not, a bill which would have given any diocese the right to ordain women if it wanted to was defeated. The General Synod did however pass a bill permitting the ordination of women as deacons, but some conservative dioceses have made it clear that such women will not be ordained as priests.

The official debate about the status of women in the Anglican Church has centred on such issues as whether there are any reasons why women should not be ordained and whether the suggestion attributed to St Paul that women should not be in authority over men should forbid their preaching in church.[8] While this is the centre of the current discussion, I shall now turn to something which is by comparison theologically uncontentious, the licensing of women as lay readers.

In the Anglican Church lay people perform a number of functions. The most important of these are, in descending order, preaching sermons, reading services, administering the bread or wine to communicants at the Eucharist or reading lessons during services. The only activities strictly theologically forbidden to lay people are the pronouncing of the absolution for sins and the consecration of the elements in a communion service. Such lay people may be of either sex, though conservative Evangelicals in the Anglican Church hold that it is improper to give women authority by allowing them to preach. We will now trace the gap between the theology which encourages women to become lay readers and the practice which discourages them.

Although the Enquiry into the Status of Women in the Church undoubtedly raised the consciousness of Anglicans about institutional sexism, it did not start the debate. The topic had already been discussed in 1971 at a National Conference on Mission and Ministry. In 1972 the synod of my own diocese passed the following resolution:

> That this Synod adopts in principle the recommendations from the National Conference on Mission and Ministry (August, 71) in regard to the ministry of women and urges parishes and appropriate bodies to implement them, i.e.: (1) Membership of Synods, Standing Committees, Parochial Councils, Boards of Presentation and all such Councils and Committees, and election, or appointment as Churchwardens, lay Canons, etc., should be open to women and men alike. It is recommended that, at least for the present, the Councils of the Church should be constituted as to encourage the election or appointment of women. (2) In the pastoral work of the Church, the abilities and the capacities of women should be recognised and consciously used. (3) The offices of Lay Reader and Lay Preacher should be open to all suitable persons irrespective of sex. Where lay people are given a specific function in public worship (e.g. reading lessons, leading intercessions) women should be given the same opportunity to minister as is given to men. Resolution 38 of the 1968 Lambeth Conference should be implemented: 'The Conference recommends that, in the meantime, National or Regional Churches or Provinces should be encouraged to make canonical provision, where this does not exist, for duly qualified women to share in the conduct of Liturgical worship, to preach, to baptise, to read the Epistle and

Gospel at the Holy Communion, and to help in the distribution of the elements.'

A copy of this resolution was given to me in 1983 by the bishop of our diocese when I went to see him because I believed that my parish church of St Paul's was practising institutional sexism. I was told that he regarded this issue as a matter for the parish to sort out.

Institutional sexism: a case study

In 1982 sixteen male members of our congregation were invited to become lay readers. Two women, with theological qualifications who had both been members of the parish council, were asked to tutor them in Old Testament studies. Neither of these women was asked to become a lay reader. This did not worry Susan Denton.[9] She was socialised to believe that males should preside in the sanctuary. She told me that she felt that men's voices sounded so much better than women's. The other woman, Ann Taylor, a scientist, was angry about being excluded. She said she felt she was being treated as a second-class citizen.

In her important book *Beyond God the Father*, Mary Daly points out that rage can be a positive creative force. She writes:

It rises as a reaction to the shock of recognising what has been lost—before it had even been discovered—one's own identity. Out of this shock can come information of what human being (as opposed to half being) can be. Anger then can trigger and sustain movement from the experience of nothingness to recognition of participation in being. When this happens, the past is changed, that is, its significance factor is changed.[10]

If it had not been for Ann Taylor the synod resolution of 1972 would not have been implemented so soon. When she first moved to our town she went to see the former bishop of the diocese to ask if she could be licensed as a lay reader. He told her that he felt that the congregation of St Paul's was not yet ready to accept women in the sanctuary. He suggested a process of gradualism. As a first step women were invited to read a lesson from the Bible at a morning service.

St Paul's congregation became used to women reading the lessons. The appointment of a woman church worker and, when she left, a deaconess, further accustomed the congregation to the ministry of women. As the next incumbent appointed to the church in 1974 was sympathetic to feminism, the participation of women in church services increased. The arrival of two licensed women lay readers from other parishes further increased the participation of women in church services. By 1975, Women's International Year, St Paul's could claim that laywomen were well on their way to enjoying the same status as laymen. The status of women further improved with the appointment of a new bishop who encouraged the deaconess to preach in the cathedral.

Although the bishop was opposed to the ordination of women on the grounds that married women could not have authority over their husbands, he was not opposed to the ordination of single women providing they remained single. He believed, however, that until there was a provision for unordaining single female clergy who married, no women should be ordained. As he had no objection to single theologically trained women preaching in church he was prepared to allow, and indeed saw it as his duty, to encourage this practice. Although the congregation was not used to women preachers, only one woman complained about the innovation. She was, however, so shocked that she left St Paul's and joined a more conservative church.

The improved status of the church women did not last long. The practice of women reading the lessons was retained, but by 1982 the sanctuary was again reserved for males. This occurred because the deaconess and the two women lay readers left the district and no attempt was made to recruit more women. It seems that the resolution of 1972 had been forgotten.

When she learnt that sixteen men were to be licensed as lay readers, Ann Taylor made an appointment to see our minister. He told her that it would not be possible for her to become a lay reader unless her nomination was approved by the other clergy and the parish council. Ann Taylor said she could not understand why this approval had not been forthcoming. She pointed out that she had served the church in various capacities. She had been a member of the parish council and had been considered to be a fit and proper person to tutor the lay readers in Old Testament studies. She suggested to the incumbent that it was wrong for the church to discriminate between men and women. She drew his attention to biblical passages which supported her position. She quoted Galatians 3:28, and also stressed that by limiting women's opportunities to minister, the church was out of touch with society. Her appeal had no effect.

I was moved by Ann Taylor's situation to become a Christian feminist. Until this incident occurred my feminism and my religion had been compartmentalised. Although I called myself a feminist I had also been blinded by the Christian patriarchal ideology to accept the sanctuary as a male preserve. A discussion about this problem with a woman who had been involved with the Commonwealth Women's Advisory Council led to an invitation to write a report on the status of women in the church. At first I felt that as I was acting in a professional capacity I should do as little as possible to disturb the social field, so when the Anglican Women's Group held a meeting to discuss changes necessary in the church, I made no attempt to influence the agenda. As I was unable to attend the meeting the president prepared a report for me to read.

The report revealed that the women were only concerned about playing their 'natural' female roles more effectively. Various suggestions were made such as sending people Get Well cards, reading to the elderly in their homes, visiting sick people in hospital, and providing transport for those in need. It was suggested that Anglican women should open their homes to those who were new to the district and that they should not confine their hospitality to churchgoers but be prepared to care for everyone. At these morning teas it was suggested that Anglican women should explain to the newcomers 'how the diocese works'. No one of course would have pointed out that Christian patriarchal ideology was operating to ensure that the ministry of women was not conducted in the sanctuary.

While most of the female members of our congregation were unconcerned about the fact that women had not been asked to become lay readers, some male lay readers were worried about institutional sexism. Several of them spoke to our minister who assured them that in due course women would become lay readers. The matter was raised in the parish council and the names of 29 women who had the necessary qualifications to be lay readers were put forward by a parish councillor, but no motion was moved.

After several months had passed and no move had been made to invite women to become lay readers, I decided to raise the issue with other church women. While I found that most were not interested in the issue—a woman who had always worked and who had been president of the local Chamber of Commerce told me that she had been brought up to believe that men should run the Church—I did find a few allies. I mentioned to our minister in a joking way that I was thinking of leading a women's revolution.

In the Anglican Church the local incumbent is in a very strong position indeed. Church administration, modelled on that of the Tudor monarchy, is not democratic. In the last resort all a parish council is entitled to manage is the church funds; other decisions are made by the incumbent. When I asked our minister why he had not licensed women as lay readers he told me that if he had done this he would have divided the parish. When I pointed out that the congregation had accepted the ministry of women before he came he refused to discuss the matter any further. However he did tell me that he personally believed that Christ can work through women: 'He's not bound to work through males.' He said he was not opposed even to the ordination of women but doubted whether a woman, particularly a married woman, should be in sole pastoral charge of a parish. He did not think this would fit in with a wife's primary duty which is to look after her husband and children.

I should emphasise that our minister has done a great deal to further the spiritual growth of women. When he first came to our parish only one small group, consisting mainly of women, as studying the Bible. By the time I interviewed him 150 people were attending Bible study groups regularly; most of these were women. Furthermore, a couple of women were studying in theological courses. But while there was considerable emphasis on the spiritual development of women, the synod resolution of 1972 was virtually ignored in our parish.

Gradually the situation began to change. On 10 July 1983 a notice appeared in St Paul's Church paper headed 'Administration of Communion'. It read: 'During July we welcome Mrs Susan Denton and Mrs Ann Taylor amongst those who participate in the distribution of communion. They follow in the tradition of former years when Louise Peters, Dorothy Smith and Jane Olsen served it.' While it could be argued that these women were following in the same tradition, their status was still much less than that of the original women. Of these Louise Peters was a fully licensed lay preacher, Dorothy Smith was a licensed lay reader and Jane Olsen was a deaconess. Furthermore, the women were being asked to accept the status of chalice-bearers, a status below that of lay reader which had been given to the sixteen men, none of whom were as well qualified as the women. While the women could read the lessons and administer communion they could not take parts of the Communion Service like the men.

The announcement in the church paper surprised Susan Denton as she had not been asked if she would like to become a chalice bearer.

When after attending a mid-week service she noticed her name on the roster, together with that of her husband, she became, she said, 'suddenly aware that there might be some good in my going up there. There might be a blessing'. However, she felt inadequate. She talked things over with her husband, who assured her that she was capable, though he admitted that he 'didn't like women up there'. On the last Sunday in July the Dentons both distributed Communion together. Susan found it an enriching experience.

The fact that women administered Holy Communion drew no unfavourable comments from the congregation. Our minister reported that he had had several positive comments. Furthermore the experience of administering Communion changed Susan Denton. She now felt she wanted to be licensed as a lay reader. She told me: 'I want the complete approval of the congregation. I don't want to slip in by the back door.' However, when a lay reader who regarded the situation as unjust took up a petition on behalf of the two women, she decided that she would prefer the back door, especially when she learned that some lay readers refused to sign the document. At her request the petition was abandoned.

After the women had acted as chalice-bearers I interviewed our minister. He agreed that as the congregation had accepted the two women there was now no reason why they should not be licensed. While no attempt was made to do this a few more women were asked to become chalice-bearers. All at first refused the offer, saying they could not see themselves in this role. However after discussion most of them accepted.

A typical example of the complicated attitudes to be found in the parish at the time came from an elderly retired man who is one of the most devoted workers in the parish. He has very definite ideas about the role women should play in the church. While not opposed to their being chalice-bearers he expressed a fear about women taking over the church. He believes women should never be asked to preach. The fact that no women were licensed as lay readers did not trouble him. He feared that women, having set their sights on getting power in commercial enterprises, had now decided 'we'll have a go at the church'.

The new women chalice-bearers were only asked to act when their husbands were available. As Ann Taylor's husband was often away she was rarely called on. Months passed and eventually Ann's husband wrote to the parish council drawing their attention to the fact that by not licensing these well-qualified women the church was demonstrating a gap between policy and practice. The parish council became concerned about the issue and in June 1984 it published the following statement in the Parish News:

> The Parish Council has discussed (over the last two months) a motion requesting licences for suitable women members of the congregation to become Lay Readers and Lay Preachers. Such requests were normally presented to the Bishop. At their June Meeting, the Parish Council decided to adopt this motion.

Thirteen further months elapsed. Finally, in July 1985, three years after the sixteen men had been licensed, five women and three men were licensed as lay readers. Part of the delay was caused by Ann Taylor's reluctance to accept the offer. She eventually declined.

No attempt has been made in this study to estimate how typical our parish might be. Undoubtedly there would be different stories to be told in different places. In some the status of women would be better, in others, particularly the parish in our diocese which bars women from sitting on its parish council, the situation would be worse. What this story does illustrate forcefully is the gap between theory and practice and the inertia of an established pattern of thought. This will not necessarily be removed merely by taking away legal barriers, even those which have prevented the ordination of women.

It is usually, though not undisputedly, said that sociological studies should be 'value-free' in the sense of merely stating facts without incorporating the author's own values. I have made no attempt in this chapter to achieve this attitude, for it seems to me that Christians must be prepared to make value judgments about what is right or wrong, particularly in the church area. I regard the position of women in the Church as unjust. However, to judge a situation unjust is one thing and to make personal judgments is another. This study has shown that it is by no means a case of clergy wishing to hold on to entrenched authority against the wishes of the laity. It contains an equally strong element of conservatism in the laity, including lay women. Perhaps in the end any attempt to apportion blame would be pointless. What the study does demonstrate is the need for voluntary affirmative action along the lines indicated by Marie Tulip in her chapter. This will ensure that the power of patriarchy is lessened.

8

Ministers' wives
Continuity and change in relation to their husbands' work

KENNETH DEMPSEY

In her recent book *Married to the Job*,[1] Janet Finch says that the part that women play in their husbands' work is a relatively unexplored issue in sociological literature. In an attempt to fill the void Finch herself offers a synthesis of the relevant research in which she demonstrates that all wives are caught up in their husbands' work to at least some degree. Using the findings from her own study of a sample of English ministers' wives, she cogently argues that their incorporation in the work of their husbands is as great or greater than that of the wives of men in other honorific occupations including policemen, politicians and doctors.[2]

In an earlier publication Finch shows that the members of her sample were highly committed to the role of the minister's wife and that they believed in the indispensability of their husbands' work to the success of their church.[3] Many of the laity I have surveyed or interviewed on the attitudes and behaviour of Australian ministers' wives would be agreeably surprised by Finch's findings. These laity believe—and deplore—that there is a growing trend for ministers' wives to be much less enthusiastic about participating in local church life and generally supporting their husbands' work than were wives of earlier generations. For example, a majority of the 87 lay leaders who participated in a survey I conducted in Victoria in 1984 said that ministers' wives were less committed to assisting their husbands in their work at the present time than they were ten years ago.

Finch's arguments are based on data collected from a sample of English Methodist and Anglican wives in the 1980s. A majority of the 30 Australian ministers' wives in the study I am reporting on here displayed a similar level of commitment to their husbands' work. The sample covers a period of some 70 years and includes six wives from the 1980s. Although it is not a representative sample it is worth noting—especially in the face of the lay point of view I have just reported—that five of the six wives of the 1980s displayed a very high commitment to their husbands' work. My sample, however, did include a number of wives who had become very disenchanted with at least some aspects of the traditional role of the minister's wife. These women resisted—usually unsuccessfully—meeting certain expectations. The failure of their 'rebellion' demonstrates that whether morally committed or not ministers' wives are caught up to a marked degree in their husbands' work. Their rebellion also illuminated a number of the factors responsible for such involvement.

The data on the behaviour of these and other wives were gathered in the course of two community studies, each of which had a socio-historical or longitudinal dimension to it. The first was conducted in the New South Wales town I call Barool and the second in a Victorian town I call Smalltown. The Barool study covers the years between 1905 and 1967 and the Smalltown study the years from 1973 until the present. During the period covered in the Barool study 26 Methodist ministers resided in the town and I was able, through interviewing, correspondence and in some instances observation, to gain sufficient data on 24 of their wives to categorise their attitudes to their husbands' work and the nature of their involvement in it.[4] During the eleven years that the Smalltown study has been in progress I have been able to collect comparable material for the wives of six of the seven Anglican, Methodist, Presbyterian and Uniting Church ministers who have resided in this town during these years. The seventh minister was a woman and unmarried. Because the similarities in the relationship of both Smalltown and Barool wives to their husbands' work are much greater than any dissimilarities I am, for the purposes of this paper, treating them as one sample. This approach is also warranted because of a number of important parallels between the two social contexts in which these 30 ministers' wives lived. Both Barool and Smalltown were centres for surrounding agricultural districts, relying on the prosperity of their hinterland for their survival. Each had a population of only a few thousand. In both cases it was farmers and their wives and, to a lesser extent, businessmen and their wives who provided the majority of active supporters and leaders for the Protestant churches I have been researching.[5]

The part played by the ministers' wives of Barool and Smalltown

All 30 ministers' wives supported their husbands in their work to some degree and at least two-thirds of them to a very great degree. Nevertheless eleven of the Barool wives were strongly criticised by at least some sections of the laity for giving their husbands insufficient support. But even these were, in fact, enmeshed in their husbands' work, often despite serious efforts on their part to reduce their involvement. Here in fairly specific terms is an account of the part that Barool and Smalltown ministers' wives played in their husbands' work.

At least two-thirds of them presided over one or more of the women's organisations of the church or parish, assisted with the Sunday school or youthwork or both, and with such fundraising activities as fetes and concerts. These things they did usually without taking over or trying to take over from local lay leaders of long standing. They often accompanied their husbands on country preaching appointments, endeavoured to be friendly towards everybody, and strove to be exemplary in their personal behaviour and to ensure that the behaviour of their children did not in any way prejudice their husbands' work.

Most served as sermon critics, confidantes and co-strategists in their husbands' efforts to accomplish such goals as getting rid of an 'obstructionist' lay leader. It seems most were sources of encouragement and reassurance in situations where organisations were often failing, congregations and financial support declining, and lay men and women were often prone to criticise their husbands' efforts. Some served on flower rosters for the church, some preached or spoke at women's meetings, and some started new groups.

Only one of the 30 wives engaged in full-time paid employment and this was only for a period of several months. Two others took part-time employment and a third gave over a large amount of time to trying to develop a career as a writer and a lecturer. All of these women continued to support their husbands' work in a variety of ways, although the woman in full-time employment was forced to give up attending meetings of the women's organisations and the woman who was trying to establish a career as a writer declined to be involved in such activities.

The two women who worked part-time said they would not contemplate working full-time because this would seriously impede their

husbands' work. I did not collect information on the attitude of all
ministers' wives to the issue of taking paid employment. It would
have been an irrelevant area of inquiry as far as the women of the
pre–Second World War period were concerned and probably for all of
the women living in Barool before the 1960s. Up till that time few
married women, especially those married to professionals, were
working. However, a number of the ministers' wives who lived in
Barool in the 1960s and in Smalltown in the 1970s said that it was out
of the question for them to take paid employment because of the
detrimental consequences it would have for their church work and for
their husbands' work.

In summary, there is a good deal of evidence to show that the great
majority of the 30 ministers' wives were heavily involved in their
husbands' work and that most sought to make that work as effective
as possible.

The costs of being a minister's wife

What is particularly interesting is that this involvement and commitment occurred despite the considerable cost to the wives. For example,
they often lived in houses that were inferior to those of many, even
most, of their parishioners, and houses which were often inadequately
furnished and sometimes in need of repair. In fact there were
problems and sometimes disruptive controversies over the parsonage,
its condition or its furnishings, during the incumbencies of at least
four of the couples in my study. For example, so appalled was one
ministerial couple over the standard of the housing provided that they
devoted as much of their energy to what proved to be an unsuccessful
campaign to have a new parsonage built as they did to any other
aspect of church affairs. A second couple sold their car to buy
furniture for what they regarded as a totally inadequately furnished
parsonage. All 30 husbands received, by professional standards, quite
inferior incomes, and because of an inadequate superannuation
scheme faced the prospect of retirement without necessarily having
the funds to buy a house.

The wives had to accept a constant and extensive invasion of their
privacy, partly because there were no time limits to their husbands'
job and partly because of its honorific nature. One minister's wife
spoke of the problems that the 'do-gooder' image of her husband
created for her:

> If I start talking to some of the women of the church about
> needing some time for myself or complaining about the
> way John's work interferes with family life I get little
> sympathy. You can hear them thinking how can she be so
> selfish when her husband devotes his life to helping other
> people? She should do everything possible to assist him in
> his work.

The invasion of privacy was inevitable because much of the minister's
'good works' occurred in the parsonage or manse or were organised
from there. Because there were no paid staff to help in the demanding
and extensive range of tasks that fell to a minister his wife ended up
doing double duty. The wives not only freed their husbands by taking
major or entire responsibility for domestic tasks and for childcare but
they also served as receptionists, hostesses and at times counsellors.[6]
In 1950 Mrs Collins, the Barool Methodist minister's wife at the time,
said when talking to some of the lay women after church one Sunday
morning: 'When I go through the gate of the parsonage I want to
forget all about the church.' Mrs Collins was enunciating an
unachievable goal. The last place it was possible to forget the church
and its people was in the parsonage. This was the place where many
church meetings were held and where the minister was most likely to
unburden himself to his wife about the frustrations and disappoint-
ments of his job. It was a provocative statement because it challenged
the prevailing arrangement between ministers, ministers' wives, and
the laity whereby the minister's wife freed her husband from household and family tasks for his demanding work. It was also provocative
because it flew in the face of the fiercely held lay belief that because
they (that is the laity) had provided the parsonage and its furnishings
they should have access to it (and to its inhabitants) more or less
whenever they wanted to.

The problems inherent in the situation of the kind I have just
been describing were exacerbated by the 'fish bowl' existence of
ministers' wives. They were living in small communities with popula-
tions possessing effective gossip chains articulated through the
many cross-cutting ties existing among community members. These
problems were further exacerbated by the fact that they lived in
a social milieu where they were expected in their personal behaviour
to be above reproach, to be friendly towards all but not to play
favourites by forming close friendships. As Finch has pointed out,
this last condition sometimes ensures that ministers' wives lead a
fairly lonely existence despite the constant parade of people through

their doors and their heavy involvement in the wide range of social activities connected with church life.[7]

There were other costs to bear as well. By marrying a minister, a minister's wife committed herself to a life of geographical mobility which often adversely affected the schooling of her children and which usually put considerable distances between herself and her relatives.[8]

Another part of the cost was the inequitable share of the workload of the church that wives invariably had to bear. In 1918 at an official farewell to the Reverend and Mrs Bruce Reddropp—a couple who had worked with great application and considerable success for four years in Barool—a famous minister of the time said: 'You don't care what a lawyer's wife is like, nor the butcher's, nor the baker's, but directly you hear of a new minister coming to town you want to know what sort of wife he has got.' Although made in 1918 these remarks capture the attitude of the laity in both Barool and Smalltown for the course of the 70 years under review. Ministers' wives were distinguished from other wives by the extent and nature of their involvement in their husbands' work. It was exceptional for any of the wives in my sample not to do far more than the great majority of the laity. Where a wife failed to, say because of illness, it was remembered and remarked upon almost 30 years later as the primary reason for that woman's husband not having an outstanding incumbency.

The reasons for the incorporation of wives in their husbands' work

In the face of the cost that ministers' wives had to shoulder, why did they centre so much of their lives on their husbands' work? There were both structural and cultural factors at work which constrained wives to participate in this way: first, the social and economic rewards of being a minister's wife; second, the presence of a strong ideological commitment to the value of the work the husband was doing and to the part a wife played in that work; third, socialisation in earlier years that ensured most wives were committed to and skilled in meeting many of the specific expectations held of them; fourth, the pressure on ministers' wives to tailor their performance to the expectations of their audience; and fifth, the manner in which their husband's work was organised, especially the fact that it centred on the parsonage or manse and had no firm time limits.

The social and economic rewards

First there were social and economic gains from marrying a minister and helping him making the job as successful as possible. The majority of the women in my two samples came from working-class or lower-middle-class backgrounds. Furthermore, only three or four of them had the necessary qualifications to pursue professional careers in their own right. So by marrying ministers these women improved their social status. This was especially the case for the ministers' wives of the pre–Second World War period when the standing of ministers was considerably higher than it was from about the 1970s onwards. There were also status gains for the wife in the context of the local church. A woman who became engaged to a young minister or trainee minister, moved as it were, from 'the back row' to 'the front row' of local church life. Within the Methodist Church the standing of wives was symbolised by the tradition of their accompanying their husbands to the front door of the sanctuary at the end of the service to shake hands with the people. A woman who was selected by a young minister or a trainee minister as a suitable partner won immediate approval in the world of the church for choosing 'the path of self-denial and service'.

There were considerable economic incentives for the wife to make her husband's work as effective as possible. Some of these too were more effective before the war; others continued to be very effective until the middle of the 1970s, and others remain effective until the present time.

In the Methodist Church for most of the first half of this century, the minister's stipend, which apart from help in kind, was for both him and his wife their only source of livelihood, was third on the list of financial commitments to be met from local funds. Both commercial bills and the levies of the central organisation of the church had to be met before the minister's stipend was paid. There is no record of any Barool minister of this period not eventually receiving his full stipend but there were instances of it being delayed for several months and in at least one case of a portion of the stipend still owing to a minister when he left Barool. Barool ministers and their wives, however, were aware of situations where ministerial couples never received their full stipend. This knowledge influenced them to work hard to make a tangible success of the local church.

Methodist ministers and their wives have always been dependent upon the laity for a house. Furthermore, before the Methodist Church joined the Uniting Church in 1977 they were also dependent upon the laity for the furnishings of that house. Any updating of household furnishings was entirely at the discretion of the local leaders. There was in Barool a tendency for the laity to adopt the practice of rewarding ministers and ministers' wives of whom they approved by paying particular attention to the parsonage and penalising those of whom they disapproved by 'letting things run down'. So, for example, plans to recarpet the parsonage during the time that I was doing fieldwork in Barool in 1966 were abandoned because the women of the Ladies Church Aid felt that the minister's wife was not showing enough interest in their organisation or in them personally. Instead of buying the carpet they bought new heaters for the church. The secretary of the Ladies Church Aid confided to me that whereas the members of the 'Aid' would have gained no personal benefit from the carpet they would gain benefit from the heaters.

Ministers always need the support of local people if their careers are to be advanced, and as a minister's wife's economic and social interests are inextricably bound up with the success of her husband's career she is also dependent on lay support for her advancement. Not all appointments within Protestant churches carry the same status or necessarily the same economic remuneration. Ministers and ministers' wives learn early in their careers that better appointments do not hang so much on showing a concern for people in poor circumstances as for ensuring that the churches in their charge are as financially viable as possible. Careers are also facilitated by expanding congregations, keeping the support of the younger members of church families and acquiring reputations for being friendly, caring and cooperative. A minister's career is furthered by a wife who demonstrates she is strongly committed to the traditional role of the minister's wife and shows skill in that role.

Career achievement was particularly important to Barool ministers in the first half of the century because their training did not equip them for any other professional career. In these circumstances, wives had a great deal to gain by working as hard as possible to make a success of their husbands' career and a good deal to lose by failing to do so. Some of the best insights into the motivation of ministers' wives for supporting their husbands during this period came from a minister's wife who had not been resident in Barool herself but who had served in a number of similar appointments and who had discussed with several Barool ministerial couples their approach to their work. She reported that like her husband and herself these

couples had done everything possible to attract people to church
because 'livelihood, future careers, and immediate happiness
depended upon the church being a successful enterprise'. She went on
to say:

> [W]e could not expect invitations to good appointments if
> we did not make a success of our present one. My husband,
> like most ministers I knew, was ambitious to get on in the
> church, so he worked very hard himself and looked to me
> to help him in every way possible. The Barool ministers
> look for the same support from their wives. We ran
> concerts, bazaars, socials and picnics, to gain sufficient
> income so that we could receive our stipend and always
> with a mind to our future career. In the appointments we
> were in during the 1930s we found ourselves in competi-
> tion with the Presbyterians for the support of the various
> office people, bank people and business people who came
> to the town. We wanted to make our church programmes
> as attractive as possible so as to gain their membership.
> We needed the financial support they would give to the
> church; we needed the lift they would give to the 'tone' of
> the church and, of course, they were particularly inter-
> esting people to have around. So I ran afternoon teas at
> the parsonage; I took up speaking at special women's
> functions, all with these ends in mind. But we were
> careful not to offend by neglecting the stalwarts of the
> church—the local farmers and business men and
> tradesmen who were our bread and butter—we could only
> succeed by pleasing them.

A decline in the standing of the churches and their clergy—the
causes of which I discuss elsewhere[9] had, by the 1950s, significantly
diminished the social and economic advantages of being a minister's
wife. However, these advantages had not entirely disappeared
because, as Finch has argued, once a woman has committed herself to
a minister through marriage she can probably best serve her own
economic and social interests by working to make a success of his job:

> [A] higher standard of living can be gained over a life time
> by being a wife than most women could achieve in their
> own right. In those circumstances it may well sound the
> most sensible economic option for a wife to invest her
> energies in her husband's work, thus promoting his
> earning potential rather than to pursue her own.[10]

This statement was especially true for the women in my study because most of them lived at a time and in an economic environment that offered few opportunities for married women to take paid employment and in a social environment where there was virtually total opposition to the notion of ministers' wives going out to work.

At the same time that the economic and social advantages of being married to a minister were being diminished probably most of the lay men and women that ministers' wives associated with were improving their position economically and socially. In other words ministers and their wives did not share in the growing affluence of Australian society to nearly the same degree as most of the leading lay families. Furthermore, as the affluence of such families increased they often sought admission to the more prestigious social circles within the community and in the process they often chose to cut their active connections with the church and its minister and his wife. Such developments diminished one of the social gains of being a minister's wife in a country town, namely close informal association with some of the fairly prominent families. Some of the wives commented on the failure of younger members of formerly prominent church families to draw them into their friendship circles. A greater number spoke with considerable feeling about the economic hardship they were experiencing at a time that their laity were 'doing well'. One put it this way: 'The lay people just gave us enough to keep body and soul together. There they were driving around in their big American cars and often we did not have enough money in the bank to pay for the latest repair bill to our old Austin. We were wearing it out for them.' Disappointment and, at times, resentment, however, did not cause most ministers' wives to give up supporting their husbands in many aspects of their work. There were many reasons for their persisting. One of the most important was their commitment to Christianity itself and to the Church as the necessary instrument of its maintenance and, ideally, expansion.

Believing in the cause

As far as I have been able to establish all the 30 ministers' wives of Barool and Smalltown were committed Christians. It appears that most sought to express their religious commitment through working for the Church and most believed that the success of the Church was essential for the advancement of Christianity and that the Church could only be successful if it had working for it good and able ministers and ministers' wives. Many of the women in this sample—especially those who had married ministers in the first-century—saw themselves as called to the full-time service of God. They believed that by marrying a minister they were able to realise this calling and at the same time realise their goals to be wives and mothers. It is important to bear in mind that there were no religious orders for women in the Methodist or Presbyterian churches for most of the period under study. Women can now be ordained to the ministry within the Uniting Church but the only full-time economically supported option for them in the former Methodist and Presbyterian churches was the position of deaconess. This was a role usually taken by a single woman and one which generally had less standing and less influence in local church life than that of a minister's wife.

The commitment of at least a majority of the ministers' wives in my two samples to their husbands' work was so strong that it is true to say that for them it was a vicarious career, a joint enterprise. For example, they made a habit of talking about 'our circuit' or 'our next appointment'. The extent of a wife's identity with her husband's career is illustrated by the following comments made by a Smalltown minister's wife in the 1980s: 'I am saddened by the approach of many younger ministers' wives who rebel against being ministers' wives even to the point where they have stopped going to church and stopped joining the women's groups. You know they don't help their husbands' work at all.' She continued: 'Some ministers have told me they don't know how their preaching is going down because their wives are not attending church so they are not getting any feedback.' This woman, who was frequently described in the parish, as 'her husband's greatest asset' organised her home so as to facilitate her husband's work. She served as his typist as well as his receptionist and hostess, regularly attended church functions and organisations, and introduced one new organisation to the church because she believed it would meet important needs of younger sections of the church community. The inextricable way in which her personal goals were mixed up with her husband's work was borne out by her teaching Sunday school so that she might have an influence on the quality of Sunday school life so that in turn her child would receive an adequate religious education. Although not officially described as such hers was, in reality, a joint career: she had made her husband's work her own.

The strong commitment this wife and many others displayed to their husbands' work probably came in large part from their

participation as young women in local churches. Here they gained
a knowledge of many of the very specific expectations that congregations, ministers themselves, and members of the Church's hierarchy
held of ministers' wives, and usually a commitment to meeting those
expectations. One can push the socialisation argument too far,
however, because there was a decline in the commitment of some of
the wives who had been active as young women in local congregations
to many of the traditional expectations of a minister's wife. Other
factors had intervened to erode the impact of early socialisation, for
example the increasing emphasis in the postwar period on the
importance of family life, of motherhood and of companionship within
marriage. Some of these wives, for example, objected to the continual
invasion of the parsonage and tried to maintain some measure of
privacy within it. The same wives insisted that they had married a
man and not a minister and were concerned to relate to their
husbands as men and not primarily as ministers. The same wives also
expressed concern over the impact their husbands' work and the part
they themselves were playing in the life of the church was having on
their children.

  In most cases the decline in their commitment to some of the
traditional expectations was not due to exposure to the feminist
movement. Only two or three of the wives who were resident in Barool
in the mid-1960s tried to advance their personal needs as justification
for not fulfilling some of the traditional expectations of them. The
Smalltown wives of the 1970s and 1980s did, of course, work as
minister's wives at a time when feminism was, so to speak, 'in full
swing'. As it happened only one of these wives gave much credence to
the feminist movement and it was only in her actions that there could
be observed a significant impact of feminist ideas.[11]

Local pressure to conform

Even where commitment to the role of minister's wife or belief in the
worthlessness of many of its traditional tasks is eroded ministers'
wives will often behave in an expected manner because the costs of
not doing so appear too great. There are the long-term costs of
damaging a husband's career and therefore one's own economic and
social interests as well as those of one's children. There are also the
immediate costs of earning disapproval of those one is interacting
with every day and alternatively the gain of earning their approval if

one meets their expectations. It is not surprising therefore, as Goffman has observed, that the character of the immediate situation and of the interaction itself (as well as external constraints) works to induce certain patterns of behaviour.[12] In the face-to-face situation there is a strong tendency for actors to match their performance to the expectations of their audience, especially where the audience exhibits a homogeneous point of view.[13] In both Barool and Small-town ministers' wives found themselves in situations where the laity adhered with great conviction to very explicit expectations of the minister's wife. The intensity of this adherence was demonstrated when expectations were breached. For example, in Barool there was an explicit expectation that a minister's wife focus her social activities on members of the congregation and not look beyond them for friendship. Barool ministers' wives knew of this expectation from their years as young women in their local congregation. The strength with which it was held in Barool was revealed on several occasions when a minister's wife offended by forming friendships with non-Methodists, especially ones of higher social standing in the community than the Methodists. A Mrs Forsyte, for example, was strongly criticised for this: 'She thought she was just too good for us. She preferred to hob nob with the elite of the district.' This was a reference to Mrs Forsyte's practice of finding her personal friends among well-to-do graziers and the town's professionals. She was also criticised 45 years after she had been in Barool by a number of my informants for not being friendly enough towards members of the congregation and for maintaining distance between herself and them by doing such things as 'failing to see us when she was out shopping'. As far as I have been able to establish this wife did not yield to the pressure the laity were placing upon her. She was, however, a wealthy woman in her own right and therefore was not dependent on the laity for her economic security. What is more, her wealth and social background enabled her to find an alternative reference group in the immediate context. Yet the Barool laity had the last word because they refused to extend the Forsytes an invitation to stay beyond their second year. This was an unprecedented action for them to take.

When the norm that a minister's wife should not work because it would interfere with her husband's work was breached in Barool by the one woman who took full-time employment, Barool people made their disapproval abundantly clear. One of the younger males of the church told the wife that she had no right to work, and to support his

point of view he drew an analogy between the wife of a farmer and
that of a minister. He said to her:

> The job of a farmer's wife is to help her husband on the
> farm and it is the same for you as a minister's wife. It is
> your job to help your husband with his work in the church
> so you should not take paid employment because this can
> only interfere with him doing his job properly. What is
> more, it stops you playing your part in the life of the
> church.

This woman did not desist, but she and her husband found it
impossible to live with the disapproval aroused by breaking the lay
people's expectations of them, and they left after only six months in
their appointment.

In both Smalltown and Barool another important expectation was
that a minister's wife should not try and 'take over' or impose
unwanted programs on the laity, especially the women. Mrs Boyd, a
minister's wife who tried in the face of gentle but determined
opposition by the most powerful woman in the Barool church to
persuade the Ladies Church Aid to increase their giving to the
churches' overseas mission stations only managed to persuade the
women to make a token increase in their contribution. The Boyds
were temporary appointees to Barool and Mrs Brown, who was
secretary of the LCA, told me that if she had known how Mrs Boyd
was going to act she would not have brought the letters from the
various mission stations requesting contributions to the meeting. She
continued: 'It is a good thing they [the Boyds] are only staying for a
few months because if they were here any longer we would have a few
'head on' clashes. Mrs Boyd made a career of being a minister's wife,
but she may have been insensitive to the fact that in the Australian
context her task was to be led rather than to lead because she had just
returned from many years in a Pacific Islands missionary appointment.

It seems that the lay women of the 1980s are often in a position to
exercise the same kind of power because a Smalltown minister's wife
who tried 'in minor ways' to wrest leadership from the laywomen was
strongly criticised and her attempts ignored.

Ministers' wives do not always comply when expectations are made
explicit or sanctions are introduced. But much of the time they do
because it is too costly to do otherwise. While they may believe that a
particular task is not worth doing or may even be detrimental to

themselves or to the life of the church they will perform it because they are committed to making their husbands' work as successful as possiblè or at least to doing nothing that will harm that work. Furthermore, they also have to cope with the expectations of their husbands. Often the husbands of the women in my sample held similar expectations to the laity. Even if a particular minister agreed that a specific expectation the laity held of his wife was unreasonable he usually preferred her to meet it because he held strongly to the view that his wife should support him in his work. Some ministers reported that they felt angered or let down if their wives failed to behave in a 'wifely' way because this made their job so much harder. The majority of ministers' wives who found themselves confronted by general disapproval of a course of behaviour they had adopted and who found their husbands were at least partially in sympathy with the lay expectations ended up meeting them. Understandably, they preferred to receive approval and goodwill rather than disapproval and ill-will from those who peopled their daily lives. So one minister's wife who believed that it was unnecessary for her to serve as president of one of the ladies' groups unhappily resumed the position because of the pressure applied to her by women of the church. She told me:

> They made it very plain that they did not like me giving up the job. I was repeatedly told that the meeting just was not working properly because I was not in the chair. They said they could not get along without me so I took on the presidentship again because my standing to one side was creating too much ill feeling and upsetting my husband.

The kind of pressure that can be applied and the effectiveness of such pressure in gaining conformity from ministers' wives is borne out by a story another minister's wife told me. This woman gave up doing something she believed was in the interests of her husband's work and the church to assume a role that she believed was less important. At the official welcome to herself and her husband the Sunday school superintendent publicly expressed the hope that she would take on the position of the superintendency of the kindergarten section of the Sunday school because as he said 'there was nobody else to do the job'. A number of other people subsequently expressed the hope that she would comply with this request. She resisted at first on the grounds that she had no experience in this kind of work and that it would interfere with her travelling with her husband to country services and seeing members of the parish that she had little opportunity to meet. However in the face of the expectation of the superintendent and other members of the congregation and pressure from her husband she capitulated. For the whole of her time in this particular appointment she resented this Sunday school work.

It must be stressed that probably most of the time most of the ministers' wives believed that the specific expectations of the laity and their husbands were worth meeting. It is also true that where they did not believe this they usually complied because the long-term costs of not doing so were too great. This was borne out by the fact that the six Barool ministers who had wives who persistently deviated from traditional expectations and who failed to modify their perform- ance under pressure, left Barool prematurely or resigned from the ministry altogether. It was clear to all concerned that these depar- tures were due to a marked degree to the attitudes and behaviour of the wives. Three ministers told me that the inability or unwillingness of their wives to support them to any great degree in their work was the main reason for their resignation from the ministry.

Living on the job

As long as a minister and his wife remain in the parish some involvement in her husband's work is inevitable for his wife. This inevitability stems not only from the operation of the sanctions that I have been describing but also because of her geographical proximity to his work and the manner in which that work is organised.

Because there are no time limits to a minister's work, because so much of it goes on in the family home and because of its sacrificial nature, wives usually find that their lives and the lives of their children are organised around their husbands' work and that they are active participants in that work. Ministers' wives answer phones, entertain visitors and at times substitute for their husbands by listening to people pour out their troubles. They try to justify to their children the chronic absenteeism at meal times of their father, his preoccupation with other people's problems when he is at home and the frequent invasion of the home by his parishioners. Even ministers' wives who are not committed Christians or who have no strong commitments to supporting their husbands in their work find them- selves caught up in that work to at least some degree because they 'live in his office'. For example, a Smalltown minister's wife for whom her husband's work 'was anything but a top priority' came to terms with meetings being held frequently in her home. She attended church much more regularly than she would have had her husband not been a minister; she regularly listened to parishioners discuss their personal problems and she tried to cope with the knowledge that many parishioners were dissatisfied with her level of involvement in local church life and were critical of her failure to give her husband more support.

Involvement in the minister's work on the part of such a wife is not a product of a conscious decision but of ad hoc reflex-like responses to requests and demands that are inevitable because she is 'living on the job'. Behavioural commitment of this kind is increased by the moral commitment most women have to making their marriages work and the knowledge that the success of their husbands' job is closely linked with success in marriage.

Taking up paid employment will obviously reduce the amount of phone answering, entertaining and voluntary counselling a minister's wife engages in but it will not totally exclude such activities. The extraordinary lengths it is necessary to go to minimise such intrusion is illustrated by the following story. This wife met the customary expectations of a minister's wife during the first few years of her marriage, but she gradually became disenchanted with playing the traditional role. So in order to escape many of its demands she took full-time employment in a town one hour's drive from her husband's parish. This gave her relief at least during the day from attending church functions and answering the phone etc., but she still resented her involvement in the weekend round of church activities, so she used the money she had accumulated from working to buy a home for herself two hours' drive from the parish. She then made a practice of escaping there virtually every weekend.[14]

It is undeniable that some of the wives in my sample deliberately sought to reduce the level of their involvement in their husbands' work and some, like the woman whose story I have just told, would have preferred to have separated themselves entirely from it. However, these women were the exception rather than the rule: the majority were strongly committed to making a success of their husbands' work, even if they did not agree with some of the specific things required of them. Many of these wives were so caught up in their husbands' work and identified so strongly with it psychologically, that in effect they had joint careers with their husbands. They were not, however, careers of equals, for the wives' roles were secondary and subordinate.

I have tried to show that even where the wives had little ideological or moral commitment to their husbands' work they were still caught

up in it to a marked degree. A number of powerful structural and
cultural constraints facilitated this. Because of the way work is
organised in this society—it is men rather than women who get the
better-paying, more secure, and more status-conferring positions—it
was in the interests of ministers' wives to further their husbands'
careers. There is also a strong cultural expectation that wives will
support their husbands in their work and put their husbands' work
before their own interests.[15] I have shown that the wives in my
sample were constrained to support their husbands in their work by
forces operating in the immediate situation and by the nature of the
interactive processes themselves. Usually wives needed the friendship and acceptance of the laity, and the laity had the ability to
sanction them economically and socially: they used gossip, joking and
persistence to ensure that wives conformed to their expectations. As
one wife said:

> It proved easier to go along with them than fight them.
> I've tried fighting and it just causes so much trouble.
> You've got to be at it all the time, you've got to win the
> same ground over and over again. While you're trying to
> make your point your husband's work suffers, your
> marriage gets hurt and the kids suffer as well. I do many
> things in the church I believe are futile and I believe that
> by doing them I deny my right to lead my own life. I don't
> like myself for doing them but there seems to be no other
> way. [This woman's husband eventually gave up parish
> work]

I have also sought to show that the manner in which a minister's
work is organised, with much of it centering on the home and its lack
of time limits, guaranteed some involvement of his wife in that work.
Even the minister's wife who bought the weekender still had to deal
with parishioners on weeknights. As Finch has convincingly argued,
there is a commitment to a husband's work which proceeds not only
from numerous acts of participating but from the personal and
familial sacrifice these have entailed.[16] A wife is also compelled by
the knowledge that various projects can be realised only if her
husband continues at his work and that for him to do this requires at
least a modicum of support from her. So commitment from ministers'
wives follows in part at least from 'having staked things of value upon
their husbands' work'.[17]

I have stressed that the costs of being a minister's wife were high.
Perhaps what I have failed to stress sufficiently is that for many the

rewards did outweigh the costs. One of the more important rewards for most of the wives in my sample was a vicarious occupational identity: In fact once married to a minister this was for most of them the only opportunity for an occupation apart from that of housewife and mother. As Finch observed in another context, 'it is the one available identity which does not confine a woman to the private domestic sphere but which offers her some kind of foothold—albeit a vicarious one—in the public domain'.[18]

The ministers' wives of the future may come to exercise much more control over their time and labour than did the wives I have been discussing. Entering the workforce is the most likely way of their achieving these ends. Many lay people have pointed out to me that while they disapprove of ministers' wives working it is a growing trend and that once firmly established it will mean that ministers' wives generally will do less in the church and give their husbands less support in the home than in the past. It must be borne in mind, however, that the possible gains coming for wives from these developments may be more than offset by the costs entailed. I say this because ministers' wives will, for the foreseeable future, live in a society organised on the assumption that it is men who are the primary breadwinners and providers for their families and that any employment that a wife takes is to be organised in such a way as to facilitate rather than inhibit her husband's breadwinning role. Wives will still be expected to support their husbands in their work and to take the main responsibility for the home and the family. They will be criticised for pursuing their own careers to the point where they jeopardise such responsibilities. Finch calls it doing 'triple duty'.[19]

If the findings of my study are a good indication then there will still be in the foreseeable future many ministers' wives who prefer a vicarious occupational identity to one of their own, for whom the gains of this identity outweigh the costs of doing 'triple duty'. In the lives of these wives the past will contend with the present and the future.

9

A clergy wife's story

MARLENE COHEN

To be or not to be is fortunately not the question. The question is what form our being takes. Pascal, Descartes and many since them have defined human essence primarily in terms of thinking capacity: only a reed, but a thinking reed . . . a thing that thinks . . . I think, therefore I am.

When God was asked for a self-description He declined to express His being in terms of faculties or achievements. He merely replied with the statement 'I am'. Human beings were formed in that image at Creation, it was despoiled in them at the Fall and it can be accounted restored to them at the Cross. We are, because He is. Our essence derives from His: He is the only ground of our being.

The implication of a divinely derived identity has been clear to me since I was fourteen. As a schoolgirl, and then from the age of sixteen as a teacher (mostly in Australia but for a short time in England), I went into each classroom and staffroom for Christ. The conversion of my headmistress was my first endeavour, while I was still a pupil, but I regretfully record that it was quite dismally unsuccessful. It took me some years to realise that it helped to care about people before attempting their conversion. A more successful enterprise, perhaps for this reason, was the evangelistic campaign I launched in my own student year, by means of the distribution of decision cards and impromptu lunch-hour talks.

Becoming a teacher gave me considerably more power to do this: within a matter of days of taking over a new class I would have everyone enrolled as Scripture Union members! I took and engineered all kinds of opportunities for witnessing to Christ and challenging others—staff and pupils alike—to follow Him also. Even transport to and from school, or a staff washroom in a boys' Prep School in England, could provide a suitable location for successful endeavour. I must often have appeared thoroughly obnoxious, but didn't realise this until some time later, fortunately by a gentle process unattended by too much guilt.

By the age of about nineteen, I had been back in Australia for some time and had become increasingly disdainful of the easy life of Christians at home. 'Some want to live within the sound of church or chapel bell: I want to run a rescue shop within a yard of hell,' declared C.T. Studd—and I.[1] The fact that this declaration involved him in leaving his wife and daughter in England for twenty years would have seemed to me then a feat of sheer nobility. I had been reading a whole range of missionary literature and had been particularly challenged by Oswald Sanders' version of the feeding of the 5000: he depicted it as an evangelistic setting with Europeans occupying all the front rows, receiving helping after helping of the bread of life while the Third World sat waiting, with little hope of even the crumbs.

The Church Missionary Society (of which my uncle had been the state secretary and my father the home secretary some years earlier) was advertising the need for a primary school teacher in Borneo and I decided to offer myself for the job. It came as a great surprise to be rejected; apparently I was too young to become a missionary. The suggestion was made that I continue teaching in Australia and apply again when I was older. I joined the League of Youth of the society and was later invited to leave teaching to become its full-time youth secretary, responsible for outreach to parishes in Sydney and throughout the state. I gathered together a team of about 70 young people (some of them men in theological training, today occupying official leadership positions in Australia and overseas), wrote a handbook, organised a training weekend and launched a program of team ministry.

Some months before this appointment I had graduated from primary to secondary school teaching and one day at an after-school prayer meeting a student asked me if I would pray for her family and in particular for her brother David. As the three of us attended the same church it was not long before she introduced us one Sunday evening at Fellowship. David joined our youth teams soon after, and on another Sunday evening—at a country service where I was preaching—he committed his life fully to Christ. We were married about a year later.

The week before our wedding we attended the society's annual summer school, as I had been responsible for much of the planning involved, with 400 people living in. At the same summer school of the previous year Bishop Stanway had asked me to go to Tanzania (then Tanganyika) as youth director for his diocese: but he told us later that it was apparent even then that I was unlikely to be free to accept.

Other than the reference to my acquiring a husband I don't think there has been any indication so far of my sexual status, and there is an appropriateness in that omission. The circumstance of my being female was an irrelevance in my ministry. At that stage of my life I was not aware within myself nor made aware by others that sexual differentiation had any bearing on usefulness to Christ. My life's theme of total ministry was pursued with the dedication of ordination. Even today when people ask me 'Do you want to be ordained?' the question can surprise me: I have truly considered myself ordained since I was fourteen. There were three components in my definition of ordination then, and they are the same three now: a personal call from God, a personal answering of the call, and a recognition of both by other Christians. Since my marriage I have suffered the bewilderment of finding the third requirement withdrawn without explanation.

The reason I now see for that withdrawal—but I did not see it clearly for about eighteen years—was not my sexual status alone but a combination of my marital and my sexual status; not only have these stood in contrast to my fundamental sense of Christian personhood, but they have been in active combat with it for the past three years, and in unconscious conflict for all those other years before! (I thank God for anaesthetising my mind from conscious realisation of that combat while our children were growing up, and while my husband was becoming established in his own ministries.)

Before our wedding there seemed to be no thought, at any official or unofficial level, of confining me in regard to ministry. Other unmarried women have found severe limitations and even humiliations placed upon them, but I happened to be in a situation where this was not so. No one seemed to think that my ministry equipment was any differently packaged or constituted because I was not male: there was no indication that the Holy Spirit indwelt me in a different way or apportioned His gifts to me according to some sexual criterion. I was allowed to be, without question. I was a source of pride and usefulness to those who knew me, as was shown by my ministry machinery being turned full on and at a speed that delighted me. There was a natural recognition that my essence was in service for Christ, that my endowment came direct from Him and that my identity derived directly from His.

After David and I were married each of these three was brought into question.

Up to a week before our marriage I was giving spiritual leadership to a large group of students, both male and female. From our honeymoon we moved into a student hostel linked with Sydney University. Though my husband was not yet 21 and was younger than some of the students, he had been appointed as Warden: as far as I remember his age had not been asked by the committee concerned, so they may have assumed that he was older, if they knew that I was twenty-three.

David was told that his duties included collecting fees, giving an after-dinner talk each weekday evening except Mondays, supervising the students' welfare and organising the kitchen and other staff. The only specific request of me (made a few weeks later) was that I check that no student be given more than one split-spoon of vegetables per meal. It must also have been implied at some stage—we forget now how it was couched—that I would fill in as cook if we had staffing problems and that I would keep an eye on the ordering of provisions and the tidiness of the students' rooms.

I realise that in this job of David's, as in all subsequent appointments, the board or person responsible for appointing him was probably reluctant to assume or expect that his wife went with him in the sense of providing an extra worker. I understand this in a general sense, but not specifically in regard to me, as it was either known at the start of each job, or discovered soon after, that I wanted to be in ministry partnership with him. We believed that God had called us into His service together, and I had thought that everyone else would see it that way. As it turned out there has never been a recognition of that partnership in the sense in which we envisaged it.

There has, however, been no official reluctance or compunction in accepting a high level of dedicated work involvement from me, so long as the work was in the blue-collar category—not white-collar, and certainly not dog-collar! The standard joke about 'unpaid curates' is remarkably apt, though I see it as a statement about status rather than about remuneration. I watched my mother occupy the role from the time I was two, with a combination of outstanding natural ability, buoyant enthusiasm and a rare quality of graciousness. Fortunately

for the church—and for her—she was never consciously resentful of
this role restriction, but anyone who knew her brother, Bert Arrow-
smith, and who knew her would have seen that they were identical
ministry machines in every piece of equipment. One of them was
turned on at high speed with constant public recognition of its
performance value and the other was left officially unattended and
barely recognised. Both, in different ways, were exploited. Exploitation by wastage is the more curious of the two—lacking as it does any
defensible rationale—and possibly the more culpable in God's view, as
we may see.

In the fifteen months that we were at the University Hostel David
gave 160 talks (with some initial trepidation as he had had opportunity to give only two addresses up to this time), received delega-
tions from students demanding more than one split-spoon of vegetables per meal—and meat of some recognisable quality—and also kept
up a full-time teaching program in a city school. I stayed at home,
helping the housekeeper unload supplies, confiscating underwear left
lying around the students' rooms and filling in on several occasions
when a cook failed to turn up. (One cook was in prison on one such
occasion but we didn't find this out until later.) I had never cooked for
40 before: in fact I had scarcely ever cooked before, except pork chops
and packet chocolate cake each time my sister's future husband came
to visit us in our flat, when our parents were in Canberra. To be faced
with the task of cooking porridge for that number early in the
morning (and while newly pregnant, as attested to by the uncertainty
of my inner equilibrium) was a challenge I still remember with
horror. Addressing a whole schedule of public meetings held
absolutely no comparative qualms for me.

I wonder why it was assumed that I would be a proficient housekeeper and cook on that scale? It has been very interesting through
the years to see what other assumptions have been made by David's
employers of the things I would do and enjoy—or should do and
enjoy.

Anyway, we joined the local church near the hostel and within a
month or so of our arrival found ourselves at its vestry meeting. What
happened there occasioned the first conscious recognition of the
surprise I must have been registering somewhere subconsciously over
the previous weeks: I can still feel it now. My being so surprised at
least demonstrates the genuineness of my self-concept at that time in
regard to ministry: it also however indicates a degree of naivety that I
can scarcely credit today.

What happened was really quite a small thing and so predictable:
the parish council was elected and no one thought to nominate me.
David's name was to be one of the first put forward (and withdrawn by
him because of the demands of his other responsibilities) and I then
expected to hear my own suggested. I was a rectory daughter with
teacher training and teaching experience, full-time ministry leadership experience and a cultivated missionary awareness: and I was
free, with scarcely anything to occupy me all day. Having been
brought up on vestry meetings, I knew that this last qualification
mattered a great deal: so many able parishioners just didn't have the
time to take on additional responsibility. The rejections I experienced
at this meeting occasioned my first conscious feeling of bewilderment
and this mind-cast was to last me for eighteen years. The way I saw it
then was that God had for some reason stopped wanting to use me, but
I could never understand what I had done to cause this. As I see it now
He had nothing to do with the restrictions placed upon me except in
turning them to good.

I should explain here that the main good has been a developing
swing of emphasis in me from the gifts to the fruit of the Spirit, from
doing to being. It was not my conscious choice but rather something
thrust upon me! My supreme self-confidence as a young Christian had
been rooted in a calm assurance of having already arrived at the
destination of my being. I sincerely believed there was no further
distance to cover. The nurturing quality of my upbringing had created
within me a self-esteem reservoir of immense proportions: the biblical
injunction not to think of oneself more highly than one ought, but to
think soberly, induced guilt in many of my friends (who emphasised
the first half) but not in me. I believed that God not only loved me but
was proud of me. It was not until last year that I understood what J.B.
Philips had apparently propounded years before, in 'Your God is too
Small', that our view of God derives subjectively from our parents'
view of us. (My daughter was preparing a talk for Fellowship and
asked me to define 'God'. I did so with aplomb as I not only knew Him
well but had made an academic study of Him over recent years. I was
therefore taken aback, and not a little incensed, when she smiled at
me kindly and explained I had exactly described my own father. We
later conducted the same experiment with a group of young people,
with the same results. Those with indulgent, nurturing parents
usually saw God this way and the others didn't.)

Another good that came from my rejection is the related conviction
that 'ministry' encompasses a vast range of spiritual activity and is of

course by no means limited to the taking of leadership and responsibility, nor best represented by it. However those of us who constitute
today's Church need to recognise that we still erroneously equate
ordination with visible ministry and therefore run the risk of imbuing
it with the highest value in spiritual terms. Leadership—a concept
also linked with ordination—does matter vitally, of course, which is
why its exercise is withheld wherever possible from women.

In my own early ministry experience, the official Church of the day
certainly chose to put me up front: any gathering of which I was part
more often than not assumed that I would be a major contributor.
Most of the Christian meetings I attended I did so as the speaker or
leader. Then suddenly it stopped. In fact the opposite occurred. From
the time of our marriage in January 1963 until May 1981, it was
assumed that I would have no leadership contribution or ministry
contribution whatever to make to any official Christian gathering of
men and women. The only time I remember speaking at a meeting
where a man was present he left before the address: he came across
during the singing of the preceding hymn and whispered 'Marlene, I'll
slip out now so you won't feel uncomfortable'. He was a clergyman of
about my own age and had only met David and me in the previous few
months. He clearly had no thought of demeaning me: he must really
have thought his presence would make me feel inadequate, whereas
his absence did so.

For eighteen years I attended church services and other such
meetings in no capacity that expressed the sense of ministry I felt.
(This would have been a minimum of about 2000 meetings.) I had lost
my 'I am' in that sense, not through any personal commission of sin
but because the Church had relocated me from the light of the Cross to
the shadow of the Fall and had done so in the mistaken belief that
God's own institution of marriage had decreed the position for me. In
the 21 years and ten weeks that David and I have been married I have
only conducted one teaching series where men were present and that
has been in the past ten weeks at a weekday Bible study.

I was too confused for all those years to do anything but keep quiet,
and keep occupied in the ministries available to me. I found real
fulfilment in discussion and prayer and still today would consider this
my primary ministry whether or not others become available to me.

Then the Anglican Church unexpectedly asked me to speak at an
Australia-wide conference on the topic 'Marriage and Family in God's
Purposes'. Not only were men present: they stayed when I spoke! In
doing the necessary biblical research I discovered the incontrovertible

biblical truth that God never intended men and women to exercise dominion over each other. The only actual statement about authority in the whole Creation material is when God gives it to man and woman together; and the authority was not over each other but over the earth. Having now seen this (and all its implications) so clearly myself I find the blindness of many of my friends in this area incredible. God never intended human beings to rule over or subdue each other and He came Himself to tell us so and show us so. Nowhere in Scripture is any person told to dominate any other person. 'Woe unto you . . . for you . . . have omitted the weightier matters—judgment, mercy and faith . . . ye blind guides, which strain at a gnat and swallow a camel/For one is your Master, even Christ; and all ye are brethren . . . neither be ye called masters: for one is your Master/You know that the princes of the Gentiles exercise dominion over them . . . but it shall not be so among you.' (Matthew 23:23–4,23:8,23:10,20:25–6) At Creation man and woman exercised joint dominion: at the Fall because of sin, the man ruled over the woman: at the Cross the power and penalty of all sin was dealt with. We are accounted restored, just as if we had never sinned. The New Testament proclaims the principle of reinstatement in three relational areas: Jew and Gentile, bond and free, male and female. The Christian Church of New Testament times devoted itself to the challenge of working out the first aspect in everyday life and ministry; subsequent generations worked on the second aspect: and our age is working on the third. Each area has been the cause of pain, conflict and schism in the Church of its time. To give Gentiles, slaves and women the status of Jews, masters and men is an undertaking of breathtaking proportions in any age.

In the 1960s the opportunity had come for David and me to go out on the mission field with the British and Foreign Bible Society. In our eleven years serving the society (six in Mauritius, three in New Zealand, then two in Africa for David alone, travelling around 42 African countries) and in both successive parish appointments, no inquiry was ever made of David or of me in regard to my ministry interests, experiences or qualifications. There was a real sense in which I had ceased to exist. The only inquiry of any kind was made six years ago, fifteen years after our marriage, in connection with the appointment to our present parish. At the conclusion of the nominators' preliminary meeting with us one of the church wardens asked 'And what about you Mrs Cohen, are you interested in church work?' There could be no more graphic way to express how much I had lost in those years that such a question could be put to me with any seriousness and with no intention of discourtesy or of patronage.

I experienced something similar to this soon after our arrival in the same parish, at yet another vestry meeting. Early in the proceedings it was explained that those who participated in discussion or voting needed to have been members there for a period of, I think, three months. Somehow it came up that even the rector's wife didn't qualify here and there was some light-hearted badinage about it. I took no part in that meeting, whereas my husband (who, it will have been deduced, had been in the parish for the same amount of time) not only chaired the meeting—with all that this involved—but selected one of the churchwardens and had the choice of an additional three Church Committee members. The feeling this aroused in me was still one of bewilderment rather than indignity, though I also remember feeling embarrassed on that particular occasion and trying to cover it by joining in the laughter. The situation clearly demonstrates once again that I had no real place, no personal location. My being had somehow been subsumed in my husband's: I had become a mere embellishment to his person and ministry.

I think now, in retrospect, that a book of Ayn Rand's brought matters to a head for me. My teenage children had given me a copy of *Anthem* for Mothers' Day in 1982 and its content meant so much to me that I have never since been able to hear Ayn Rand criticised without leaping to her defence (though a part of my mind cannot defend that defence!). *Anthem* is the story of a land where the word 'I' had long ago been forbidden and was now forgotten, and the book closes with the glory and pain of its rediscovery.

I asked an artist in our parish to adapt the cover of the book for me for use as a visual aid at women's meetings. I was on the circuit—and so grateful to be—as a speaker for an international women's convention group. One of their rules was that no men were to attend the meetings: this resulted from the genuine conviction that a woman should not have authority over a man. I agree with this contention—it being also a biblical injunction—but not with the belief that any such rule is concomitant to it. As I have commented before, I have four ordained Anglican clergymen in my immediate family—an uncle, now deceased, a father, husband and brother-in-law—and I have heard each of them preach several times. On no occasion has it occurred to me that any of them was speaking on his own authority.

The adapted cover depicted a woman with arm upraised, exulting in her freedom: but instead of a clenched fist her hand was open and relaxed and instead of a 'mighty Colossus' stance we had her on her knees! I have adopted it as my autobiographical comment, a statement of my own 'I am'.

My son has just commented, as I am writing, that Coleridge described the primary imagination as a repetition in the finite mind of the eternal act of creation in the infinite 'I am'. When Christ died He set me free. His blood cleanses me from all sin, even the sin of Eve, and I will no longer be held to account for it. I am free indeed and will stand fast in my liberty. But I also intend to try to obey the associated injunction that I must not use my liberty as an occasion to serve my own interests. Before I left school my French teacher, who was a committed Christian, gave me a little French New Testament with the biblical inscription 'The Son of Man came not to be ministered unto but to minister and to give his life a ransom for many'. She must have spotted that I was having trouble over English synonyms for the word 'ministry'. Jesus undoubtedly saw ministry as service, a total self-giving. I wonder why theologians of repute even today still equate 'the ministry' with authority.

Theologians are particularly sensitive, I've discovered, when any of the Church Fathers is brought into question in regard to the status of women. Undoubtedly this results from a fear that if their accuracy is undermined in one area it will risk the whole, but this need not be so. Another fear could be that church history may be found to affirm what many women today assert, that Christian men consider Christian women to be ontologically inferior to them, in a spiritual sense as well as any other. As the Church we should face the fact that the following men have made the following statements: Augustine (of Hippo): Women were not made to the image of God; Tertullian: Women are the Devil's gateway; Aquinas: Women are mis-begotten males. A modern Church Father may justifiably be assumed to be summing up the ancients in his declaration 'A Woman is ontologically subordinate to a man'.[2] She is unconsciously regarded as somehow unworthy, even as unclean.

The uncleanness of women in Judaism has been a subject of fascination for me since reading the Mishnah a few months ago. A Jewish woman delivered of a female child is unclean (and then in process of purification) for double the period of a male child. Samaritan women are considered menstruous from birth. No woman can be a witness in a court of law, and so on. In particular there is an emphatic equation of virginity with chastity: loss of virginity entailed loss of personal value. This concept of soiling has been fostered throughout the centuries in religious and secular writings and it is, I think, a core—though unrecognised—concept in our own churches today.

Jesus deliberately broke the law in regard to uncleanness. He did so in connection with a Samaritan woman (speaking to her about herself, let alone theology), a menstruous woman and so on: and He deliberately did so in public. He even chose a woman whose lifestyle had been uncleanness to be the first evangelist. His intention is unmistakable. He considers no one unclean. He has made us all clean, every whit.

There is a curious dichotomy in some traditions of Christian thinking about womanhood. Virginity is ennobled and so is motherhood, but the inevitable conflict between the two remains a source of some regret. Perhaps the real sequence of that view is this: (1) Virginity symbolises purity, (2) loss of virginity is a taint, as sin is, (3) a woman will be saved from her 'sin' by bearing children (as in 7 Tim. 2:15). Pope Paul VI put it more euphemistically: 'True women's liberation is in recognition of a woman's vocation to be a mother.' In fact, Jesus sees it very differently—which is predictable: like Father like Son! He refused to allow personal worth to have any residence in status, role, function or performance and He made this particularly clear in regard to women. When He was congratulated on His own mother's performance of her function—'blessed is the womb that bear thee and the breasts which thou hast sucked'—He replied 'No, rather blessed are those who hear the will of God and keep it'. To Martha, who was performing her expected function, He made the point again: 'Mary has chosen the better part which shall not be taken away from her.' Christ's Church today is still taking away some of that better part from women, and doing it in His name. Talents are being buried in the ground in the mistaken belief that such an activity is doing God service. To bury one's own talents is bad enough; to bury other people's talents—and to legislate for the process to be enforced—is alarmingly worse.

True women's liberation lies in men's recognition of a woman's freedom to be: true Christian women's liberation lies in Christian men's recognition of a woman's freedom to be, in Christ and in her calling to ministry. Though the Bible nowhere elevates motherhood (or fatherhood) to the highest rung of ministry, Christian principles and common sense would dictate to me that it should for some years be a primary ministry for both parents. In fact the Bible seems to hold fathers more than mothers responsible for how children develop. I have never understood the clumsy division of labour whereby missionary parents or others in 'full-time' service can feel called to neglect their own children in order to save other people's children. Of course they don't see it as neglect: they openly operate on the policy 'if I do God's work He will look after my children'. But God's work *is* our children. Once again there is often a confused ontological distinction whereby children are seen as extensions of the parent and therefore any focus on them can be a form of self-interest.

Being a parent is a primary ministry (for those who of their own free will and believing themselves to be in God's will, have taken on the role), but it is not a full-time occupation. As He has given us gifts of ministry, so let us minister, whatever that ministry may be. The Holy Spirit[3] dispenses ministry gifts regardless of sexual criteria.

When Bishop Dain and two other clergy combined their efforts to launch us into the married state he chose a text of obvious suitability: 'They two went on.'

What actually happened however is that David started and I stopped. As far as the official Church—the whole body of men and women in Christ—was concerned I stopped for eighteen years. Then in two successive years I was asked to be a keynote speaker at National Anglican conferences. The other speakers at those conferences came from established ministry spheres, so after the conferences were over they again went on: and I stopped again. I had no avenue to go on in.

In 1983 I applied for a licence to preach in our parish and within the diocese. (I obtained my BD in 1981 and am presently enrolled for an MTh. My program of study over the years has been a lifeline: I became an extra-mural student with London University the year after we arrived in Mauritius.) It was decided not to grant the licence, and one reason given was that 'it would not be in the best interests of David's future ministry'.

How can two go on if only one of them is permitted any movement? And why was only one ministry being considered when two people with ministry gifts and experience were involved? What God hath joined was being put asunder by men—men of God—not with any intent to destroy or to hurt, but in the sincere belief that no other option existed. I again stopped. As part of a new policy adopted by our archbishop, I was however licensed to preach one year later in August

1984, and I now preach once a month as part of our preaching team. It has not been easy to minister with freedom to a congregation that knows my suitability for such a ministry has been in question and that my licensing has been a matter of dispute.

` My husband has shared my bewilderment at each stage, because his private validation of my teaching gifts has been in conflict with the fairly consistent invalidation of them by the official Church.[4]

10

God and pronouns

RICHARD FRANKLIN

Christians have nearly always assumed that the appropriate pronoun to use for God should be 'He'. But this has been part of a much wider set of linguistic conventions, which ultimately reflect a whole way of thinking, a way which is often today called a patriarchal ideology. This way of thinking is questioned these days in many contexts for many reasons, and the questioning necessarily has an impact on religion. I am not in this chapter concerned with all the subtle ramifications of this change, but only with how it is reflected in our choice of pronouns.

Let us begin with non-religious contexts. There is a problem in referring to people in the ordinary third-person context while remaining gender-neutral; for example in advising school children we might want to say, leaving dots for the difficult part:

> If anyone wants to be an engineer . . . need(s) to choose maths in . . . courses.

The traditional way to handle this (for example in Acts of Parliament) is to say that 'he' covers both male and female. So we say:

> If anyone wants . . . etc., *he* needs . . . etc. in *his* courses.

Today, however, people increasingly protest, and surely rightly, that this inevitably suggests we are really talking only to the boys. Suppose we try to emphasise both genders by altering 'anyone' to 'any boy or girl'. We can then no longer say:

> If any boy or girl wants . . . etc. *he* needs . . . etc. in *his* courses.

113

And though it may be tempting for its feminist shock value to use 'she' instead of 'he', this is obviously open to the same objections.

Of course there is a grammatically correct way out, namely 'he or she':

> If any boy or girl wants . . . etc., *he or she* needs . . . etc. in *his or her* courses.

But this soon becomes intolerably clumsy, so people easily slip back into 'he'. Sometimes we find 's/he'. The trouble here is that we do not know how to pronounce it (except as 'she or he'). Moreover with cases other than the nominative we must presumably use 'him/her' and 'his/her', which again gets intolerably clumsy. Again we may try systematically to use the plural:

> If boys and girls want . . . etc., *they* need . . . etc.

However, not only can continual plurals get as frustrating as 'he or she's', but the trick will not always work. Suppose we want to go on:

> However at least the first one of them who later changes . . . mind will be able to switch to languages later

then we have the same problem as before.

Let us grant, however, that for skilled users of English the situation is at best an irritation, to be avoided by a handful of circumlocutions. The real problem is that most users are not really skilled, and the difficulties encourage slipping back into 'he'. There are at least two reasons for avoiding this. The first is that more and more people are annoyed by what they feel is sexist language. The second, and even more important, one is the *unconscious* influence on our thought of how we *unthinkingly* speak. We need to change bad linguistic habits for good ones, so the unconscious influences will go in the right direction. So we need a gender-neutral form of words which will continually, though covertly, remind people that they really mean both sexes. Unfortunately, English just does not have such a form.

To those who are skilled enough not merely to use English but to reflect on it, there might seem a good case here for inventing a new set of words, and then trying to get them accepted, just as 'Ms' has been largely accepted. We might try some composite form of 'he or she', such 'heshe'. But how would we pronounce it? 'H'she', 'hee-shee', 'heesh'? Then we would have to cope with the other cases, presumably by such forms as 'himmer', 'hiser', 'himmerself'. A better way might be to select the vowel that 'he' and 'she' have in common. (We already have the single vowel 'I' as a pronoun.) For 'him or her' and 'his or her' we could capitalise on the fact that the feminine has only one form, so we could again drop the 'h' and write 'er'. The result would be:

> 'he or she': 'e' (as in 'see').
> 'him or her': 'er' (as in 'earnest').
> 'his or her': 'er'
> 'himself or herself': 'erself'

In this way we introduce only three new words to cover all the uses of 'he', 'she', 'him', 'her', 'his', 'hers', 'himself' and 'herself'.

However I do not think any such proposal would be accepted. In the first place, though English absorbs hundreds of new words every year, they are substantive words, typically tacked on to our existing vocabulary to cover new circumstances. A change to our structural words, part of our basic word stock used in innumerable different contexts, is extremely difficult to establish. These forms would also be unacceptable because they sound like non-standard forms with the 'h-' dropped and have associations of ignorance and lack of education. Second, when such changes do occur, they are rarely the result of discussion by skilled and reflective language users. Rather there is a gradual shift among the whole linguistic community for which no one person is responsible, and a new usage begins to emerge. The skilled, who tend to be purists, often condemn it as improper (slang, neologism, ungrammatical, etc.). If it fills a real need, however, it will become accepted. Then what is legitimate purism in one generation becomes sheer pedantry in the next. For though we are entitled to protest for a while, in the end correct English must be what English speakers say.

I think this is happening now. People are exploiting the happy accident that the plural third-person pronoun is gender-neutral. So they increasingly say,

> If any boy or girl wants . . . etc., *they* need . . . etc. in *their* courses.

For this we pay a price. The singular verb 'wants' and the plural 'need' now both refer to the same subject, namely 'any boy or girl'. But such protests, I think, are purism on the way to becoming pedantry.

So much for non-sexist forms in ordinary contexts. If the tendency I discern succeeds, it will have both advantages and disadvantages for the problem of religious language. The advantage is that the less sexist our ordinary language is, the more the problem of talking about

God as 'He' will stand out, and so the greater will be the pressure for change; unconscious linguistic habits, that is, will now be pressing for a change instead of against it. The disadvantage, however, is that the previous solution will not work here. Clearly God cannot be 'They'. So what are we to say? 'It' is too impersonal; simply to substitute 'She' would again at best have feminist shock value; so we seem stuck with 'He'.

Unfortunately there is no one answer to this problem which suits all cases. However one device does stand out as giving maximum relief. The central problem, after all, is with liturgy. For it is above all in worship that difficulties are most deeply felt by those who find traditional language loaded with unacceptable patriarchal overtones. The device is: wherever possible—and it is nearly always possible—turn all third person pronouns into the second person; that is, replace speaking *about* God by speaking *to* God. So 'He' is replaced by the gender-neutral 'You'.

There is ample precedent for this. Again and again the psalms, for example, switch from second to third person and back, often in the same verse. Here is a random sample, using the translation of the current Anglican *Australian Prayer Book*:

> In the hour of fear: I will put my trust in you.
> In God whose word I praise in God I trust and fear not.
> (Ps. 56:3–4)

> I will sing your praises O my strength: for God is my strong tower. (Ps. 59:20)

> The river of God is full of water: and so providing for the earth you provide grain for men. (Ps. 65:9)

Hence when we find passages with third-person pronouns, we can simply convert them to second person, as in the previous examples. Consider:

> O shout with joy to God all the earth: sing to the honour of *his* name and give *him* glory as *his* praise.
> Say to God 'how fearful are your works: because of your great might your enemies shall cower before you. (Ps. 66:1–2)

Here we can convert 'his' and 'him' into 'your' and 'you', without defeating the purpose of the psalm in any way. In fact in this case it makes the first verse more consistent with the second.

Such a change is in no way obtrusively 'feminist'. In fact it not only
has ample biblical precedent, but seems positively valuable in its own
right. For it reinforces the basic truth that our primary attitude to
God should be one of prayer, and that talk *about* God which is divorced
from talking *to* God is always potentially sterile.

This device cannot always be applied mechanically. Where it
cannot, sometimes other equally simple changes may be effective.
Thus people increasingly object to the use of 'man' or 'men' to mean
humankind. In the phrase in the Creed, 'for us men and for our
salvation', 'men' is best simply omitted rather than being replaced by
'humans'. Again, where 'He' or 'Him' cannot conveniently be replaced
by 'You', we can often repeat 'God' rather than use a pronoun.

None of this should be mistaken for a solution to the deep,
underlying theological issues discussed in this book. For at bottom
what is at stake is our whole understanding both of God and of
ourselves. These ultimately cannot be divorced. If we are to think of
God at all we must use human images, while Christian views about
human nature cannot ultimately be divorced from views about God.

In our self-understanding, we have been accustomed to think of
human characteristics as typically 'male' or 'female'. The 'male' ones
would include: taking the initiative; being in control; standing firm
against pressure; reasoning rigorously by making sharp distinctions
and tracing out their implications. 'Female' ones would include:
nurturing; yielding and gentleness; intuitive insight; seeking consensus rather than defining differences. Despite, or perhaps because
of, the vagueness and open-endedness of these lists, they play an
important role in our thinking about ourselves and each other.
Increasingly this is seen by many as inappropriate stereotyping. The
new picture of human personality and individuality is different in at
least two ways. First, we seek more freedom of choice for individuals
in their roles in life. Let husband and wife decide for themselves who
will be the main breadwinner; why should not a man have the
primary task of bringing up the children while his wife is the main
provider? Second, there is a new picture, not only of the legitimate
areas of choice, but of the ideal of human personality. Many now
admire a more androgynous pattern. Men, they hold, should not be
ashamed of showing traditionally 'feminine' gentleness and sensitivity (which can be combined with all necessary firmness). Women
should not be ashamed of showing traditionally 'male' decisiveness
(which can be combined with all necessary concern for others). For
spiritual progress makes possible—in fact it largely consists

in—achieving a 'fully rounded' personality which successfully harmonises characteristics that from a lower level appear opposites.

For Christians, these issues inevitably spread ultimately into their views about God and the Divine Nature, and about the authority of their revelation. The God of the Bible appears, at least initially, as a heavily 'male' figure. Quite apart from the exclusive use of 'He', the terms used (metaphors though they may admittedly be) are also typically 'male' in their imagery: God is Lord, King of Kings, Judge of all men (including presumably women), Shepherd, etc. And how far, many Christians ask, are we at liberty to question this picture?

This is no place for a detailed discussion, but a few points may serve to balance the assumptions that have been held so unquestioningly by so many for so long. For new and exciting vistas of biblical interpretation develop, involving both the nature of God and also male–female relationships. Thus, in the Old Testament, though the commonest terms to address God suggest the 'male' emphasis, it is striking also, when we look for it, how much 'female' emphasis there is on God's nurturing, tenderness and compassion. Again, the development of the notion of Wisdom, which is always portrayed as feminine, seems to approach startlingly close to the Logos, the second person of the Trinity, by whom all things were made.[1] As for male–female relationships, the role of great female leaders such as Deborah may be seen as indications of how God has always broken through the patriarchal stereotypes of society to show that leadership as well as devotion can be irrespective of sex.

In the New Testament, much discussion is needed of why Jesus chose 'Father' as his central term for presenting his picture of God to his contemporaries. However clearly it is not meant to give a specifically 'male' picture of God. For, as only one example, when Luke tells the parable of the shepherd searching for the lost sheep, where the shepherd has always been seen as an image of God, he immediately follows it by that of the woman searching for the lost coin, where equally clearly the woman represents God (Luke 15:3–10). As for male–female relationships, not only does Jesus, in strong contrast to his age, repeatedly treat women on a complete spiritual equality with men, but there is the great declaration in Galations 3:28, quoted by several writers in this book, that in Christ there is no difference between Jew and Gentile, slave and free man, or man and woman.

What we should do about these questions is a further matter, where much thought—and experiment—is needed. However, as a simple and immediate step, we could look for undeniably biblical notions which reflect the 'female' rather than the 'male' aspects of God. One obvious one would be God as Nurturer; no one could deny the total orthodoxy of the notion that God nurtures the world and us. When, therefore, we use the commonest of all terms for God, namely 'Lord', we could balance this clearly 'male' notion by regularly addressing God as 'Lord and Nurturer'.

Beyond this simple proposal lie others which would certainly disturb many Christians as much as they would help others. A central one is whether we are prepared to balance Jesus' chosen metaphor of 'Father' with the other aspect of parenting, and so address God as our Father and Mother. Such linguistic changes are not trivial, but reach to the heart of our understanding of the divine nature.

It is for individual Christians to judge whether and how far they feel called by the Spirit to introduce such challenging changes. However the point of my present suggestion is just that we can separate those linguistic changes which are theologically contentious from those that are not, and we can implement the latter immediately. Specifically, we can avoid using 'He' of God, chiefly by changing to the second person, and we can balance the clearly 'male' orthodox metaphors such as 'Lord', by joining to them unquestionably orthodox 'female' ones such as 'Nurturer'. These simple proposals could, first, bring some immediate relief to those who find much current worship painful—sometimes painful enough to drive them away from the Church altogether. Second, there is the importance of sheer linguistic habit. It would be something if we could create linguistic habits in worship which left open, rather than begged, the central questions which Christians must eventually decide.

11

Affirmative action in the Uniting Church 1977–83

MARIE TULIP

It is a surprising thing that the Church, often regarded as the last bastion of male domination, should have been one of the first institutions in Australia to undertake what would now be called an affirmative action program, yet this happened in the Uniting Church. And it has been highly successful. Women now make up at least a third of the membership of nearly all committees and councils of the parish and congregation, and a third of the lay membership of presbyteries, synods and the Assembly, and their committees. This increased participation of women has built up women's self-confidence, changed men's attitudes, and transformed the style of many meetings. Property and finance committees, and specialised committees of the assembly and synods, are slower to change. Elders' councils on the other hand tend to have more than the required one-third women.

The increase in the number of women on decision-making bodies does not of itself change the power relation between women and men, and the Church is clearly still controlled by men in many areas of its life. However, the fact that women are now beginning to transform the life of councils and committees, and also to enter the ordained ministry in greater numbers, demonstrates, to themselves and others, that religious authority is no longer a male perserve.

The slight shift in power in the Uniting Church in Australia needs of course to be seen as part of a wider social movement in which women have been challenging male domination in many areas of Church and society both here and in other countries. It is a shift from almost total male domination of the structures and authority patterns of the Church toward structures and styles that include women and reflect women's experience. The change has taken place both symbolically and also in hundreds of specific local situations all round Australia. It is, I believe, a movement of the spirit, breaking entrenched patterns, opening up the Church to fresh options, bringing new life.

We now know how common it is for women to be written out of history, and already claims are being made that men deliberately adopted these changes in the Uniting Church out of the goodness of their hearts. One of the aims of this chapter is to set the record straight.

The historical context

At its Inaugural Assembly in June 1977 the Uniting Church in Australia took the historic step of adopting in its constitution and regulations clauses which sought to ensure the significant representation of women in all its decision-making bodies. It was a brave and surprising step for a church to take, the only one to have done so in this country where churches are still widely regarded as reflecting male supremacy.

This chapter seeks to tell the story of this struggle for change, to assess what it achieved, and to explore future prospects. As one of those involved in the events that led up to the constitution, I write as an interested participant, not a detached observer. I have of course tried to canvass as wide a range as possible of opinions and experience of members of the Uniting Church on these issues.

The timing is significant. When the Uniting Church was inaugurated, the regulations concerning women were to remain in force for six years, that is until June 1983. As that period has now come to an end I believe it is important for an account of what has happened to be written while it is fresh in people's memories.

Discussions directed towards church union have taken place among various churches in Australia since early this century. By 1971 three churches, the Congregational Union of Australia, the Methodist Church of Australasia, and the Presbyterian Church of Australia, had progressed far enough to have drawn up a Basis of Union. By 1974 they were in the final stages of drawing up a constitution and regulations for the new church they were to become, to be called the Uniting Church in Australia. The body responsible for drafting the constitution and regulations had 21 members and was called the Joint

Constitution Commission. All its members were male, and came from the upper reaches of the legal and administrative hierarchies of the three churches. Another body, the Joint Constitution Council, had 75 members representing women and men from each of the three churches in all the States of Australia. Being larger and more widely representative of the different aspects and groupings of church life, the council was much easier for the people in the congregations to relate to and be in touch with. It was this larger body, the Joint Constitution Council, that was responsible for deciding policy. The smaller Joint Constitution Commission expressed that policy in proper form in the constitution and regulations and in other ways. By the end of 1974 the Joint Constitution Commission had done a lot of groundwork and was ready for the larger Joint Constitution Council to come together and express its mind on many constitutional matters that would determine what form the new Uniting Church would take. The first meeting of the Joint Constitution Council was to be on 1 November 1974.

Many women were aware of the limited role and status of women in the three churches, and wanted to make sure that the structures of the new Uniting Church would enable women as well as men to participate fully. There was a sense of hope and urgency, of an opportunity for action of the kind that comes only rarely. We wanted the participation of women in the Uniting Church to be an item on the agenda of the Joint Constitution Council at this first meeting on 1 November 1974.

The previous year, in 1973, women from all the major denominations had come together to form the Commission on the Status of Women of the Australian Council of Churches (NSW), and a great deal of the pressure for change that was coming from women in the church was brought to a focus in this body. A packet of writings on feminist theology was published and read with widespread enthusiasm. A seminar series on women was held in the city. Consciousness-raising groups were formed, a resource collection was begun, and a national conference was held on Women's Liberation and the Church.

In mid-1974 the commission conducted an Enquiry into the Status of Women in the Church, the central findings of which were pinpointed by Sabine Willis, its director, in her introduction when she observed: 'Despite women's considerable physical presence in the Church their representation on decision-making bodies is miniscule. When funds are allocated, constitutions changed, theology discussed, the women are largely absent. In short, there is an enormous imbalance in the numbers of men and women serving on decision-making bodies in most churches, and many capable women deeply regret this.'[1] Many women who were seeking changes within these church structures hoped for a new church and new possibilities with the formation of the Uniting Church.

Meeting of Uniting Church Women, 3 August 1974

It was in this atmosphere of hope that the Commission on the Status of Women of the ACC called a meeting of Uniting Church women on 3 August 1974 in the Epping Congregational Church Hall to discuss the participation of women in the Uniting Church. The aim was to clarify and express women's views while the constitution was being drafted so that the structures of the new church could reflect the renewed hopes of women for full participation. Those invited were the State secretaries of the Congregational Women's Union, the Methodist Women's Federation, and the Presbyterian Women's Association; the fifteen members of the Joint Women's Committee made up of representatives from the women's organisations of the three denominations; the members of the ACC Commission on the Status of Women; and some other interested individual members of the three churches. All were asked to pass the invitation on to any other interested women.

Thirty-five women came to the meeting, including members of all the above organisations. Two women were to speak, and then draft proposals for a submission on the place of women in the Uniting Church were to be discussed. There was an air of excitement and anticipation, and of some risk. Women who were leaders within the church structures and women who were interested in women's liberation and the Church were meeting for the first time and finding common cause. Betty Marshall spoke about her visions for a church in which 'the time of isolation of women within the organisation is ended, and the time of participation has begun', and she went on to say: 'The Constitution Commission of the Uniting Church has been appointed and has already written a preliminary document—while we are assured that women have been taken into account there is no woman on this Commission'. Marjorie Spence spoke of her experience as the convenor of a committee of the NSW General Assembly of the Presbyterian Church, a male-dominated body in which in 1973 out of a total of 538 members, only eight were women. By a vote of the assembly Marjorie was allowed to present the report of her committee, but only after several members had objected and one called her an 'outsider'. She said:

> To say that a Communicant member of the Church was an outsider was to express a truth for that is just how I felt and how the structure of the Church intended me to feel . . . I felt betrayed by a hard master—the Church. It requires from its servants hours and hours of voluntary, sacrificial time and effort and allows them to carry the responsibilities involved without providing for their rights.

The submission

The meeting then turned its attention to the draft proposals for a submission on the place of women in the Uniting Church. After a great deal of discussion agreement was reached on the recommendations of the submission and it was unanimously adopted. It consisted of a preamble arguing that while there were virtually no biblical, theological or legal barriers to the full participation of women in the life and ministry of the Church, there were very real barriers in the traditions and structures of the Church. It went on to say that it is not enough to remove discriminatory laws and procedures. 'For the true integration of women into the total ministry of the church, positive steps will need to be taken to overcome the habits and stereotypes of centuries.'

The submission asked that the following eleven recommendations be adopted by the Uniting Church and that regulations be worked out to ensure they become part of the church's practice:

1 That at least 60 per cent of the members of presbyteries, synods, and the Assembly be lay people, and that all age groups be represented.

2 That at least 50 per cent of the lay members of parish councils, presbyteries, synods, and the Assembly be women, so that these bodies may be truly representative of the church membership.

3 That the committees set up by these bodies include at least 30 per cent women and that women be given equal opportunities in leadership.

4 That administrative and staff positions at all levels be open to women and men, and special efforts made to recruit women in order to overcome the present imbalance.

5 That positive steps be taken to actively seek out and encourage women to become candidates for the ordained ministry.

6 That the participation of women in the theological processes of the Church be actively encouraged at all levels, including teaching in theological colleges.

7 That care be taken to use all-inclusive language (i.e. the use of such terms as 'men and women', people, persons) on all occasions and in all documents, including liturgies, rituals, and orders of service.

8 That the Church take positive steps, with the necessary support staff, to prepare and encourage the women of the Uniting Church for involvement in the life of the Church and of society and for the recognition and development of their potential as people.

9 That times of meetings be arranged so that full lay participation is possible.

10 That lay participation in all aspects of the Church's life, including worship, pastoral care, education programs, developing church policy, and general church administration, be encouraged so that full use is made of all lay resources.

11 That a limitation on the consecutive years of service of a member of any Assembly committee be seriously considered in an effort to widen opportunities for participation and for continuing renewal of the decision-making areas of the Church.

The meeting requested the Commission on the Status of Women to convey the submission to the members of the Joint Constitution Commission and to its executive officer, asking him that they also be placed before the Joint Constitution Council. The meeting also asked that the submission be incorporated in the newsletter *Countdown* and be publicised in church papers, and that representatives of the women be able to attend the next meeting of the Joint Constitution Commission to present the submission in person.

Responses to the submission

At the end of the women's meeting there was a great feeling of achievement and, though many would not have used the word, of

sisterhood. We felt the submission was important and well thought
out, and it was supported by many of the most highly respected
women in the three churches. However, while we did not expect the
male office-bearers and church representatives to agree with everything in it, we were quite unprepared for the deep resistance we were
to encounter.

Where we had hoped for the widest possible dissemination and
discussion of our proposals, we found when the Uniting Church Office
replied to us that they were unwilling to circulate our proposals or to
give them any publicity or even to give us the names of members of
the Joint Constitution Council to whom we had hoped they would be
sent. Nor were they willing to allow our three representatives to
attend a Joint Constitution Commission meeting to talk to members
in person. Women were evidently perceived as posing a greater threat
to male power and control than we had imagined.

The Joint Constitution Commission met on 10 September 1974 and
decided that they would bring to the attention of the Joint Constitution Council the matters raised in the submission, and send copies of
it to the Australian presidents of the women's organisations of the
three churches. We felt, however, that it was essential for members of
the Joint Constitution Council to have a chance to actually read the
submission and also for some of the men who were members either of
the commission or the council to meet some of us so that we could talk
through the issues involved. Without an actual meeting we felt there
was no chance of our proposals being taken seriously. We therefore
decided that as the Uniting Church Office would not accede to our
requests we would ourselves send the submission to Joint Constitution Council members, and invite them to a meeting to discuss the
issues with the women making the submission. We had to use our
informal networks to find out who these members were in each state
and their addresses.

Meeting of some members of Joint Constitution Council with Uniting Church women, 18 October 1974

The meeting was on 18 October 1974 in the Chatswood Methodist
Church Hall. Twenty-one of the 35 women who made the submission
attended, and seven of the 75 members of the Joint Constitution
Council, two of whom were women who had signed the submission.

Opinions and feelings about our recommendations were thoroughly
aired and discussed, and we got to know each other fairly well. There

was not then, and had never been, any disagreement about the aims of women participating fully in the life and ministry of the Church (as already laid down in the Basis of Union, paragraphs 13, 14, 15), or about general principles that special efforts should be made to include women in staff positions, in the ordained ministry, in theological study and teaching, in the language of the Church and all other aspects of the Church's life. However, as soon as we suggested how these principles might be incorporated in the constitution and regulations of the Church there was a complete block.

We felt we were getting precisely nowhere with our submission. It was a classic case of male resistance and stalling. Our arguments for a set proportion of women were not answered with reason but with comments as to their being 'impractical' or 'unnecessary' or 'women would be taking the places of the "best people"' and so on. The attitude of the men, unable or unwilling to take us seriously or to enter into real discussion, made us angry and sad. And they were the men who had been sympathetic enough to attend.

Towards the end of the evening the constant stalling of the men eventually provoked the women to anger and brought the meeting to a crisis. I think that, together with the number of committed women there and our obvious seriousness, it was this strong expression of our anger that made this meeting a turning point in the whole struggle. It called the men's bluff, and I believe they realised they had to take responsibility for either including women by a percentage system, or excluding them with unsupported and therefore empty words of goodwill. It also galvanised the women into a deeper commitment to the struggle. All the women I spoke to afterwards said they came away from the meeting more convinced of the need for percentages than ever.

To give some idea of what we were arguing and of how stirred we were, it seems worth quoting here from a statement I wrote as a response to that meeting. It was circulated to the members of the Joint Constitution Council as a further preparation for their November meeting when they would be coming together for the first time to decide matters of policy for the Uniting Church. We wanted their voting to be based on as full as possible an understanding of what we were asking. The situation as we saw it was as follows:

> At present there are very few ordained women in the three churches in Australia. In N.S.W. in 1973 the Congregational Assembly had a fair proportion of women but the Presbyterian Assembly had 8 women and over

530 men, and the Methodist Conference had 33 women and 520 men. What is going to happen in the Uniting Church, particularly if members of councils are chosen on the basis of one minister and one lay person per parish/ group of parishes/group of presbyteries, etc.? We are worried that the one lay person will almost always be a man. It is then even more vital to guarantee that a certain proportion be women.

It is sometimes asked why more women do not offer as candidates for the ministry. The ordained ministry at the moment looks for all the world like a male club, and unless the church can give some sign of its good faith to women, it is not surprising that women do not come forward. Including a percentage of women in the church councils would be a credible sign that women's experience and gifts are valued in the church community as much as men's.

After the meeting, a Presbyterian woman said, 'As far as the church is concerned I'm just hanging on till 1976, hoping the Uniting Church will be different'. Another Presbyterian: 'My Church has never asked me to do anything'. A Congregational woman: 'I got so mad hearing all those women begging the men to allow them to be part of the Uniting Church. We have to struggle to be accepted as baptised members of the church'. A Methodist: 'I'm more convinced of the need for percentages than ever!'

Given this context, we argued strongly for our views, believing they had special relevance for the Uniting Church and its Basis of Union:

We believe the only way to ensure full participation of men and women in the Uniting Church is by having set proportions of men and women on the various councils. The questions we are putting to the Commission and Council still haven't been answered.

It is said that a system of percentages would be too rigid and confining. But a system of percentages is accepted to guarantee certain proportions of lay and clergy and the same sort of system could be used to ensure participation of women.

It is felt that the change towards fair representation of women will come about naturally, without percentages being stipulated. This has not been the experience of any group that has tried to break the middle-aged male clergy monopoly on church government. For example the battle for equal lay representation was won in the Reformed

Churches at the time of the Reformation, and hundreds of years later the proportion of lay persons still has to be constitutionally guaranteed. For years the Methodist Church has been talking about equality between men and women but the representation of women in church government has remained at the level of tokenism. In 1973 the N.S.W. Methodist Conference passed a resolution one morning that women should be given higher representation on committees including the Standing Committee. On the same day 6 outstanding women were nominated but only the previous 3 members were elected. Presbyterians have more recently overcome the legal barrier to ordination of women as elders and ministers and believe there will be a gradual increase in participation of women. If they believe this in good faith why is there such strong opposition to the proportion of women being indicated in the Constitution? We feel it should be there as a safeguard.

The Basis of Union clearly states that the Uniting Church will provide for the exercise by men and women of the gifts God bestows upon them. How is the Constitution to do this except by setting out percentages?

Meeting of Joint Constitution Council, 1 November 1974

The Joint Constitution Council held its first meeting at Naamaroo on 1 November 1974, with many important matters to be discussed and decided. Friends of the women's submission, women and men, negotiated it through the difficult rapids of counter-argument, meeting tactics and a full agenda. The vote when it came was in favour. Reporting later on the many decisions of the Council, the *Sydney Morning Herald* (5 December 1974) chose to headline the women's issue, 'Quota for Women in Uniting Church', as also did the *New Spectator* (20 November 1974). Both papers gave good reports of the decisions, the *SMH* reporting as follows:

Women will constitute at least one-third of the lay representation of councils and committees in the proposed Uniting Church in Australia.

This has been recommended by the Church's constitutional council, despite misgivings that to 'talk in figures' was contrary to the spirit of Christianity.

The one-third principle will apply for six years. It is
hoped that after that time selection of women will require
no compulsion.

But old attitudes die hard. The *New Spectator* quoted a Methodist
male delegate who commented, 'We will have to watch in cases where
women are not available to fill the suggested quota. Otherwise we
might have Grandma coming down to presbytery or synod meetings
just because Grandpa happened to be elected. We don't want to
encourage the idea of wives accompanying their husbands'.

The actual decisions as reported in the minutes were as follows:

Submission re Status of Women

It was resolved:

1   That the Council expresses its concurrence with the
    principles underlying recommendations 4 to 11 in the
    Submission, and points out that the first part of No. 4
    is already provided in the proposed Constitution and
    Regulations, but that the remainder of what is sought
    in that and the following recommendations are admi-
    nistrative and policy matters requiring decision and
    implementation by the councils of the Uniting Church
    when constituted.

2   That the Joint Constitution Commission be asked
    either by amending the necessary regulations so as to
    require and permit, or by some other means seek to
    ensure, that for the first six years of the Church's life
    at least one third of the lay members of each Council
    be women.

3   That this Council recognising the principle embodied
    in the Basis of Union that women should be given
    equal opportunities with men to exercise the gifts
    which God bestows upon them, urges the Joint Consti-
    tution Commission to ensure that provision is made by
    every possible means to facilitate the full participation
    of women in every aspect of the life of the Uniting
    Church.

The women who made the submission were delighted. We regarded
the acceptance of a set proportion of women as a significant victory on
the way towards full equality of women and men in the Uniting
Church.

But we were also disappointed. Our submission had recommended
that at least 60 per cent of the members of councils be lay people, and

at least 50 per cent of the lay members be women. In fact the constitution requires that only 50 per cent be lay, and that of this 50 per cènt one-third should be women. So in fact, recognising that over 95 per cent of the clerical members are men, the required proportion of women is one-sixth of the total, or 16 per cent, whereas our submission sought 30 per cent—a very significant reduction.

The second major qualification was the addition of the six-year time limit.

The third qualification is apparent in the detailed wording of the requirements in the regulations for membership of the congregation councils and committees, parish councils, presbyteries, synods and the Assembly, for each of which the words 'if practicable' or some similar phrase appear. In addition, the Council declined to make any specific provisions relating to recommendations 4–11 of the submission.

So it was far from a clear victory. Yet we understood only too well the Church's resistance to change, particularly on this issue of relations between the sexes which affects everyone so intimately and so deeply. After 2000 years of male domination in the Church, with past attitudes still so deeply entrenched, we were delighted with what we saw as a step forward, a change in the pattern, an opportunity for growth.

The question still to be answered was, were the proposals so watered down as to be ineffectual? Were the qualifications so serious as to have made the whole thing a token gesture? Were we back where we started, with the real power structures of the Church, the decision-making bodies at all levels, still effectively in the hands of men?

How the regulations worked out

The six years for which the regulations concerning women were to be in force are now over. It is disappointing that some assessment was not made by the Church before the expiry date so that an informed debate could have been engaged in and a decision made on whether the regulations should continue or not. When I undertook this study the rather strange silence had been broken only by a NSW minister quite openly rejoicing that the regulations would have a limited life. A survey was undertaken a few months later by women in Victoria which showed that 79 per cent of the laity of the Uniting Church, but only 44 per cent of the clergy, felt the regulations should continue.

In March 1983 the Commission on the Status of Women of the Australian Council of Churches (NSW) agreed to sponsor the present study. Leaflets were circulated widely and large advertisements were placed in all the state newspapers of the Uniting Church. The response was immediate, enthusiastic and gratifying. Letters, some short, many long and detailed, came from all states and territories except Tasmania, and express a wide range of experience and opinion. Of over 60 replies, 78 per cent are from women, 22 per cent from men. Considering the passions and conflicts so easily aroused by this subject, even more perhaps in the Church than in society generally, I was delighted that so many were ready to grasp the nettle. The results are not necessarily representative of the membership of the Uniting Church, but they are broadly based enough for assessment to be made of what the legislation achieved.

The general pattern that emerges is that at all levels of church government and in most geographical areas the regulations were accepted and complied with. Sometimes it was with enthusiasm, sometimes with reluctance, but with few exceptions a serious effort was made to include women in the proportions set down.

Most correspondents saw the effect on the Church as a large and worthwhile increase in the participation of women. At first many women were too shy or self-deprecating to come forward, and many men and some women showed various degrees of opposition, but as these initial obstacles were overcome, it 'became part of the thinking to include women'.[2] Later, after four or five years, the numbers of women started to slip again.

There is a widespread feeling that the regulations achieved their aim, and a sense among many contributors that the balance between women and men on councils and committees is now as it should be. Many others however have a sense of unease that although women's participation has greatly increased, the underlying attitudes and structures of male domination remain.

Patterns of response

There are three main patterns of response expressed in the letters, although there is considerable overlapping. A small group, fewer than 10 per cent, are opposed to the regulations or think they made no difference; a second much larger group thinks the regulations brought about important changes and that the present situation is broadly satisfactory; a third group, about the same number as the second group, also thinks the changes have been important and beneficial but considers they should go further.

The main objections to the regulations, as reflected in the first group, are that they somehow interfere with God's will, that the people in 'top' positions should be men, that regulations might lead to people who are not the 'right people' being on committees. However, very few of the correspondents made these objections, and often they supported the regulations in other ways in their letters, and had been quite willing for women to participate at all levels of church government.

The large second group, representing, one feels, a large body of opinion in the Church, sees the regulations as having brought about a significant change for the better. Most problems have already been sorted out. Although there is a vague sense of threat to men, and fears that some may leave, most men tolerantly accept, and sometimes even welcome, the increased participation of women. Women themselves are in general enthusiastic about it and are benefiting from it. Very little change in meeting style or procedure was noticed or expected by this group, but there was a general feeling that the increased contribution of women had enriched the whole Church. Now that the old cycle has been broken and a new pattern of participation established, many people in this group appear to consider the regulations no longer necessary.

The third group also think that the legislation has brought about significant and desirable change but in contrast to the second group they think that the change is not deep enough or securely established. Where the second group look more to past changes and what has already been achieved, the third group look with a more critical eye at the present and at possibilities for the future.

Where the second group are glad for women to have a bigger slice of the cake, the third group want a different cake. They do not think it is enough for women to take part in the Church on the old terms. To them, full participation of women requires that the patriarchal structures of male domination and female subordination be transformed into a new relationship of equals.

Reflections on the present situation

A minister, recognising that more women are on committees, asks what has this achieved. 'In many instances,' she says, 'women are not able to be assertive enough to make any input, either to a cognitive discussion or in changing the emphasis of a meeting.' In other words, women are present at meetings but are not powerful enough to

challenge the male style, supported as it still is by superior numbers
and the weight of tradition. It is not that women are in some way
weak or incapable, or still in need of some sort of extra education or
experience; rather it is that the governing bodies of the Church are
still controlled by men.

The figures of the General Assemblies of the Uniting Church since
union support this view of the present position. At the First (Inaugural) Assembly in June 1977, women were 31 per cent of the lay
members and 17.5 per cent of the total (nearly all the clergy being
men); at the Second Assembly in 1979 the percentages were 40 per
cent and 21 per cent, and at the Third Assembly in 1982, 41 per cent
and 19.6 per cent respectively. That means that the regulations were
fully complied with (in fact there were slightly more women than the
required 33 per cent of lay members) and yet we still have a situation
where for every one woman at the Assembly there were four men. And
in 1982 all the officers of the Assembly, and all the chairpersons and
secretaries of Assembly commissions, councils and committees except
one were men. Looked at in this way I believe we can still say that the
legislation has been a success, but it is important to see what has been
achieved and what has not. Certainly the old pattern has been broken
and more women are on decision-making bodies, and this has found
ready acceptance in the Church. But it does not mean that the
Uniting Church has stopped being a male-dominated institution or
that women and men now participate equally. For those interested in
real sharing of power and responsibility, the legislation has been a
beginning, but there is still a long way to go.

There is, I believe, a certain danger in the view of many church
members that everything is now all right and the regulations can be
dropped. They underestimate, I believe, the strength and momentum
of male power in the Church. This is not necessarily to blame men, but
to say that the system will not change unless deliberate steps for
change are taken, and men have a stake in this, just as women do.
Extending the term of the regulations may be only one of the possible
appropriate ways forward, but unless the Church takes some action in
the light of the present situation, the slide backwards which some
women have already identified may accelerate.

What is the present situation? Certainly it is important not to deny
the gains made (and referred to earlier). But it is also important to
look at the whole picture. Let us look first at where women still
encounter obstacles to full participation and then at where breakthroughs have been made.

Undergirding the continuing numerical superiority of men on many councils and committees (for example the Assembly, as described above), there is still the whole weight of the patriarchal tradition and symbol structure of the Church. Although some genuine attempts at change are being made, most references to God are heavily male, language in church documents, liturgies and hymns is strongly sexist, authority figures (for example, clergy) are nearly all male, theology is still male-centred, and so on. All these things are changing, but little headway has been made so far, and each change requires a lot of work and energy from women.

Several people referred to the way tradition expresses itself in male networks. Established over many years, they tend to be self-perpetuating and are a problem when it comes to nominating women. Highly qualified and experienced women expressed disappointment that they were not asked to do anything related to their special qualifications and skills, though they were asked by the Church to do other traditionally feminine things. Meetings are still set up in a way which excludes some women and makes it difficult for others to attend. Many women continue to be alienated by the rational, competitive meeting style, in which men monopolise the talking and put procedure over content and the interests of people, while other women and men are more hopeful as they identify ways in which women's style is gradually, if slowly, transforming what they see as the dry bones of male meeting procedure.

The hurt involved for women who go on challenging old patterns is well expressed in the following letter:

> I've been reflecting on how I feel in my own parish situation. Initially we tried hard to ensure that approximately one third of the members of the parish council were women, although it was achieved only by appointing a greater number of women from one of the two congregations making up the parish. Five years later when an executive of the parish council was appointed, its six members were all men. When I raised this at a meeting of our congregation earlier this year and sought to move that the congregational meeting request the parish council to do something about it, I was quite unprepared for the hostility which my motion engendered in the meeting. I was told that such an action would be divisive within the parish council, that it had only happened because all of the officers of the parish council were men (as though that explanation was good enough). As an aside one person

suggested we didn't have to worry any more about what the regulations said about having one third women as the time in which that was to take effect had now expired! I can still recall how awful I felt in that meeting when my motion was carried by one vote and a subsequent motion, to which I agreed, was passed that no action be taken on the result. This experience at a local level and others have made me feel alienated from some members of the congregation that I have known for a long time and at the moment I am feeling very ambivalent about becoming involved in the institutional church.

The continuing strong influence of the masculine and feminine roles underlies many of the present hurtful attitudes: 'There is still discrimination against women mainly due to attitudes and expectations which are slow to change and difficult to alter. Women are still expected to act like women; to be outspoken is laudable and "prophetic" in a man, "aggressive" in a woman. Business matters are still the province of men, who are deferred to in most councils of the church.' One woman wrote of her desperation at being discriminated against in her work and then the relief of a particular accepting community, grateful for the reforms of the women's movement. She said that 'aggressive' women make her feel 'shivery and squirmy', though at the same time without realising it she was appreciating the benefits they had brought about.

Many women feel excluded from the church community because they are outside the traditional 'ideal family' pattern. One woman who was divorced said the church women expressed sympathy but no real understanding. Another said the sexist attitudes of the church men prevent the Church from reaching the families (for example single-parent families) who need it in her area.

Several people said that women feel confident locally, for example at congregational and parish level, but 'insecure outside this area'. 'At Presbytery many women are regular in attendance but with little to say.' 'Few women speak at Synod although amongst the lay delegates women would predominate.' It seems that where women are strong enough to influence meeting style, that is, locally, they quickly gain confidence and contribute well. Where men predominate, at synod and the Assembly and above all on the specialised committees and boards, men keep control and women keep quiet—or refuse to be nominated. There is a tendency to blame or exhort women, but it might be more appropriate to change the structures and style so that women feel comfortable and secure enough to participate. As one women said, 'so many women have developed the confidence once they have the opportunity'.

Only two men mentioned their own effort to change roles. One sees himself as a pioneer when he picks up a teatowel at church functions—and let no one underestimate the courage needed to break role-patterns. The other, who has been 'attempting to encourage all to use inclusive language' says that 'by some men I am seen as a betrayer of my sex!' Well, if breaking sexist language and other structures of domination is seen as a betrayal, perhaps it is time a few more men became traitors!

It is clear that the battles are still there to be fought. But I want now to turn to the signs of hope, the breakthroughs. And I believe that women have indeed begun to make a difference.

The fact that women are present on the committees and councils means that the committees are already different, and there have been a great many comments on changes towards a more humane, personal, social, caring style, with less competition, more consensus, and the power to see that 'ideas have legs'. The rate of change is too slow for some women, too demanding of the energies of others, and some fear the slide is now backwards. But women *have* staked their claim, and change has become visible.

In the second place, women are beginning to overcome their fear of power, bred in us since Eve was framed, and to give up the manipulative way of using power through someone else. As women come out from behind the scenes to exercise power directly on committees and as officers of those bodies, they are beginning to create role models for younger women, as also are the growing but still small numbers of women ministers. I believe it is true that authority is still tied to maleness in the Uniting Church, and that this will continue to be the case while most ministers are men. However, if 35 per cent of students at the United Theological College are now women it is clear that, at this deep level of authority patterns, change has begun to happen. It represents a shift in power at the symbolic level in the Uniting Church.

The same shift seems to be happening in relation to women elders, and it is interesting to speculate on why women are choosing the elder role. It uses women's traditional gifts of nurturing and caring, but in combining them with an avenue for participating more creatively in worship, and also with the oversight of the spiritual life of the congregation, it links and integrates them with the symbolic and the decision-making powers of the Church. So it becomes for women the free choice of a high and responsible avenue of service, rather than their being slotted into the traditional doormat role. A second reason may be that it gives women a way of expressing their gifts more directly than the slow, difficult, equally valuable role of serving on and transforming committees.

The picture that emerges, especially from the third group of letters, is of a church very ready to welcome women onto committees and councils, and to accept in general the many obvious changes and benefits this has brought. At a deeper level the Church is still male-dominated and -controlled. Most men are happy with the status quo and seek to perpetuate the structures and styles that suit them. Almost all initiative for change in this area comes from women and is accepted or met with passive or covert resistance from men. Often this resistance may be unintentional or even unperceived, simply the momentum of the powers that be. The changes have been welcomed by women and in some cases have been deep and significant enough for women to become aware of their own relation to power in a new way, and to have a transforming effect. Some women are sad, disappointed or angry at the Church's reluctance to give up its attachment to the old roles, or are simply fatigued from carrying the torch for so long, and are choosing to move out rather than go on with a fruitless struggle.

Future prospects

Looking back, we can recognise that several factors were important in the success of the regulations on women. First, the enormous initial impetus from women and the continuing collective energy of women; second, that the regulations were based on important beliefs of the church and clauses in the Basis of Union; third, that the proposals became part of the formal legislation of the Church and were then supported by male leaders; fourth, that society was also moving in a similar direction at the time; and fifth, that a new structure was coming into being, so people were prepared to try a new way of balancing the sexes at the same time.

Now, six years later, the Uniting Church has begun to settle down and people have come to terms with the regulations in various ways as we have seen. There is still an apparent reluctance to see the relation between the sexes as a power relation. 'Harmony' seems more important than further struggle, so the gains made by great effort are accepted, redefined (for example as inevitable or natural), and then everything is seen as having reached a satisfactory balance. Conflict is avoided rather than faced and worked through. But we have seen that there remains a lot of discrimination and dissatisfaction in the Church. The advances are real, but limited and precarious. The Church has a choice to go forward or to slide back. The weight of patriarchal tradition is strong and the processes of change take a lot of work, energy and good will. To press on now requires another major effort. After its pioneering venture one can only hope the Uniting Church will take up the issue again and carry it forward.

Several correspondents talked of possible ways ahead, including directories of women, and 'some kind of support system for women who feel that they are being ignored or demeaned in the church'. Some argue against keeping the regulations, others, like this clergyman, argue for them: 'Because it remains possible for men to exclude women and rationalise their actions, there needs to be a re-affirmation of the policy and an extension of its terms. Otherwise there will be some return towards the previous situation. A sufficient sanction could be to require each committee, council, board etc. to report to its Presbytery or Synod on the proportion of women in its membership.'

One woman believes 'the world is far ahead of the church in providing and accepting a changed role for women in social decision-making'; another asks, 'I wonder whether the experiences of secular organisations in affirmative action programmes have some relevance for the Church'.

Taking an opposite tack, an old campaigner and very active elder suggests a program of non-cooperation: 'I feel that further energy expended in ensuring that the Regulations remain would not be worth the time involved—having established a pattern I think it will continue as it has, which hasn't been wholly satisfactory. We could concentrate on encouraging women to bring about change through a different, non-competitive mode of operation. Refusal to cooperate and withdrawing support when decisions are made without proper consultation with women or where we are not adequately represented would be more effective than having a regulation which can be ignored. One parish in this presbytery has four ordained ministers and four lay representatives attending presbytery meetings and not a woman among them in the six years since union.

My own feeling is that the Church should move forward on as many fronts as possible, depending on where women choose to put their energy. I think that regulations do serve as a brake on the expansionist nature of male power, and are therefore worth keeping. Let's not lose the hard-won ground already gained! But as quotas can so easily be got round in subtle or even blatant ways, I would suggest also the setting of future targets, for example that decision-making bodies should represent the composition by sex of the congregation, the targets to be formally adopted by the councils of the Church, together with specific programs and strategies for moving towards them.

Second, the Church has as yet put virtually no money into this area, crucial for its future health. I would suggest that full-time appointments be made, perhaps two women in each state, to initiate and encourage the support action along the lines of all eleven recommendations of the women's submission in 1974.

But perhaps our best hope is still the profound and hopeful restlessness of women.

A disappointing postscript

In 1983, at the end of the six years for which the regulations were in force, the Assembly allowed them to lapse. At the following Assembly in May 1985 the NSW Synod moved that the regulations be reintroduced. The motion was lost, and the mood of the Assembly, as shown in other decisions also, was clearly against the participation of women in decision-making bodies of the Church. Our earlier optimism about the willingness of the Uniting Church in Australia to move out of its conservative and patriarchal mould was unfortunately ill-founded.

12

A quixotic approach
The women's movement and the Church in Australia

VERONICA BRADY

Don Quixote has always been one of my heroes not because he mistook windmills for giants or prostitutes for princesses but because he insisted on believing in the possibility of giants and princesses. Times of social change are times of tension, confusion and misunderstanding. Warring ideologies can be as destructive, perhaps even more so in a psychic rather than physical sense, as warring armies. The Women's Movement, the struggle that is to readjust the position of women in a changing world, a struggle which involves contesting injustice on the one hand and clarifying the notion of woman and the place she has in the world on the other, is part of this conflict of ideology, the result of the seismic historical upheavals of this century. In talking about any aspects of the Women's Movement therefore it is important first of all to get clear what we are talking about and where the argument leads us. But it is even more important in dealing with 'Women and the Church in Australia' because the combination of the word 'Church' with the rest of its phrase is particularly complex, particularly provocative. Let us first of all then get clear what I shall be talking about when I use the word.

As the Oxford Dictionary tells us, 'Church' has two kinds of meanings. It means something objective, 'a building for public worship' or 'the ecclesiastical organisation'. But it also means something subjective, 'the Christian community collectively', a community gathered together in the faith, hope and love that arises out of the Gospel, the Good News, of the story of Jesus. In talking about the 'Church' and 'Woman' in Australia or indeed anywhere it is important to keep this distinction in mind because external appearances may not always be true to the inner reality, which is the essential. But since these appearances probably concern most readers of this book I want to begin with them, and since I am myself a member of the Roman Catholic section of the Church I shall mainly be writing about the face that church presents to the world.

As far as current perception goes, the Catholic Church is the great enemy of feminism and this not only in the eyes of non-Christians. Christian feminists like Rosemary Reuther and Mary Daly in the USA and Barbara Thiering and Jean Skuse in Australia[1] have made out an eloquent case for the dehumanisation and even 'neuroticisation'[2] which have all too often been the consequence of official church policies like the opposition not only to contraception, divorce and abortion, but also to careers for women. By and large as far as the Australian Church is concerned woman's place seems to be in the home, her primary and perhaps only role to bear children or else to become a woman religious. The option to remain single has a very dubious place, though middle-aged spinsters prove their worth as sacristans, church sweepers, flower-arrangers, and if old or unattractive enough, as priests' housekeepers. As for the woman religious, even though she would seem at first to have a special place within the institution, that place is generally as second-class citizens whose function is, it seems, to provide a cheap and docile workforce as teachers and nurses. Especially in parish schools, the nun is expected to do what the parish priest decrees, meekly and without question, to treat him with deference and wait on him—if Father comes to dinner he must never be allowed to do the washing up. There are grim stories told of priests totally insensitive to the emotional and physical needs of sisters in remote country parishes, just as there are equally grim stories of the celibate male's lack of understanding of sexual needs and problems in marriage. All this may be caricature, but caricature takes off from a basis of fact and nothing is gained by denying the undeniable. Equally it is hard to defend Rome's resolute opposition even to consider the question of the ordination of women—in theological terms an open question—and even harder to stomach the recent decree that women are no longer to be allowed to act as readers in the celebration of the liturgy, a decree which one can only suspect arises out of the notorious misogyny of medieval theologians who regarded women as ritually unclean, thus showing themselves to be disciples of Plato for whom the body and bodily functions was something unclean rather than of Jesus of Nazareth whose dealings with women were remarkably free for his time. For him indeed women were equals, a fact which lead a sometimes unsympathetic Paul to proclaim that in the Christian community there should be no more distinctions of Jew and Gentile, slave and free man, male and female but that 'you are all one person in Jesus Christ' (Gal. 3:28). All this is unfortunately very familiar. But merely negative criticism is seldom fruitful. It is possible, I believe, to be positive about the relations between the Catholic Church and women.

To tackle first of all the question of the Church's attitude to sexuality in general, and to contraception, and abortion, to divorce and extra-marital sexuality in particular. There is no doubt, as we have said, that the ban on all forms of contraception apart from the rhythm and the Billings method has forced many Catholics to have more children than they wanted or could cope with, emotionally as well as financially, and turned some women into mere childbearing machines. Yet sexual freedom is an ambiguous concept. Susan Sontag has argued recently:

> Merely to remove the onus placed upon the sexual expressiveness of women is a hollow victory if the sexuality they become free to enjoy remains the old one that converts women into objects . . . This already 'freer' sexuality mostly reflects a spurious idea of freedom, the right of each person, briefly, to exploit and dehumanize someone else. Without a change in the norms of sexuality, the liberation of women is a meaningless goal. Sex as such is not liberating for women. Neither is more sex.[3]

Compulsory sexuality, whether it be heterosexuality or, as some extreme lesbian separatists would have it, homosexuality, can be as tyrannous a subjection to physical necessity as uncontrolled fertility. If one of the goals of the women's movement is liberation from this subjection, then the Church's ideal of chastity is by no means as negative as it has been said to be. The word has gathered unfortunate overtones, it is true, and is all too often associated with repression, ignorance, fear and frigidity. But the notion that sexual expression should be governed by respect for the other and for oneself and that it is not the only or even the best way of loving is a positive one. So too with virginity. Against the neo-Freudians the Church asserts that it is possible for some people to be mature and loving without the experience of genital sexuality. There are neurotic celibates, of course, but there are also large numbers of celibate men and women in the Church who are normal loving human beings. Ideology is particularly dangerous here. 'Woman' is not just a sexual category— indeed sexuality may well be the linchpin of gender inequality—and to challenge the idea that one becomes a woman through the experience of genital (as distinct from psychic) spirituality is to advance rather than retard the cause of women. If it is true, as Julie Kristeva suggests, that groups define themselves according not only to their relation to the means of production but also to the means of reproduction, then chastity offers an alternative to the exploitative mode of our society and to the conflictual model of existence.[4]

This brings us to some consideration of the context of our discussion, Australian society. Whether or not it is true, as Barbara Thiering alleges,[5] that Australians generally have a 'deeply crippled self-image' it is incontestable that Australia is intrinsically involved in the capitalist world system and, perhaps more contestable, that our ways of thought and behaviour are affected by this system. By and large it seems to be assumed that the task of schools is to train people as workers and consumers and thus to accept the sexual stereotyping that directs boys in the direction of the maths and sciences and thus to positions of power and prestige in technological society and girls elsewhere, on the premise that their task is to be beautiful rather than brainy and thus ultimately objects of men's pleasure. Sexuality is an ambiguous concept but it is at least arguable that in this kind of usage it is part of the capitalist consumer ethic—certainly the female body has become a necessary element in marketing.

In objecting to this exploitative aspect of sex, the Church is perhaps doing what it did in the Graeco-Roman world when it opposed prostitution and the systematic degradation of women which went with the exaltation of the spirit at the expense of the body. Though most feminists have little sympathy for the Church's concept of woman, it does give woman a very important place. Indeed the Church is traditionally seen as a woman, the feminine if you like, in relation to the fertilising power of God at work in creation, and Mary the Mother of Jesus as the most perfect of all believers. Convent schools in Australia may have much to answer for, but at least they put before girls an image of the independent woman not only in Mary but also in women saints like Catherine of Siena who in the name of God ordered the Avignon Popes back to Rome, Teresa of Avila who talked as an equal with nobles and princes, Mary Ward the seventeenth-century Englishwoman who founded an order of nuns who were to be as free to live in the world and serve its needs as the Jesuits were, Catherine McAuley whose followers went with the migrants who crossed the world to Australia, America, Africa and so on to look after the poor, the sick and the ignorant or that great Australian,

Mary McKillop, who founded the Josephite order to educate and care for the people of the outback. It is even arguable that in the nuns who taught them many girls recognised independent women who as teachers, nurses or social workers had a career in their own right. Long before the twentieth century, there were feminists like Mary Ward, for example, who replied to the priests and bishops who wanted to condemn her idea of a community of liberated women. Their argument was that women were necessarily inferior to men, less intelligent and thus unable to present Christian doctrine or to cope with temptation. Thus they needed to be protected, set apart behind the high walls of a cloister. To this Mary Ward responded:

> There is no such difference between men and women [she retorted]. Fervour is not placed in feelings but in a will to do well which women may have as well as men. Women may do great things, as we have seen by example of many saints who have done great things and I hope in God it will be seen that women in time to come will do much . . . This is truth, this is verity, to do what we have to do well. Many think it nothing to do ordinary things. But for us it is a great deal . . . This is all I have to say at this time; that you love verity and truth.[6]

Australian society by and large is an aggressively masculine if not macho one, but the Church's image of the woman at least gives woman a place and a significance over and above her role as mere sexual object, housekeeper or producer of children. Even the emphasis on motherhood and the family make her a powerful and valuable person, someone to whom the male must defer and whom he must honour, and contemporary women are beginning to rethink their attitudes, accepting that mothering may be seen, as Mary Beth Elshtain puts it, as 'a complicated, rich, ambivalent, vexing, joyous activity'.[7] Recognition of this fact goes along with the repudiation of the old dualism with which we have been saddled in favour of an 'account that unites mind and body, reason and passion, into a comprehensive [view] of human subjectivity and identity', thus creating 'a feminist theory of action that, complicatedly, invokes both inner and outer experiences'.[8] The sacramental world of the Church also presupposes this kind of unity and it is thus not so surprising that many of the pioneering generation of feminists like Bella Guerin, one of the first women to graduate at the University of Melbourne, as well as many more recent feminists like Germaine Greer or Susan Ryan, have been products of convent schools. Brought up and trained in single-sex schools they did not have to define themselves in terms of masculine expectations. There was more room for them to discover what it meant to be female as something positive, not just as not-male.

This kind of discovery has not been so important so far in the Women's Movement in Australia, where the great task has been to contest social injustice, to rebel against pervasive patterns of subordination, limitation and confinement, and see to it that women are given their rightful opportunities in public life, allowed to have careers, as members of parliament, doctors, lawyers, academics and so on. In this task there is still a long way to go, but at least the pass has been won. The next stage, however, is more problematic. On the one hand women who have achieved some social power are in danger of being co-opted, becoming 'courtesy males' or at least of being perceived as doing so, while on the other hand, many feminists, especially the lesbian separatists, are withdrawing from political involvement. As its founders saw it, however, the Women's Movement does not involve surrender of the public sphere, the sphere of culture and civilisation, but neither does it involve losing one's sense of self as feminine, possessed of a special mode of existence. Feminists elsewhere have become increasingly aware of this dilemma and this has led to the call for a feminist theory. Susan Griffin, for instance, poses the question: 'What if all our efforts towards liberation are determined by an ideology which despite our desire for a better world would lead us inevitably back to the old paradigm . . . of warfare?'[9] If it is true, as Simone de Beauvoir has said, that woman has been defined by the male gaze, has been the mirror image of his desires, then it is necessary now to begin to define the feminine, its mode of being and forms of power and to consider the ways in which we are to modify the hitherto dominant masculine mode and power structure. What is needed, in other words, is not so much a model of contestation, of hatred of the male as enemy but 'a passionate desire to heal suffering . . . a vision of possibility, a desire to know the whole truth [about human existence], and understand and know what is obscured or what has been forgotten, to take in the unknown'.[10]

In Australia in particular the feminine mode has been obscured. Whatever it means, it can be associated with the land and with the dark side of the self, the intuitive and the instinctual, all of which Australian culture has tended to neglect, clinging to the fringes of the self as to the fringes of the continent.[11] My contention is that the words to describe and thus to activate this dimension are words and images which are essentially religious, which have to do, that is, with realities at present unseen. Feminists elsewhere, in the USA particularly, are increasingly becoming aware of the need to take possession of this area, to define what it means to be woman as such, not just as not-man or even as anti-man. How many women today are like Laura in Elizabeth Harrower's *The Watch Tower*, who still felt 'like someone on a runaway train, events [flashing] by like stations, with no reference to her at all'[12] or like Glen Tomasetti's heroine in *Perfectly Ordinary People*. One cold Monday afternoon cleaning the bath she is suddenly aware of herself, getting old and still 'thinking useless thoughts' and, getting out of the bath, looks at herself in the mirror on the door of the medicine chest and says aloud, ' "There's no progress around here" '.[13]

This word 'progress', of course, is the crucial word in any discussion of the Women's Movement, especially now when many of its earlier goals seem to have been more or less achieved. Unable to create an Archimedean point outside the world, we must now begin to find and make our own some centre of value within the self, 'scanning the beacons that flare along the horizon', as Adrienne Rich puts it, 'asking whether any of them is our lighthouse'.[14] If much of our Australian culture involves a radical forgetting of the traditional values, the Church, despite everything, still keeps alive at least one of these beacons, a sense of the transcendent and thus of the absolute value of each individual not for what she/he possesses or has achieved in material terms but for her/himself, a sense which thus gets beyond sexual stereotyping. If that person is free who is no longer constrained by forces which alienate her from herself, whether these forces be external, economic, social or even political, or internal, physical or emotional needs, and can thus do what she wants, the secret of freedom may well be found in this sphere of interiority, in the spiritual dimension, the sphere of the 'sublime "I" ',[15] the sphere which is no longer governed by nature or the state. Similarly Christian teaching has never been really sympathetic to crude masculine notions of power—hence Nietzsche's and Schopenhauer's charge that Christianity is effeminate. A feminist discourse will need to develop its own concept and language of power and may well find both concept and language in the Christian tradition of non-violence and of symbolic expression.

And so we return to Don Quixote, to the importance of challenging definitions of reality and of value which tend to restrict, confine and oppress. Women in Australia may have made important gains, but it

is at least arguable that the way forward for the future lies in
exploring the nature of her feminity, not in accepting the status quo
but transforming it. Consciousness-raising, after all, is a matter not
only of coming to know different things but of coming to know them in
a different way. In the general deconstruction of reality which follows
from experiencing it inwardly and affirmatively, woman may discover
her full significance. With its emphasis on the intuitive, the ecstatic
and the symbolic the Church may well be woman's best ally in
discovering this significance, directing us away from narrow merely
rationalistic and utilitarian definitions of reality and value to explore
inner, female space. In turn women then may recall the Church to
its true nature, to become the place of inwardness and thus of
freedom.

13

The feminisation of structures in religious orders

ANNE McLAY

Religious orders of women within the Roman Catholic tradition have typically been female replicas of the male models. Men have written or corrected their constitutions. In some instances men have assumed the role of Higher Superior or, more commonly, have acted as spiritual director, fulfilling their role in an active way. Many female religious orders have been founded as a kind of subsidiary arm to the more important and more privileged clerical order.

This has been but a reflection of the normal status of women. Women are still the most burdened in any contemporary poor society. Women still have little say in our own religious and social system, in our government, economics, defence. We do not have to be Marxist to see validity in Friedrich Engels' naming the subjugation of women as the first relationship of oppressor–oppressed, or in his further claim that it is the foundation of all other class and property relations.[1] Jesus had changed this, giving women dignity and equal leadership roles. But the Church, as it developed, was pressurised by Roman law and Graeco-Roman social practice in the opposite direction, and women became unequal again. This movement towards inequality was strengthened by the ambivalence of Paul's attitude to women within the Christian community. On the one hand, he affirmed their equality (Gal. 3:28); on the other, he severely restricted their active participation in public worship (1 Cor. 14:34–5). He opened up a new independence for women by including them in the call to celibacy (1 Cor. 7:8). Yet this meant that women who did marry became confined to the household, in which reigned a descending hierarchy: God—man—woman (1 Cor. 11:3).[2]

Rosemary Reuther explains this first exploitative relationship thus: 'From the dawn of history the physical lightness of woman's body (which has nothing to do with biological inferiority) and the fact that the woman is the childbearer have been used to subordinate the woman to the man in a chattel status and to deprive women of the leadership possibilities and the cultural development of the dominant group.'[3]

Religious women escaped, in some ways, from male dominance. In New Testament times women were often leaders of house churches. In later decades, deaconesses were usual. As convents were established, nuns were able to win great freedom from the clerical male establishment and to create a rich feminine culture. In one way, they did this by becoming 'male' in so far as they existed in relationship to God, not to father or husband. Thereby they could escape many of the implications of their femininity, and could perform extraordinary feats of public service.[4]

In Australia, for example, they built hospitals and staffed them, almost without any help from the diocesan churches. They administered and staffed an extraordinary number of schools and, once again, frequently built them unaided by the official church agencies.[5] They have been among the forerunners of social work with their homes for various kinds of disadvantaged children and adults, and in these latter decades have moved out into many diverse kinds of pastoral and social ministries, including that of action for social change. It has been an achievement largely unsung by both civil and ecclesiastic society, for these religious women somehow do not really belong to the official institutions of 'state' or 'church'.

I am a member of a fairly typical—and 'successful'—nineteenth-century religious congregation of women devoted to the spread of God's Kingdom of love through the service of the needy. As our name indicates, we engage in the works of mercy, spiritual and corporal. Though we have some affinity with the Irish Christian Brothers founded some few years previously, the Sisters of Mercy are not a female arm of a male order. Yet, like most of the female congregations established at that time, a bishop's influence was critical to the type of society we became. Our foundress, Catherine McAuley, was spending her inherited wealth in setting up a house of refuge for young women at risk in the Dublin slums. She did not want her small band of helpers to become a religious congregation, fearing the restrictions on their service that this would entail. However, Archbishop Daniel Murray of Dublin finally persuaded her that the work would not otherwise endure without this official church sanction and regulation. He had quite a lot to say in the writing of her constitutions, even

deleting a section written by Catherine on the sisters' cheerful yet
sweet gravity of manner, apparently considering it too 'feminine'.
Having been amended by the archbishop in this and other ways, the
constitutions were then sent to Rome where a totally clerical Sacred
Congregation finally approved them.[6]

Until such time as each new Mercy foundation comprised seven
professed sisters, the local bishop was empowered by these constitutions to 'nominate the Mother Superior, and the other principal
officials of the Convent'. He himself was named as the highest
superior, under the Holy See, of the communities. In Queensland,
Bishop James Quinn (1861–81) continued to act in this way, taking
liberties not allowed to him even by the Mercy rule. He made and
remade superiors at his will, long after the number of professed sisters
was more than seven. He changed staff, sometimes against the
decisions of the convent superiors. He altered internal arrangements,
innovating and changing conventual customs. Through his decree,
their internal government developed in a direction other than that
envisaged in Ireland. At the command of the bishop, the Queensland
Sisters of Mercy departed from the monastic form of separate independent religious houses as intended by Catherine, and were transformed
into a diocesan-centralised unit. He deposed Mother Vincent Whitty,
the first Brisbane superior and a woman of amazing vision and
courage—so outstanding, in fact, that the Dublin Chapter of Mercies
had refused to let her volunteer to go with Quinn to the newly
separated colony of Queensland, saying they could not spare her.
Quinn would not take no for an answer and prevailed on Cardinal
Cullen of Dublin to overrule the women's decision. Yet a few years
later he deposed her from office for being 'too lax' in government.[7]

Mother Vincent Whitty and Mary McKillop, founder of the
Australian Sisters of St Joseph, each in quite different ways successfully refused to be subordinated. Mary McKillop had extraordinary
burdens to carry imposed by more than one Australian bishop. Her
protest was often public, and in Queensland she withdrew her
members rather than agree to Quinn's demands.[8] Mother Vincent
preferred to avoid any public break with the bishop or withdrawal
from the diocese. Her character was such that she could do this and
still preserve her own quiet serenity. The Brisbane Sisters of Mercy
grew in strength and virtual independence under her continued
informal leadership.[9]

But women like Mary McKillop and Mother Vincent were rare
creatures. On the whole, the women seemed to have little will to effect

fundamental changes. Many generations of young sisters, including my own age group, were guided in the spiritual life by Jesuit retreat directors and Jesuit confessors. The prevailing model was a severe interpretation of the Spiritual Exercises, often harsh in a way not intended by their author Ignatius. The result was certainly a disciplined, aggressive approach to spirituality, more appropriate to the army model of the Society of Jesus than to women's communities.

One result of this male influence in the development of the female orders has been the adoption of the patriarchal structures of Western society. Among the consequences has been a violence that many women religious seem to have to do to themselves to fit these largely 'masculine' structures. Given the ideal of religious life prevailing for a long time, namely, that it is a lifestyle commanding one's loyalty to the smallest detail of daily activity, whether physical or mental, the violence could be at times almost total.

This is not to say that many women did not live happy and fulfilled lives within the structures. But something had gone wrong and there was suffering, some of it perhaps unredemptive, much of it undoubtedly unnecessary. Institutions of themselves can be Christian or unchristian. Structures can help or hinder our proclamation of the truth, our service of people, our building of community. There is the beginning of an awareness among us, I sense, that we women religious need to find structures and procedures for our institutional living which more truly embody our natures as women. In this chapter I shall try to explore this question of 'feminisation' of structures, and shall refer particularly to the structure of General Chapter, highest organ of government in a religious society. It is a very tentative exploration, coming out of my own reflection on my own experience and prompted by my role as member of the general council of the Brisbane Sisters of Mercy. It is a beginning exploration and I hope the reader will accept it as such.

For those readers not familiar with the inner workings of a religious order, let me first describe some traditional practices which most contemporary religious can remember. A religious order's structure is democratic at its highest level, in so far as the structure is based on government by top officials elected in General Chapter by elected delegates of all the professed members. However, until recently, the democracy ended there. The highest superior was assisted by a 'vicar', next in order of importance and power, followed by the rest of the governing council (two or three usually), who were definitely lower on the hierarchical ladder. Local officials were appointed by the top person or group. Often positions or functions were given to or belonged by right to the 'seniors by profession'. In our congregation the Mistress of Novices and the Bursar General were automatically members of the council. The combination of councillor, superior and spiritual teacher in the one person of the Novice Mistress gave her for most young people in formation an overwhelming aura of sacredness. As one sister at a recent gathering of over-fifties reminisced, 'She was God'.

In every house of the congregation, the sisters sat in order of seniority at table, in chapel, in the community room. Bedrooms and other 'goodies' were received in order of seniority. On visitation of poor homes in the local area, one of our traditional works of mercy, the senior led the prayers while the junior carried the basket. This is but one small application of the principle which defined much of our behaviour.

All in all, maintaining the structure seemed at times more important than developing the Kingdom. While such regulations allowed large organisations to function in an ordered way and without too much overt conflict, it was often at great cost to the individual. The base was control and domination. The discipline was at times surprisingly similar to that of an army—traditionally a male organisation in our society. Justice not mercy could easily prevail. People had little real participation in making decisions which could affect their lives to an enormous extent. Instead of the uniqueness of the human personality being nurtured and nourished, many were forced into a common mould, and they often cracked. Work became the final product for quite a few, the source of their identity. Efficiency of service, competence, productivity rather than people and their needs seemed part of their *raison d'être*. There was stress on corporate identity, with the habit (dress) as the cherished symbol. The heart seemed ignored. Women who seem more at home in the smaller informal family-style unit than in the highly regulated anonymous large institution existing to produce the goods of holiness or service or whatever, readily became resentful and angry, or apathetic or depressed.

When the structures were finally made more flexible, in the wake of Vatican II, the hidden rebellion dissolved into many departures from religious life. The men were also affected—for the structures they had built ignored, I believe, the 'feminine' within themselves. Men may have seemed freer than women in using the structures, and I have no tightly constructed proof that such structures were inherently 'masculine'. Yet they were structures built up largely by men and copied by or forced upon women. They are consistent with those of our traditional patriarchal society, and counterparts still survive in civil life.

Rosemary Reuther and Judith Vaughan present arguments that seem relevant here. Vaughan, using Reuther, argues along these lines:

> A hierarchically structured society establishes some persons or some groups of people above others, and gives them the power to define all others in relation to themselves—an essentially dehumanizing situation. Those who are lower on the scale thereby have to define themselves in relation to their superiors. Relationships of mutuality and interdependence are impossible. Alienation from others and from one's true self is the final result.
>
> If, then, the first—and fundamental—social relationship of exploitation is the male/female relationship, then the male is easily seen as the superior on the hierarchical scale, and the female the powerless, dependent, passive one. While this relationship of woman to man has undergone some changes during the centuries, for example, from 'inferiority' to 'complementarity', the basic inequality exists. One group of people in power (men) are able to define another group of people (women) over against themselves.
>
> Women have been conditioned to accept their dependence and powerlessness. Men and women are prevented from relating to and co-operating with each other as equals in the creation of society. Women are kept by our social structures from interfer[ing] with the real business of running the world.[10]

I cannot yet say to what extent I accept the feminist arguments; but I do know from my own experience that structures such as I have described were alienating to most of the women living under them. The manner of living that they imposed appears to have involved some inner contradictions especially repugnant to women. The structures can be termed, I believe, 'masculine' rather than 'feminine'.

It must be said at this stage that 'masculine' and 'feminine', as I use them in this chapter, are not interchangeable terms with 'male' and 'female'. 'Masculinity' and 'femininity' belong to both men and women. The man, however, is dominantly 'masculine' and the woman correspondingly 'feminine'. The whole person, nevertheless, has developed both sides to his or her personality. While many of our masculine and feminine traits may be culturally determined, I accept, however, that some are inherently uppermost in our nature as a man or a woman, and that we have to work to develop the other side of our self. Women appear to prefer a mode of judging through feeling, men through thinking. Women emphasise nurture, compassion, sensitivity within human relationships. Men emphasise competition, mastery, control. Women seem naturally more receptive, men more aggressive. Women intuit, men reason. A general case, at any rate, can be made for such distinctions. Whether they are inherent or cultural in origin, I find them acceptable so long as they do not lead to diminishment and are not seen as obligatory or exclusive. Our rationalist Western society as a whole is masculine, and our education has left latent many of our non-rational, feminine traits, whether we be male or female. We are seeing one effect of this masculine imbalance in the religious order structures which have been described.

I would like to develop my argument concerning the need to 'feminise' our structures by examining what has happened to the General Chapter of Religious Congregations of women within the last three decades, that is, since Vatican II. The General Chapter is an amazingly democratic organ of government to have persisted through long years of enculturation of religious orders by a society based on autocracy, whether feudal or monarchical. In early groups such as the Benedictines, the chapter was used for regular review of the monastery's life, and the youngest member was listened to as reverently as the eldest. In all groups it was the organ of election of the major governing officials and, theoretically at least, set broad directions for the future. By Vatican II it had become, in practice, often just an electing body. Vatican II introduced the notion of a special renewal chapter, with at least two long sessions. Its purpose was a thorough overhaul of aims and practices and manner of living. The special chapter took years of preparation and of putting into operation. For most women religious, it meant learning new techniques based on the rules of parliamentary debate and/or the principles of business management. They wrote submissions, elected delegates, learned to debate on the chapter floor. Small house meetings and large group assemblies were held to generate and discuss data. Committees and research groups were formed; first, second, and third drafts of position papers were written. Commissions or task forces carried the position papers through the debating process until they were accepted as

statements of the chapter by the elected delegates. Constitutions
began to be revised in the light of a re-examined original charism or
spirit. They were rewritten, initially at least in the traditionally legal
form. Renewal became a way of life, a spirituality almost.

But there was also hostility to some aspects of the new learning.
The formal, adversary style traditional to parliamentary debating or
even the more newly developed techniques of business management
were self-defeating for many women. They were valuable techniques,
but something was not quite right. Once again there seemed to be
occurring a violence to self and to relationships. A kind of paralysis
often set in. Or at other times, an overaggressive reaction resulted in
hostility. History seemed to be repeating itself, and we did not really
learn from our mistakes when we came to the chapters of the 1970s
and early 1980s. The models being employed were worked out by men
and taught to the women by men, who also guided the process of many
of the sessions. Women were still assuming their traditional passivity
in the face of their guides in the spiritual life. The models developed
by the men brought religious together in large groups. This seemed to
be particularly alienating to women, most of whom work more
efficiently in smaller informal settings. Again a kind of violence was
subtly accompanying the large group assemblies, at least those
concerned with debate and discussion. A kind of power play indirectly
held sway. A sense of powerlessness in many individuals resulted, and
a reluctance in the group to take responsibility for itself.

But the beginning of a reaction among the women was also
becoming clear, a reaction which is one manifestation of the wider
Women's Movement in society. This latter may be described as
probably the most significant social movement of our time.[11] One of
the directions it is now taking is the perception of a need for both
women and men to readdress the feminine within us and to build
structures accordingly. Some Catholic writers, who also subscribe to
the view that this is the most important movement of our day,
attribute it to the power of the spirit of Wisdom.[12] There has been a
movement of Wisdom through the centuries, and the breakthrough is
occurring in our own day and foremost among women. Wisdom in the
Old Testament is always feminine. The Wisdom literature of the
sacred books shows God constantly dynamic, creating all the time,
working from within, rooted in our human situation, flowing outward
and inward, nurturing and ordering all things well, bringing an
exchange of life and of love. Jesus' mission comes out of God's Wisdom
and is recognised through his growing discernment of the Spirit of

God working in his own life and in the lives of those around him, particularly the 'little ones', the poor, the powerless, the rejected. Among the 'little ones' of his society were the women. With his complete personality Jesus could relate to women equally as to men. Jesus' urgent, all-consuming sense of mission, his compassionate awareness of those who were suffering through any kind of oppression, his willingness to endure, to let go, to persevere, to challenge—however the Spirit called him at a particular moment—these characteristics are reflected in much of the contemporary Women's Movement, especially where Christian women are involved.

This is what I hear such women saying: we need a more holistic, non-violent approach; an approach which nurtures and nourishes the human beings affected; a decision-making process which works from within the situation; a process which means being open to others, not dominating but seeking consensus among all those whose lives will be touched; a process which gently probes the interior of the human psyche and devises ways to discern the Spirit within our psyche and within the events around us. Perhaps women, including religious women, had to experience the frustration and the anger of trying to operate within masculine models, had to feel restricted by the tight structures of debate and analysis and decision-taking, had to push themselves to the limits of their energy and find it led to non-productivity or to the ordering of details and minor tasks rather than to finding visions and nurturing people. Only then, perhaps, could they reach that degree of consciousness which could say 'Let's work out our own models, models that do not discard what is valuable in the masculine but which more completely suit our nature as women'— models, in fact, which are holistic, all-rounded.

As my contribution to that task, I would like to suggest two steps towards the feminisation of any structures in religious congregations of women, and more specifically, of the structure of a chapter. They are not new, but I think it may now be time to try to clarify what we have been intuitively moving towards. Therefore, I would suggest that, first, we need a new model of knowledge, a new concept of knowing and understanding; and that, second, we need a new model of association, a new concept of the kind of environment or climate in which we operate together.

A new model of knowledge would take due account of the 'feminine' aspects of our intellect, those non-rational abilities which Western society has tended to ignore, indeed, has tended to dismiss as irrational. The rational, logical tasks of collecting and analysing data, and of making syntheses to detect trends and form generalisations are vitally important and an essential part of a holistic model of knowledge. But they comprise only half the model. There is also an intuitive approach to knowledge, which grasps by wholes and is often, and probably usually, for a woman, connected with a feeling approach to decision-making. It is the part of the intellect which gives play to the imagination, to creativity, and to the aesthetic elements in human living. The emotions are indispensably interwoven, and it is this that makes many highly logical thinking people dismiss intuition as 'the way in which women think'—or rather 'don't think'—and hence as inferior. Yet it is essential, for both men and women, to develop both sides of one's intellect if an integrated approach to knowing and to living is to be reached.

Many writers assert that there are biological as well as psychological factors indicated.[13] The faculty of reason or logic is seated in the left hemisphere of the brain. Some neurologists and psychologists say that men are naturally more specialised than women, concentrating on the rational or logical approach to decision-making, less holistic in the operation of their brains. Intuition, as part of the non-rational (*not* irrational) dimension of the human self, is connected with the right hemisphere of the brain, with what is called 'feminine consciousness'. It is also the seat of the aesthetic element of human existence, expressed and communicated through different art forms.

Not all philosophers and scientists have refused to recognise intuition as a valid way of knowing. There is an anecdote told about Albert Einstein, when he was asked to describe the theory of relativity simply. He replied: 'I cannot do what you request. But if you will call on me at Princeton, I will play it for you on my violin.'[14] Plato taught that when modes of music change, the fundamental laws of the state change with them.[15] The right hemisphere of the brain, the seat of 'feminine consciousness', is the locus of musical expression. What scope do we give to music in our days of law-making during Chapter, or of law-interpreting in our local house meetings? Can we come to the point of permitting understanding to come through feeling? Of providing channels for this to take place? Can we allow our emotional life, individual and communal, to lead us to deeper understandings?

I can imagine the alarm that those last questions may arouse in some readers. So I would like to repeat again that it is a *holistic* approach which is needed. I would suggest that we women religious need to explore non-rational techniques of data collection, to round out or to complement the rational techniques presently employed. I

would suggest that non-rational techniques of achieving understanding of the data collected can also be devised. I would also suggest
that women religious pay more attention to the vital role that the
emotions play in all our decision-making and to the fact that feeling
as a way of making judgments (that is, on the basis of values) is for
many women a preferred way.

What might this mean in practice? Let me explore the possibilities
for the Convocation or formal opening of the chapter, the calling
together of the community for the sacred event. This is done normally
in some form of a large assembly. Reports of the administrators are
read. Position papers may be prepared. A few members—but only a
few—have the confidence to respond in the large group. Some information is given; a lesser quantity is received. No one is particularly
satisfied. Several are alienated by their non-participatory status, or
by their inability to use those channels of communication which are
opened to them.

I am not suggesting that we give up preparing reports. Such are
appropriate to a holistic model of knowledge. But I do suggest that we
not forget our deep need for symbol—the language of intuition.
Symbol is basic to music, art, dance, celebration and worship. Symbol
is intrinsic to metaphor and story, dreams and twilight imagery.
Could Convocation, then, comprise the telling of the story of the
group, the ritual acceptance of its present reality, and an imaginative
interpretation of the future? Perhaps this might be more revealing for
many women, providing both data and understanding, and new light
on the more rationally conceived reports. Stories can be told and
ritualised through oral witness and symbolic presentation. The value
of oral testimony, for example, is being rediscovered by historians,
many of whom are now stating that oral witness can be more reliable
than the written word. Lyndsay Farrall's experience in Papua New
Guinea led him to the realisation of the validity of oral testimony.[16]
One of our local Mercy communities recently told stories around a
camp fire in the backyard, and were amazed at the understanding it
helped the group reach. Stories seem to take us back to the very heart
of reality, including our own. The young people who founded a
commune in the Californian mountains rediscovered this ancient
truth. Barbara Dean, one of them, writes:

> We also live without television and movie theatres. And
> like many others who have been in that situation, we tell
> stories. Constantly, and over and over, to anyone who will
> listen . . . Some stories have been told so many times that

they have achieved near mythic proportions. Especially
when one of these comes up again, and especially on a
night like this, I realize the importance the stories play in
our lives, the sense of almost epic meaning and connection
they impart. Storytelling somehow makes who we are and
what we are doing real, in the very ways that matter
most.[17]

Our story can be told through the symbolism of dance, music, art, as
well as words, and, very fittingly for an institution such as a religious
order, through the corporate symbolic action of ritual. The telling of
stories, sharing not just information but also our faith-filled interpretation of the events of our lives, can help develop a layer of prayer
about us, an awareness that God is with us and at work in all kinds of
situations. If religion, contemplation, mysticism, is a right-brain
activity; if imagination and intuition are 'feminine' traits, then we
can more easily bring them to life by creating and participating in our
own social dramas.

Westerhoff explains the role of ritual in our corporate lives.

Ritual is a social drama which embodies the experiences
of a community . . . Through the power of symbolic actions
we order our experience; through the use of symbolic
narrative we explain our lives. Ritual operates on those
levels of existential reality that undergird the conceptual.
Importantly, ritual points to and participates in that
primordial truth which is located at the expanding edge of
our horizon of knowing, in the affections and the intuition,
not common sense or reason . . . [I]t is in our symbolic
actions—our rituals, our social dramas—that we experience the ultimate meanings and purposes of life and our
lives.[18]

Movement is an essential element in corporate ritual. Creative dance,
as with other art forms, can 'awaken the right lobe'.[19] Dance was very
much part of Old Testament worship; it can be a bridge from the world
of intellect to the world of imagination, helping us grasp in deeper
ways the meaning of religious concepts and see the world in a novel
light. De Sola and Easton tell a story which seems pertinent here:

Once, at a liturgy celebrated after endless discussion and
argumentation, when it seemed that there would be yet
more verbalization all through the liturgy, the
unexpected happened. During a momentary pause, a

> young man arose and dramatically entered the open space
> before the altar. Then, without a word, he mimed, danced,
> and acted out a moving comment on the morning's con-
> flict, cutting through with strong gestures all that was
> unessential. A gasp of astonishment passed through the
> congregation; it was reminiscent of other times when the
> Holy Spirit seemed to suddenly move and be present in
> unexpected ways, causing all to take note and be
> changed.[20]

Perhaps our community can find a richer meaning for ourselves and a truer vision of God through dance, music, poetry? It is not fortuitous that the final draft of our constitutions are written in a poetic style akin to free verse, and that other groups are writing theirs in similar style. Perhaps we could give special care and time to the type of worship and other celebrations we have during Chapter, allowing them to give play to our 'feminine consciousness'. Perhaps we could also test the power of symbolic dramatic action, as did the Old Testament prophets teaching their truths—and reaching a deeper understanding themselves—through symbolised action. So, too, do the women of the contemporary peace movement, and the women in the American Church movement.

We must remember also our urgent and continued need for a 'still point'. We need to take a lot of time to pray and reflect together, to listen to the spirit of Wisdom within. We need to schedule real time for quiet, real time for nurturing ourselves. It would seem that the act of creation, of inventing, of making something new, must occur at the still point. It comes out of the mystical element in human life, of the non-rational or intuitive, of right-brain or feminine consciousness. The moment of breakthrough, moreover, happens most often at a moment of meditation, or relaxation, or contemplation. There is a leap of the imagination, a touch of the divine Wisdom, and its knowledge is transmitted. The whole of the intellect is required in the preparation for this one moment of breakthrough to something new. But if we are too busy to reflect, to contemplate, to relax, to pray . . . is that moment of breakthrough even possible?

The second thing I would urge is that we need a new model of association. We need structures based on a non-violent way of relating, of nurturing self and caring for one another, of empowering through friendship. We need a climate of being at home with each other, a different texture of our action together, our corporate decision-making.

A recent book on women in politics in Australia comments on their 'informal, participatory and consensual style unlike the formal, adversary style traditional to Parliament'.[21] We have a need to listen to one another, truly listen without getting ready our own repartee. Many of our women are ill at ease in the 'formal, adversary style' or even at preparing formal recommendations. Perhaps the more intuitive members could tell their stories and leave it to those with the skills of logic to shape into relevant data or proposals. I suspect that some such simple cooperative technique would eliminate the harmful sense of powerlessness. A sense of the need to wait and to listen would be required from others.

Maybe consensus would be a more holistic mode of decision-taking than majority vote. Chapters of recent times have talked about 'participative government', 'participatory structures and procedures'. Some steps have been taken to put these concepts into effect. Yet we still have a long way to go if those whose lives are affected by structures of government and procedures of administration are empowered to be involved in and take responsibility for the decisions made. An attempt to achieve real consensus among all the members in some of the most important decisions for the congregation would be a long step on the way. But decision-taking by consensus requires patience and time. A vote may solve the necessity for making a reasonably quick judgment, but it may be a compromise that satisfies no one, or else a tyranny of some over the rest. In times of real conflict a vote may pass a law without real agreement reached, without being a true expression of who we are and how we want to live together. Sometimes, to reach consensus, discussion must be dropped. We must retire into our 'still point'. Finally a decision may be reached which we can all accept, and which allows for personal growth within a context of genuine harmony. At other times a decision may not be reached. The community is not ready. Our Chapter may have 'ragged edges'. Some issues may be left on hold until the level of energy to resolve them is high enough.

This is the way of empowerment. We enable each other to respond with total sincerity to God's Word in our lives. Leadership in this context is giving each member the power to participate and to decide. Leadership is for emptying ourselves, letting go. Leadership is for each one of us. This is the friendship model of Jesus. Jesus shared what was in his heart with his disciples, whom he no longer called servants or slaves but friends.[22] Friends know one another's business. Friends grow to think alike, to do things the same way, to make decisions in like manner. Friends give each other energy for their corporate mission. Sometimes it is easier to be a servant than a friend. A friend dies for his or her friend. Jesus gave his friends the symbol of his total self-sharing—the Eucharist. He wanted his friends to do likewise, to be friends of one another. All this can be very difficult. It can be especially difficult in times of disagreement, when the common vision seems in jeopardy. But Jesus' concept of friendship means supporting one another in discerning God's action in our lives; being aware of the movements in the group; growing to be more real with each other, surfacing the underlying issues and staying with them however painful. It demands that we build a climate of trust and non-violence as the context for our communal deliberations.

That may well be the contribution religious women can make to today's growing femininity of our Church and our society—the discovery of new ways of living and working together in an organisational mode that lets each of us contribute, whether we be man or woman, with the whole of our being.

14

Implications of the feminine and masculine in pastoral ministry

EDWARD MORGAN

The history of pastoral care in the Church is documented as largely a description of care exercised by men, mostly ordained or monastics, on behalf of either men or women. It is true that there have been examples of anointing with oil as far back as the early centuries of the Church's life by lay people, either male or female, as well as by bishops and priests.[1] Historical documents also refer to unordained men and women who have been known as charismatic healers; for example, Queen Anne of England (d. 1714), the last of English royalty to practise healing.[2] However, for the most part, the notable names in the literature of pastoral care are those of ordained men.

None of this is surprising in view of the reality that the appointed and recognised pastors of the Church have mostly been men. Now that ordination is more open to women, pastoral care is being practised more extensively by ordained women on behalf of either men or women. In addition, the laity—both men and women—are often assuming new roles in the Church, including the pastoral role. Therefore it is appropriate to consider the implication of the masculine and the feminine in pastoral ministry. While it would seem that the focus in this consideration might turn entirely to the feminine aspect, since females are 'new' to the pastoral scene, we must remember that, although pastoring has been done by males, this does not mean that sufficient attention had been given to the masculine aspect of this ministry. We have much to discover about both the feminine and the masculine.

For our purposes, 'pastor' will refer to the pastoral person, whether clergy or lay, male or female. The terms 'pastoral care' and 'pastoral ministry' can be used interchangeably, and both indicate a level of ministry different from simple Christian caring. Pastoral ministry does mean Christian caring, but at a level which includes the authority of the Church, competence in pastoral skills, and the presence of certain personal qualities in the pastor.

The special nature of pastoral ministry

The implications of masculinity and feminity need special considera- tion with regard to pastoral ministry as compared to priestly and prophetic ministries. The latter two ministries tend to be expressed in formalised and public settings of liturgy and preaching, and the theological issues as well as practical considerations of gender have been extensively defined. Whether an ordained woman can represent Christ in the Eucharistic celebration, and whether an Amos-like denunciation of sin will be taken seriously when delivered by a woman, are questions being resolved by contemporary testing. However, in priestly and prophetic roles, the impact of the personal factors of masculinity or femininity are somewht removed from the people being ministered to—by distance, or perhaps by the wearing of vestments, by the presence of a number of people, and by the expectations inherent in the ministerial role.

On the other hand, pastoral ministry tends to be done in private; the pastor is in physical proximity to the other person; touching is likely or may be part of the ministry itself; emotional tension is high; there is a helper–helpless implication which means vulnerability of the person who is ministered to; and in general both emotional and physical intimacy are heightened. This is not to say that theological convictions and practical considerations are irrelevant, but the personal dynamics of ministry come to the fore, and the pastor's masculinity or femininity will have an immediate impact on the person being ministered to—and his masculinity or her femininity will have an immediate impact on the pastor!

The foregoing is not meant to imply that it does not matter whether the pastor is ordained or a lay person, male or female. In a situation marked by inherent intimacy, an ordained male pastor has a certain distance established between him and, say, a female hospital patient, just by the fact of ordination. At the same time, ordination gives a certain permission to intimacy because it is perceived as 'safe'.

Thus the effects of masculinity and femininity are conditioned to some extent by the fact of ordination. A lay female pastor who ministers to a male hospital patient may find that intimacy is inhibited by the fact that her role is atypical (in current practice) and she may not know the man as well as an ordained pastor would know one of the flock; yet intimacy may be enhanced by the patient's natural acceptance of a mother figure's care in the sickroom setting.

The masculine and the feminine

Our approach to the implications of masculinity and feminity in pastoral ministry will be made through the theory of the psyche developed by Jung. According to this theory, a person normally develops with a dominant sexual ego-identity, either male or female. This part is the conscious self. However, within each person there is an element of the opposite sex, a contrasexual core referred to as the anima in the male personality and the animus in the female.[3] In the male, the anima exists in the psychic unconscious and personifies the contrasexual elements which express certain so-called feminine qualities. Ulanov identifies these as 'tenderness, sensitivity, devious-ness, seduction, indefiniteness, feeling, receptivity, elusiveness, jealousy, creative containing and yielding, and understanding'. In a female, the animus exists in the psychic unconscious and personifies the contrasexual elements which express certain so-called masculine qualities—'capacity to penetrate, separate, take charge, initiate, create, stand firmly over and against, to articulate and express meaning'.[4]

Jung differentiates between shallower and deeper layers of the psychic unconscious. The former is the personal unconscious, con-taining 'repressed memories and traits which can be recalled to consciousness and experienced as belonging to the ego'.[5] The deeper layer, called the objective psyche, contains archetypes, instinctive psychic drives of an objective, non-personal, universal nature which express themselves as 'a living system of reactions and aptitudes that determine the individual's life in invisible ways'.[6] The anima and animus are among these archetypes. Represented mythologically, the anima archetype is represented in 'stories having to do with the eternal feminine in all its forms'[7]—for example, the Great Mother—while the animus archetype may be met as the Great King or in many other forms. How the contrasexual archetype functions is described briefly by Ulanov: 'it operates unconsciously and auton-omously within the psyche. It often seems to have a life of its own which frequently conflicts with our clear intentions and values. Thus, to the conscious ego the anima or animus seems to be an impersonal "other" that confronts the ego from outside itself. Somehow the ego must learn to bring this force into connection with its own personal identity.'[8]

We are now approaching the relevance of Jung's theory of psychic structure to pastoral ministry. As an example, consider a male pastor with his dominant sexual ego-identity and masculine characteristics. Within him is a feminine core, the anima, introjected into his unconscious from significant females in his childhood—mother, sister, etc., culturally conditioned, and affected by the biological realities which differentiate him from females. So he is not simply a male; he is a male with femininity within. The function of the anima is to mediate the contents of the objective psyche (the deeper unconscious) to the man's conscious ego—that is, to put the man in touch with his capacity to focus upon and express his feminine qualities.[9]

If, however, the anima is unknown to or ignored by the conscious male ego, it is unconsciously projected on to people of the opposite sex.[10] The man then sees in the woman not herself but himself, but since his projection is unconscious, he is unaware that he has a false image of her. Meanwhile, since she is a female with a masculine core, her animus, she may or may not be projecting her animus on to him. If she is, then the two are not really meeting each other; they are meeting themselves in each other. If, on the other hand, the man 'recognises that his anima is not identifiable with the woman upon whom it is projected, but rather belongs to himself and requires that his individual ego relate to it',[11] he will be on his way towards the fulfilment of one of Jung's basic precepts—that personal wholeness is achieved only by full awareness of one's contrasexuality. The man will then have both his masculinity and femininity to bring into the presence of the other person.

Since we are taking the position that females as well as males will be involved as pastors, it should be emphasised at this point that what has been said about a male and his anima can also be said about a female and her animus. A woman with a clear female ego-identity will bring a richness to her pastoral ministry if her animus is brought into connection with her conscious ego; then she will have both her femininity and her masculinity to bring into the presence of the other person.

The implications for pastoral ministry

A female hospital patient suffers pain of apparent organic origin. The source of the pain cannot be determined with certainty without exploratory surgery; but exploratory surgery is not guaranteed to reveal the source. Medication and diet may alleviate the symptoms but may not effect a real cure. The patient is suffering, but she assumes the martyr role, bearing bravely this undeserved affliction while holding no malice toward anyone. She is able to recite the alternatives the doctor has outlined, but she couches her recitation in terms of being willing to go along with whatever 'they' decide, expressing hope that surely someone will extract the solution from a hopeless morass of possibilities, all too complex for her to cope with.

Suppose that the pastor is a male, either ordained or lay. It would be appropriate for him to offer the healing ministries of prayer, possibly the laying on of hands, and the elicitation of a positive attitude in the patient toward the healing process. The pastor would also attempt the guiding function of pastoral care by helping the patient to sort out and weigh the alternatives in terms of their practical effects, present and long-term. Ministry might include helping the patient to deal with her avoidance of responsibility for decisions about her treatment.

As a male functioning out of his dominant sexual ego-identity, the pastor may become very analytical, probing for details about medical procedures, what the doctor said, gathering data, and pushing for a decision about what to do on the basis of 'logic'. If the pastor had a negative introject from his own martyr-type mother, his anima might express itself toward the patient as an irritated impatience with her all-enduring *laissez faire* attitude and confused response to the options presented to her. Further, her dependency on 'them' for making a decision about her treatment may trigger in the pastor his aversion to the dependent ('feminine') side of his own makeup, resulting in his further assertiveness toward the patient to overcome her dependency, take charge of her life, make a decision, and be ready to accept the consequences! If the pastor's ego is not aware of these dynamics, his ministry to the patient will probably be objectified, unsympathetic, and overly directive.

If, on the other hand, the pastor, while ignoring his masculine characteristics and ways of responding, is connected on the conscious level with his anima, his analytical, goal-oriented abilities will be balanced by feminine qualities and responses. Speaking and acting tenderly, he can bring the feeling dimension into the sickroom. (At some level of consciousness the patient may realise that she needs tenderness and may criticise the pastor inwardly for not demonstrating it.) The pastor will be able to differentiate between his mother as martyr then, and the patient as martyr now, and thus to respond more sympathetically to exploring the context in which the patient's decisions must be made: what about her family circumstances? how can imagining the future illuminate certain options? how much of the distress is physical pain and how much fear or anxiety? Thus the pastor will gently encourage the patient to get in touch with her whole self, including, possibly, her animus' expression of the masculine desire to be fearless and self-sufficient ('I can handle this martyrdom'), and the desirability of taking responsibility for crucial decisions about her own life.

The description above indicates that when the pastor sets the feminine-in-him free to join the masculine-in-him in ministry, he is not demonstrating a learned pastoral skill. Instead, his ministry to the patient is a natural expression of pastoral masculinity combined organically with a pastoral femininity which he recognises and welcomes, not as an alien visitor from outer space (actually, from inner space—his unconscious), but as a genuine and valued part of his complete being, brought consciously to light and life and honoured by its use on behalf of someone in need. Ulanov describes this relationship of a man with his femininity this way: 'To establish contact with his anima, a man must trust her as though she were an actual autonomous, inner woman who cannot be controlled or dismissed but must be met as a person.'[12] Likewise, the masculine in a female, her animus, must be met as an actual, autonomous, inner man who cannot be controlled or dismissed but must be met as a person.

Let us now look at one of the common denominators, dependency, which appears as a factor in various pastoral situations, to see how the masculine and the feminine might play an important role. Some common pastoral situations are:

1   a bereaved person who is the object of sympathy because of his loss;

2   a hospital patient or nursing home resident who is confined and who experiences physical and emotional disability;

3   an elderly shut-in who cannot accomplish tasks or enjoy activities formerly managed with ease;

4   a new resident in the community who is an outsider to established social groups and who does not know 'the system' of the community;

5   a counselling client who is by definition someone in need of help.

In each situation there is a dependency in the sense that the person is not as self-sufficient as he or she used to be, and/or might be at some time in the future. In other words, there is an implied and/or actual cry for healing, sustaining, guiding, reconciling, or a combination of those four functions of pastoral care. What place, then, does the pastor's masculinity or femininity have in ministering to the other person, whom we shall refer to as 'the dependant'?

The dependant may present the pastor with a perfect balance, in which sense of dependence corresponds exactly with the need which actually exists. Or, the dependant may be unaware of actual dependence, or may refuse to accept its reality, and may present the pastor with an unrealistic self-assurance or even a rather hostile facade. At the other extreme, the dependant may respond in a clinging, helpless, infantile way, giving the pastor the message that needs are far greater than they actually are.

If the pastor is a woman, she may need to be particularly aware of the 'Great Mother' archetype lurking within her. As Ulanov notes, '[t]o be able to say no to another's need . . . is notoriously difficult for a woman'.[13] A sort of pastoral masochism can result from an inability to say no to certain needs expressed under certain conditions by other people. The pastor walks the second mile so often that her feet bleed, when actually this seemingly pastoral attitude may simply reinforce the dependant's dependency and prevent the steps needed for growing independence. The pastor is adroitly taking care of this need to be needed. Or, if a female pastor meets resistance in the form of denial of needs when in reality needs obviously exist, and if the female pastor is not in touch with her animus, she may try to intrude (phallically) through the resistance presented by the dependant, in which case power replaces tenderness as the motive for ministry.

If the pastor is a man, particularly if he is ordained, the 'Great King' ('Saviour') symbol may be the danger which corresponds to the 'Great Mother'. Or, the dependant's expressed needs—realistic or unrealistic—may trigger the pastor's own fear of having needs (rejection of his 'feminine'), resulting in overly energetic problem-solving and need-meeting by the pastor.

Two brief illustrations from my professional associates further indicate how the masculine and the feminine have pastoral implications. A man whose teenage daughter had a severe sexual trauma did not share this problem with his male pastor, but did reveal it to the pastor's younger, less experienced female curate. The male chaplain at a military hospital told a female student chaplain that she would see a lot more tears on the wards than he did. And she did. (The patients were almost exclusively male.)

What implications are suggested by these illustrations? First, a man's anima may be more easily set free to express itself in the presence of a female pastor, that is, men are more willing to reveal their 'weakness' to a woman than to a man. Second, if females attempt to model pastoral approaches after more masculine styles, they may defeat the very openness in communication they wish to establish. Third, male pastors who nurture their own anima may be better able to put males to whom they minister in touch with their feminine dimension and thus their wholeness of self.

Masculine and feminine in the Garden of Eden

The fulfilment of God's purpose in creation is expressed in his desire to 'make man in our image' (Gen. 1:26). One way of stating the goal of pastoral ministry, therefore, is the attempt to restore or to sustain the image of God in another person whenever that image has been fractured, defaced, or impaired. The functions of pastoral ministry are aimed at restoring wholeness, mending brokenness, and preserving the image of God in man.

Scholars have pointed out that the Hebrew word for 'man', *adam*, is a generic word which differentiates mankind from the animals. Thus, in the P creation narrative (Gen. 1-2:4a), 'man' or 'mankind' includes both male and female. We conclude that both man and woman are created equally, though differently, in God's image. As Sapp puts it, 'in contrast to the J account, man and woman are created simultaneously in P with no hint of temporal, much less ontological, superiority'.[14] Furthermore, God's creation of male and female is 'very good' (Gen. 1:31).

The Creation narratives testify that man and woman are complementary; neither one's life is complete without the other; God's image is fully revealed only when both male and female are present. And God places them in a community of two, 'the community derived from God, the community of love glorifying and worshipping him as the Creator'.[15] In this community, man and woman are to love by enjoying the gifts of each other and by affirming in each other the image of God which is there. They have a personal relationship, but until after the Fall, there is no pastoral ministry since the image of God in each is intact. But when pastoral ministry is needed, it will be

equally the responsibility of man and woman; and each—created in
God's image—will be equipped equally for the fulfilling of God's
purposes.

In the Garden of Eden, we have our first look at the masculine and
the feminine. The J creation narrative (Gen. 2:4b–3:24) is very
descriptive of the personal relationship between man and woman, and
between mankind and God. Yet it appears that masculine and
feminine characteristics are found in both man and woman. Man, for
example, is portrayed as obedient, even passive. He goes where God
puts him and does not do what God says he should not (2:15–17). He is
also emotional, capable of a spontaneous, intimate expression: 'This at
last is bone of my bones . . .' (2:23). Impulsively, and without weighing
the consequences, he succumbs to temptation (3:6, 'and he ate').
Reluctant to face the consequences (like a man!), he tries to hide from
the Lord and is swift to rationalise his cowardice and unhesitating in
casting blame on the woman. Some of his actions come from post-
fallen and some from pre-fallen states, but man is portrayed as having
a definite feminine dimension. The masculine dimension is seen in his
evaluative and decision-making aspects, as he gives names to the
living creatures and decides that none is a fit companion (2:19–20).

Woman is portrayed as intellectually alert and aware of the limits
of her creaturehood as defined by God. She knows which tree is off-
limits and which ones are not. Appreciating the complexity of the
situation, she is engaged in wrestling with options, principles, and
risks. Eating from the tree of the knowledge of good and evil is
prohibited, but since God created the tree to produce fruit good for
food, he must have intended the fruit to be eaten. Woman takes
charge and decides. In these respects, she demonstrates characteristics more usually associated with masculinity. Yet her femininity is
there—she appreciates aesthetics—the tree is lovely. Further, she has
higher motives, the yearning for wisdom. On a much higher plane
than man's impulsive disobedience, woman is 'the victim of the desire
for infinity'.[16] Of course, in her fallen state she is no better than
man—she, too, tries to hide from God and to shift responsibility from
herself by blaming the serpent.

Outside of the presence of the Holy Spirit in human interactions,
the most crucial single factor in the effectiveness of pastoral ministry
is the person of the pastor. In the Creation narratives we find a
variety of personal characteristics (though not a complete catalogue
by any means) which can be affirmed as important when one person
ministers to the needs of another in a pastoral way, and these

characteristics are not restricted to males or females; a pastor, either male or female, clergy or lay, may exhibit any of these characteristics. Where present they can be nurtured and strengthened; where weak or absent, they may be compensated for or developed. We may identify the characteristics as follows:

1   to be aware of one's own needs
2   to know proper boundaries
3   to exercise self-discipline
4   to be capable of emotional responses and bonding
5   to be able to evaluate objective data
6   to know one's own motives
7   to be able to make decisions and to abide with the consequences
8   to assume responsibility for one's own actions
9   to be sensitive to one's surroundings
10 to have a perceptive mind
11 to wish for and to seek a deeper knowledge of God and his ways
12 to think about and to do what is good for the other person

Adam and Eve were not only husband and wife. They were pastors to each other. Had they ministered pastorally to each other as God intended, we would not need all of the tending and mending which pastoral ministry today requires to restore the image of God in men and women.

One final observation has to do with the shame felt by man and woman when they became aware of their nakedness after the Fall. Their sin was pride, of seeking to become 'like God' (3:5), not a matter of sexual consciousness. As God had created them, man and woman had a full awareness of their own and each other's sexuality, of their respective masculine and feminine natures. They knew that each needed the other, and they accepted this complementariness. Terrien states that man and woman after the Fall 'are ashamed of one another'[17] Bonhoeffer, on the other hand, attributes the shame to the man's and the woman's 'reluctant acknowledgment' of their limitedness[18]—the grace of complementariness is transformed by sin into a self-centred resentment of each one's incomplete nature, of each one's desire to be complete without the other.

A somewhat different interpretation would allow the truth of both positions while restating the issue in different terminology: in the Fall, man became ashamed of that part of his total self represented by woman (his feminine part of completeness—his anima), and woman became ashamed of that part of her total self represented by man (her masculine part of completeness—her animus). Thus it is part of the recreation of the image of God in man that he recover an unashamed affirmation of the feminine in himself, and of the image of God in woman that she recover an unashamed affirmation of the masculine in herself.

The pastoral ministry has been exercised predominantly by ordained or monastic males on behalf of the laity, either males or females, and this has resulted in a quite natural lack of concern about the effects of masculinity and femininity in the pastor and in the one who is cared for. I wish to propose that because of the particular character of pastoral ministry—personal, by nature relational, often intimate, private, and emotion-laden—it is especially important to discover the effects of masculinity and femininity in this ministry. The Jungian theory of the human psyche provides a framework in conjunction with which to make this exploration. The male pastor in touch with his anima and the female pastor in touch with her animus will be better able to do pastoral ministry because they can affirm femininity along with maleness and masculinity along with femaleness. A more whole person is better able to help another person to become more whole. For the pastor, the second great commandment could then be interpreted, '. . . love your neighbour as you love yourself, including that part of yourself which is your contrasexual element'.

15

Christian conversion and the feminine

TONY KELLY

First, a definition of terms. By *Christian conversion* I mean the fundamental dynamism of Christian existence. No one is once and for all 'converted'. One follows the Way of Christ by embarking on a journey, the existential journey of faith, hope and love. To be always open to the truth of what one believes in, to the full promise of what one hopes for, to the unrestricted goodness of what one loves, to fullest collaboration with those with whom one believes and hopes and loves—all this means a continuing process of conversion.

No one is converted alone, not for long, anyway. To be converted, turned out of oneself toward that Universal Love revealed in Christ, is to be turned toward others who, one way or another, support or occasion one's growth in conversion. Typically, these others are our sisters and brothers in the Church, the neighbour who represents Christ calling us to a special love, and even the enemy who tests the realism of the unconditional love one is supposed to be living. It is always a conversion mediated by being with others, and interacting with them, in shared prayer and celebration, in mutual love, in common concern for an ever wider world, in dialogue when one meets differences, in conflict if rejection or persecution be one's lot. In one way or another, we interact to inspire and challenge to a greater individual and communal conversion.

Conversion is a movement into what no eye has seen nor ear heard nor the human heart conceived. Though we move within a mystery of grace, it still 'has not yet appeared what we shall be' (1 Jn 3:2). We never lay hold of the full mystery of God—whom no one has ever seen (Jn 1:18); nor, it would appear, can we ever exhaust the fullness of our shared humanity, made, as it is, in the divine image: 'Let us make

man in our image and likeness . . . male and female he created them'
(Gen. 1:27).

Conversion, in our context, then, is an ongoing communal development from what is opposed to Christian authenticity or less than what
should be, to what accords with such authenticity and promotes it: in
this case, *the Feminine*.

What do I mean by *the Feminine*? I am not unaware of the number
and complexity of the issues connoted by this word. It is a problema-
tical term. It might seem too vague to those concerned directly with
'womens' issues'. It might seem too bland for a 'feminist viewpoint'. It
will probably be understood as too psychological and interior in view
of the decisions to be taken by those who are concerned with a more
inclusive humanity and a greater Christian wholeness.

Nonetheless, I will keep it. It at least points in a direction. Perhaps
there is some merit in not wanting to define *the Feminine* too quickly,
but to let its meaning emerge in its proper originality and persuasive-
ness. At the least, it is an emblematic term for that new depth and
breadth of creativity demanded by any alert Christian commitment
today. And, as I hope to make clear, it is a dimension of conversion
particularly urgent in this precarious and challenging present.

The Feminine, be it an essential human dimension or a particular
human value, occurs in different ways to different people. In one
sense, it does not occur as the most urgent issue of the day. I would see
that as the very survival of the human race—given the growing threat
of thermonuclear destruction, the unimaginable scale of world
poverty and starvation, the oppression of whole nations by inhuman
regimes, the ecological crisis, the murderously unjust distribution of
the world's resources, the arms race: all the elements that put into
jeopardy our human future, and call forth a common responsibility.

At such a point of crisis, an insight into the value of *the Feminine*
(however elusive it might remain) occurs. For one thing becomes
clear: the world as we have known it is coming to an end. One way or
another, it is ending: if we don't change, it will end in some enormous
self-destruction. If we do change for the sake of human survival and
development, it will be in the making of a world in great contrast to
the way things are now. For the world that is passing has been, by and
large, brought into existence by the thinking and decisions, the plans
and the actions, the exploits and exploitations, the conquests and
conflicts, the morality and philosophy of men. In the public world of
history, it has been a world largely populated by men. They were the

main actors on the world stage, recorded in a history written by men about men for men. If women did appear, it was, at best, in a supporting role; or because, by accident or genius, they did what men did, remarkably well. More usually, be it in art or religion, philosophy or science, government or education, conflict and exploration, they were behind the scenes.

Admittedly it would be silly to overload this general statement (however true I believe it to be) with a further generalisation implying that women were innocent and men were villains. For, on the one hand, women often consented to and inspired the self-destructive course of history. On the other, there was in this 'man's world' an abundance of goodness and heroism, grandeur, beauty and achievement; and above all, the beginnings of a justice that was waiting for its day. Men did love in their own way: they loved the Helen whose face launched their thousand ships. They loved the Eve who was their helpmate and mother of their children. They loved the Mary who was the mother of the Saviour of the world. They loved the *Hagia Sophia*, the Holy Wisdom, who intimated herself to them in flickering visions of something infinitely luminous, gentle, compassionate and all-comprehending which could never be enclosed or controlled within scope of their world (Ws. 8:1–9:6). Their love was, however, marked with a failure: by idealising their women out of their world, they disallowed the creative presence of the real women of the world in the formation of what they assumed was theirs, by right or responsibility. They did not hear the unsettling question that women implicitly stood for, and often explicitly put: is all this really the best that we human beings can do?

Yes, we loved. But if we are to continue to love, it must be on other terms, terms far more inclusive of the creativity, dignity and sheer reality of women than we had dreamt of before.

But now as we stand on the brink, all of us, with men offered the knowledge that their limited best was not good enough, *the Feminine* emerges as an essential dimension of any future we might share. If our first breath is a prayer of hope that a human future will be given us, our second breath utters a request, at once timid and desperate, to the women in whom some passionate unfamiliar spirit is stirring: For all our sakes, can you teach us to sow peace where we have reaped, harvest after harvest, of war? Can you teach us to rejoin the totality of the human race even though we have collapsed into hopeless, competitive divisiveness? Can you teach us wisdom to use all this power science has discovered for the common good? Can you lead us to a Holy

Mystery which, despite all, might give meaning and hope, even though we have come to a dead-end in a bleak, God-forsaken no-man's land?

Such, then, is one way in which *the Feminine* emerges in male consciousness. It occurs at that limit where men, individually and communally, know that they are limited, especially in the face of an uncanny and threatening future. To this degree, it occurs as an act of hope, and a plea for forgiveness—it does not mean a new phase in the idealisation or divinisation of women. God remains God. But any act of hope in God today seems to send us back to an exploration of our fundamental biblical faith. That reveals that God is present in our world in the full grace of our humanness, not in some half-human version of it: 'Let us make human beings in our image and likeness . . . male and female he created them' (Gen. 1:26,27).

For men to experience the question of *the Feminine* in the way I have tried to evoke it, has this advantage. If *the Feminine* is an essential aspect of hope for the future, men are, as it were, defined into the emergence of *the Feminine*, as relying on it, needing it, being led by it, finding themselves through it. Thus it does not occur in the destructive way of one more alienation in the current breakdown. It is rather a sign of life and new beginning.

What is at stake is the whole of humanity and its future. The liberation of *the Feminine* is an expansion within history toward a more hopeful and whole humanity.

To put it more simply, I see it not as what *they* (women) are telling *us* (men), but what *you* (women—personally addressed) are calling all of us to discover together—precisely at the point where an uncritical and half-human masculinity has come to the end of its resources. This is far from being a negation of male worth. I am not advocating some form of psychic or historical sex-change. No, I am envisaging a more hopeful and, indeed, more playful, exchange between the sexes, where, at the beginning of something quite new in human history, women will be free to speak and act and lead. What we need is a truly human conversation. In such an exchange, men will not feel that they disappear if they listen or if they are led. For they will be hearing a more richly human word, just as they are being invited into a fuller expression of their masculinity within a more integrally human world. 'Affirmative action' is not emasculation. It is humanisation. Of course, it means letting go of the narrow isolated styles of former sex roles. That will be hard. But so are the deeply destructive violent ways of the present, hard. There are no easy options. Hope can never envisage its outcome. Here, as elsewhere, 'it has not yet appeared what we shall be' (1 Jn 3:2). To that degree, it is experienced as a risk. Nonetheless, men and women will, one might predict, still keep on making love. Do they have anything to fear if it is more personal?

Conversion *and the Feminine*, in this present context, comes to mean, in practice, conversion *to the Feminine*. No one would dispute that this is a complex and many-levelled movement of heart and mind, with the implications of both a journey inward and outward. As a religious word, 'conversion' implies primarily a turning to God, a new relationship with the ultimately Holy. But that level of faith has intellectual and moral components: intellectual, because it is not a conversion to anything at all, or to nothing, or to an illusion, but to the ultimate truth which faith apprehends; moral, because any relationship to the Holy affects one's being and action in the world: 'If God so loved us, we ought to love one another' (1 Jn 4:11).

Further, because such a conversion has religious, intellectual and moral components, it necessarily deeply affects one's psychic being, how one feels about oneself, one's worth, one's destiny.

Conversion to *the Feminine*, then, includes at least these four interrelated levels of further openness: the religious, the intellectual, the moral, the psychological. It enlarges that historical horizon which, for centuries if not millennia, has limited our cultural experience of God, privileged the masculine in our understanding of reality, locked our morality into the ethical concerns of a male-centred world, and made women feel their identity to be somehow dependent on, and subservient to, the male—in whom the true glory and splendour of the human condition was presumed to be embodied.

It is not usual in the vast literature on *the Feminine* to find these four levels distinctly or comprehensively treated. For that reason, in what follows, I shall offer some account of each of them. Whatever *the Feminine* means, or however one might come to define it, a great deal will be lost if it is not recognised as a dimension of our experience of God, a question of objective truth, an issue of a more global morality, and an appropriation of a more wholesome psychological integrity.

Religious conversion to *the Feminine*

Here it is a matter of negating a notion of 'God' elaborated in exclusive patriarchal and male terms to affirm the Holy Mystery through a more inclusive symbolism, both female and male. The True God is not a patriarchal idol but the One in whom our most complete humanity finds its hope. Anyone in the Judaeo-Christian tradition who has given any thought to the matter has always known that God is beyond any objective expression. The Mystery is neither 'he' nor 'she' nor 'it', but the 'You' that fills the horizon of life. This 'You' means, loves and enables our communal and individual being and freedom, in life, in death, and beyond death. The only language finally worth anything is interpersonal language, 'I' and 'we' addressing and listening to the 'You' in whom we exist and blossom into being. Still, even the greatest mystics eventually speak. And when they do, they are faced with the problem of how to mean, in word and in ritual, who it is that loves them. Typically, they go through the whole repertoire of human experience if their words are not to fail altogether, calling God 'friend', 'father', 'mother', 'spouse', 'saviour', 'rock', 'fortress', 'life-giver', 'fire', 'breath' . . . But words are carriers of meaning, and meaning arises out of the experiences of history. So it is of some importance, for those who live in the tradition of biblical faith, to take notice not only of the words that are the vocabulary of that tradition, but to the experience out of which such words arise.

The biblical tradition is manifestly marked by a powerful patriarchal culture. That is a matter of fact. What is a matter of surprise is the manner in which biblical faith breaks free from such a culture to express new divinely willed possibilities for human existence. It is a matter of regret that we have been so slow to follow such a lead.

On the level of scholarship, we could hardly do better than to follow Elizabeth Schüssler-Fiorenza's researches. I cannot reproduce her scholarship here, but the following quotation indicates the direction of her thought:

> Although Jewish (and Christian) theology speaks about God in male language and images, it nevertheless insists that such language and images are not adequate 'pictures' of the divine, and that human language and experience are not capable of beholding or expressing God's reality. The second commandment and the unspeakable holiness of God's name are very concrete expressions of this insistence. To fix God to a definite form and man-made image would mean idolatry. Classical prophetic theology, often in abusive language, polemicized against the pagan idols and thus rejected goddess worship, but it did not do so in defence of a male God and a patriarchal idol. By rejecting

all other gods, prophetic theology insisted on the *oneness*
of Israel's God and of God's creation. It therefore rejected
the myth of the 'divine couple', and thus repudiated
masculinity and femininity as absolute ultimate divine
principles. But in so doing, it did not quite escape the
patriarchal understanding of God, insofar as it trans-
ferred the image of the divine marriage to the relationship
of Yahweh and Israel who is seen as his wife and bride.[1]

But there is another tradition in Israel's effort to evoke the meaning
of its experience of the Divine. This is usually called 'Wisdom
Theology', in which the dominant characteristic of God is *Sophia*
(wisdom), not only a feminine word, but one connoting many aspects
of *the Feminine* (for example, mother, bride, beloved, sister, healer,
creator, artist . . .). This style of monotheistic theology is not intent on
distancing itself from pagan nature-religions and fertility cults. It is
an inclusive theology. It attempts to evoke the all-pervasive, all-
comprehending and creative presence of God in all histories and
cultures—even if 'She' dwells uniquely in Israel.[2]

This Holy Wisdom is a compassionate Spirit (Ws. 1:6). She comes to
the one who prays, 'bringing all good things with her' (Ws. 7:11). Of
all such graces, 'she is the Mother' (Ws. 7:12). She is 'more beautiful
than the sun . . . she reaches mightily from one end of the earth to the
other, and orders all things well' (Ws. 7:29–8:1).

Fiorenza comes up with the plausible suggestion that Jesus understood his ministry, and even his identity, in the light of this Holy
Wisdom 'who is vindicated in all her children' (Lk 7:35):

> The Palestinian Jesus movement understands the
> ministry and mission of Jesus as that of the prophet and
> child of Sophia sent to announce that God is the God of the
> poor and heavy laden, of the outcasts and those who suffer
> injustice . . . he stands in a long line and succession of
> prophets sent to gather the children of Israel to their
> gracious Sophia God. Jesus' execution, like John's, results
> from his mission and commitment as prophet and
> emissary of the Sophia-God who holds open a future for
> the poor and the outcasts and offers God's gracious good-
> ness to *all* children of Israel without exception. The
> Sophia-God of Jesus does not need atonement of sacrifices.
> Jesus' death is not willed by God but is the result of his
> all- inclusive praxis as Sophia's prophet.[3]

Take for example just two instances of the character of the God
Jesus involves in his 'all-inclusive praxis'. Jesus invokes God as *Abba*

and acts in the power of the Holy Spirit, to inaugurate the new human
family of which he is the centre: ties of blood or social stratification
are of no account, but 'whoever does the will of God is my brother and
sister and mother' (Mk 3:35). Any patriarchal classification of human
beings is excluded: on the human level, there is no mention of
'fathers'! Second, in his injunction against patriarchal roles, Jesus
underscores the reality of the community of equals which the
Kingdom of God brings about: 'Call no one rabbi . . . father . . . master'
(Mt. 23:8–11).

Relying on Fiorenza's scholarship and the work of many others who
move in the same direction, it is possible to conclude that Jesus
invokes God as *Abba* (Father), in his unique idiom, not to justify
patriarchal structures and relationships, but precisely to contest such
enslaving human classifications.[4]

Another fruitful approach to freeing 'God' from fixated or congealed
male imagery is to consider the character of the Holy Spirit. There
may be some future in envisaging the Christian experience of God as
implying the formation of a new humanity: Jesus is the new Adam
(hardly unbiblical; see 1 Cor. 15:45) with the Spirit as the New Eve,
possessing and inspiring Israel, Mary and the Church, forming this
new humanity with all the virtualities of maternal, spousal and
virginal love. For the Spirit, in Christian understanding, is pre-
eminently the Gift. This resonates with a certain maternal
symbolism, for as one writer puts it, '[n]othing on earth is "given" to
us as our mother is: she personifies love in its most disinterested,
generous and devoted form'.[5]

So, despite this extremely cursory indication of the play of feminine
and masculine symbols in our relationship to God, and of God's to us, I
hope this much might be clear. Any continuing religious conversion
must be free to explore the whole range of sexual symbolism if our
experience of the Holy Mystery is to be genuine. If through male and
female symbolism we celebrate the God of our humanity, it must
make a difference: our sexuality will be more totally and playfully
engaged in the experience of Ultimate Love, with considerable
advantage to woman, man . . . and God!

Intellectual conversion to *the Feminine*

Conversion to God is not a turning to unreality. It means taking a
position in a real world in the light of the ultimate truth and meaning
disclosed in the experience of faith. Now, if such a faith has

(re)discovered dimensions of *the Feminine* in Ultimate Reality, the integrity of that faith provokes a more intelligent and critical exploration of the meaning of *the Feminine* within one's philosophical and scientific tradition.

It is at this point that we discover the masculine bias in the classical traditions of philosophy which have usually nourished the expression of faith. Such key figures in the history of Christian theology as Augustine and Thomas Aquinas inherited and transmitted a powerful Greek philosophy (Plato and Aristotle) which did less than justice to the reality of *the Feminine*. For a full account of this I would refer to the research of Kari Elizabeth Borresen.[6] In Greek metaphysics, form and act were identified with the male principle, while the female mode of being was always depicted as 'un-formed', the material component, the passive, receptive principle. Higher reason contemplating the eternal was identified with a male nature, and lower, practical reason was identified with the feminine. In the various theological transpositions that occurred in the light of this philosophy, (though it was always acknowledged that men and women were of equal *spiritual* dignity) the male was more immediately made 'in the image of God', since the male principle was the active one, and male nature was the most perfect form of human nature.

It is true that no serious thinker today (let alone anyone with a knowledge of modern biology) would take this model of relationships between the sexes very seriously, despite its long and powerful influence. On the other hand, to conceive of the female–male relationship in terms of an easy, uncritical mutuality or complementarity does not really close with the issue either. This is often the language of men and women who are beginning to see the problem. What still remains obscured is that women are offered a complementarity to the male in a male-dominated or 'androcentric' world.

What we need, and what is beginning to take place, is a rethinking of human sexual existence in which the woman, for example, is not a half-human being (even 'the better half'), not just a complement to the male, but a feminine person possessing an irreducible value in her openness to the transcendent, the undefinable fullness of existence, whether or not she exists in a particular category of relationship to a man or not. There is something absolute, that is, not relative, to the male, in feminine existence which has to be recognised before female–male relationships can be a true meeting of persons. I have found a number of examples of how this is beginning to be explored in an impressive way.[7]

Moral conversion to *the Feminine*

Christian faith assents to the true in order to promote the doing of good. 'Whoever does the will of God is my brother and sister and mother' (Mk 3:35). This moral dimension of conversion to *the Feminine* is to some degree obvious and reasonable—an issue of straight justice, human rights, the abolition of anti-feminine structures and attitudes. But, it seems to me, the Christian authenticity that prompts us to risk all for the sake of the Kingdom of God demands another level of response from women and men, but in different ways. This turns on that essentially Christian activity of forgiveness.

Let it be noted that the real meaning of this kind of forgiveness does not reside in a soft-hearted, soft-headed smoothing over of the evidence of real evil—a kind of pretence that it never was really evil in the first place. Certainly, Christian forgiveness is about an unlimited hope in the triumph of an ultimate mercy and healing; but this is realistically expressed in naming and recognising evil for what it is: the confession of sin in oneself and a call to repentance with regard to others. It is part of a process by which we refuse to let ourselves, or others, be eternally defined by failure, malice, wrongdoing of any kind—'Father forgive . . . as we forgive . . .'.

In our present context, if we are to envisage a new level of creative and hopeful communication between women and men, the issue of forgiveness has to be faced. For men, first of all: 'Bless me, Sisters, for I have sinned!' It is not an attitude or an expression readily suggested to men in a man's world. It appears utterly foolish and weak. It feels like giving in, and it does amount to giving up the way things (however inhumanly) were. But it is on such a foolishness and weakness that the mystery of new life has always been based (1 Cor. 1:20–26).

This does not imply a pretence that each man has been guilty of all the violence, exploitation, humiliation and oppression that women have suffered from men throughout history. But it does imply that each individual does exist in a mysterious archetypal solidarity with the members of his or her sex—a matter that women today seem to understand more clearly than men. Here I am thinking of the enormous significance of 'the significant women' who have inspired new possibilities in the lives of thousands of their sisters.

So, as he speaks for himself and in solidarity with all his brothers, I think it is time for each man to find the freedom to ask forgiveness of the women with whom he finds himself in conversation. Popes need to do it, politicians need to do it; so do husbands, priests, brothers, friends, doctors, lawyers, teachers . . . This is the one act that really expresses for us men a commitment to, and a hope for, something radically new. If I see it only as a futile humiliation, then perhaps it is time to ask myself how precarious, despairing and isolated my world has become.

Admittedly, it is a hope and a risk, not a command or a requirement—let alone a subtle strategy for disarming feminine anger or for taming the passion for the as yet undefinable 'new'. Still, need it be a manipulation for men to hope that they will be forgiven? On a few occasions, I have tried to express this much: unless women do forgive (eventually) they will not have the unique healing and creativity that comes from forgiving: they will be more trapped within themselves than any single act of male malice could bring about. Without forgiving, they will always be reacting against the past at the expense of acting for the future . . . Unless women find the freedom to forgive, won't they merely parallel all the inhumanities that men have been guilty of?—seeking for power, acting without loving, regarding the opposite sex as inimical and inferior, a means for providing heirs or extending possessions, as an occasion of sin or a means of recreation?

Forgiveness makes a more hopeful humanity possible. I suspect, too, that it is the secret source of humour, that ability that so many women have to tease our solemn male posturing into a more real communication, so to suggest a sense of proportion, of what is human and what could be so . . .

Psychological conversion to *the Feminine*

Because this conversion implies a new dimension in one's relationship with God, because it implies a new exploration of reality, because it demands a new hopeful and healing moral stance, it implies a new quality of self-possession. It affects one's sense of self and one's estimate of the worth of that self. For this conversion is not only a movement outward but a journey inward, to reclaim and to 're-member' the fuller self that an uncritical or un-Christian masculinity has forced us to disown.

Since Freud was conspicuously incapable of expressing or perhaps appreciating *the Feminine*, it is Jungian psychology that pretty well dominates this 'journey inward'. In terms of specifically Christian conversion, one significant aspect of 're-membering' the human psyche is the recovery of Christian history, especially in its origins. This takes place in instances as diverse as the sheer recognition of the status and number of women in the early Church at all levels of leadership;[8] the revolutionary liberating attitude of Jesus in regard to women; the Gospels' presentation of women as 'first among the faithful' in the occurrence and the quality of faith;[9] and the pervasive use, in the New Testament, of feminine symbolism to describe the divine–human relationships.

I can do no better than refer the reader to Fiorenza and Moloney on these matters. The point is that biblical scholarship is providing us with a 'dangerous memory' of the presence and worth of *the Feminine* in the original Church, both in symbolic terms and in the history of the actual women who were 'mothers of the church'. A willingness to remember the past in the collapse of the patriarchal present, and to accept that memory as a grace and an invitation amounts to a psychological conversion.

Notes

Introduction

1 Tony Kelly *Seasons of Hope* Blackburn, Vic.: Dove Communications, 1984, p. 95
2 Miriam Dixson *The Real Matilda* 2nd edn, Penguin Australia, 1984, p. 241
3 Jill Conway 'Gender in Australia' *Daedalus* 114, 1, 1985, pp. 343–68
4 Dixson *The Real Matilda* p. 241
5 *Magdalene* 4, December 1982, p. 13
6 Dixson *The Real Matilda* p. 241
7 *Enquiry Into The Status Of Women In The Church: Commission On The Status Of Women* Australian Council of Churches (NSW), 1974, p. 4
8 Dixson *The Real Matilda* pp. 241–42
9 ibid. p. 242
10 *In Unity* 32, 1, 1985, p. 12
11 Dixson *The Real Matilda* p. 242
12 To be passed a bill must receive approval from two-thirds of the bishops, priests and laity voting separately. Though a majority were in favour, it failed these requirements
13 Hester Eisenstein *Contemporary Feminist Thought* London and Sydney: Unwin Paperbacks, 1984, p. 60

1 Woman and the Church: Her story

1 Aristotle *Generation of Animals II*, 732a, 738b, 727b, 729a, 731a
2 Tony Kelly 'Restoring the feminine in our image of God: Liberation from the half human' *National Outlook* July 1983

3   ibid

4   ibid

5   Elizabeth Fiorenza 'You are not to be called Father: Early
    Christian history in a feminist perspective' *Cross Currents* 29, 3,
    1979, pp. 301–323

6   P. and D. O'Farrell 'The status of women: Some opinions in
    Australian Catholic history' *Bulletin of Christian Affairs* Special,
    1977

7   Walter M. Abbott SJ (ed.) *The Documents of Vatican II* London:
    Chapman, 1966

8   B. Pitman, B. Johnstone, H. O'Leary, I. Hay, A. O'Hagen
    'Current Focus: Declaration on the question of the admission of
    women to the Ministerial Priesthood' *Compass Theology Review*
    II Winter, 1977

9   Robert Banks 'The early church as a caring community and some
    implications for social work today' *Interchange 30*, Sydney: AFES
    Graduate fellowship, 1982

10 Irene Brennan 'Women in the Kingdom of God' *The Month: A*
    review of Christian Thought and World Affairs 13, 12, 1980
    pp. 414–17

11 Banks 'The early church as a caring community'

2   The role of the Church in the education of girls and women

1   Constance Parvey (ed.) *The Community of Women and Men in the*
    Church Geneva: World Council of Churches, 1983

2   William Barclay *Educational Ideas in the Ancient World* London:
    Collins, 1959

3   James Donaldson *Woman: Her position and influence in Ancient*
    Greece and Rome and among Early Christians London: Long-
    man's, Green & Co, 1907

4   ibid. p. 158

5   Tertullian *De Baptismo cxvii and Ad Uxorem*

6   See also Lina Eckenstein *The Women of Early Christianity*
    London: The Faith Press, 1935

7   A.F. Leach *Educational Charters and Documents* Cambridge:
    Cambridge University Press, 1911 and A.F. Leach *Schools of*
    Medieval England London, Methuen, 1916

8   John Lawson *Medieval education and the Reformation* London:
    Routledge & Kegan Paul, 1967

9 Eileen Power *Medieval English Nunneries* Cambridge: Cambridge University Press, 1922

10 Leach, *Educational Charters and Documents*

11 Sheila Fletcher *Feminists and Bureaucrats* London: Methuen 1981

12 H.C. Barnard *The French Tradition in Education* Cambridge: Cambridge University Press, 1922 and S.J. Curtis and M. Boultwood, *History of Educational Ideas*, London: University Tutorial Press, 1966

13 W.A. Campbell-Stuart *Quakers and Education* Epworth: Epworth Press, 1953

14 ibid

15 June Rose *Elizabeth Fry* London: Macmillan, 1980, chapter 1

16 Aubrey Richardson *Women of the Church of England* London: Chapman & Hall, 1908, p. 137

17 For further reading on the Sunday School movement, see *Letters of Hannah More* London: Bodley Head, 1925; Charles Birchenough *History of Elementary Education* London: University Tutorial Press, 1938; Richardson *Women of the Church of England*; L.B. Walford 'Hannah More' in *Four Biographies* London: W. Blackwood & Sons, 1888, for introductory material, and M.G. Jones *Hannah More* Cambridge: Cambridge University Press, 1952

18 See for example Josephine Kamm *How Different From Us* London: The Bodley Head, 1958; Barry Turner *Equality for Some* London: Ward Lock Educational, 1974; Josephine Kamm *Hope Deferred* London: Methuen, 1965; E. Raikes *Dorothea Beale of Cheltenham* London: Constable, 1908; Barbara Stephen *Emily Davies and Girton College* London: Constable, 1927; Sarah Burstall *Frances Mary Buss* London: SPCK, 1938

19 *Christian Observer* 1812 pp. 738–41, First report of the *National Society for promoting the Education of the Poor in the Principles of the Established Church throughout England and Wales*. The National Society was, with the parallel British and Foreign School Society founded by Lancaster (a Nonconformist), the main systemic provider of elementary education until the state took over in 1870

20 'On Lord Sandon's Bill' in *The Church Quarterly Review* April–July 1876, vol. 2, London

21 R.L. Archer *Secondary Education in the Nineteenth Century* Cambridge: Cambridge University Press, 1928

22 Cheltenham Ladies College Magazine, 1906
23 Raikes *Dorothea Beale*
24 Blanche Clough *A Memoir of Anne Jemima Clough* London: Edward Arnold, 1903
25 Fletcher *Feminists and Bureaucrats*
26 Peter Anson *The Call of the Cloister* London: SPCK, 1964
27 ibid. p. 138
28 ibid. p. 303
29 *Church Quarterly Review* 1876, pp. 60–61
30 Eileen M. Byrne *Equality of Education and Training for Girls* Brussels: Commission of the European Communities, Studies, Education Series 9, 1979
31 It is not generally recognised that statistically, women and girls are at present 50.8 per cent of the world's total population and men and boys 49.2 per cent. To classify women as 'a minority' is as inaccurate statistically as it is conceptually

3 Sexism and fundamentalism

1 C.M. Clark *History of Australia* vol. 1, Melbourne: Melbourne University Press, 1968, p. 75
2 Gabriel Herbert *Fundamentalism and The Church of God* London: SCM, 1957, p. 17
3 Patricia Grimshaw 'Women and the Family in Australian History' in Elizabeth Windshuttle (ed.) *Women, Class and History: Feminine Perspectives on Australia, 1788–1978* Fontana-Collins, Australia, 1980, pp. 37–52

4 The ordination of women: On whose side is the Bible?

1 For supporting evidence for this summary of New Testament teaching about women see my book *Women and their Ministry* Melbourne: Dove Communications, 1977, chapter 1 (henceforth *WTM*)
2 This is explained later in the essay in the discussion about the teaching on the subordination of women.
3 In any case the argument that the twelve apostles are the prototype of all future ministers is without substance. A valiant attempt to prove this was made in K.E. Kirk (ed.) *The Apostolic Ministry* London: Hodder & Stoughton, 1946, but despite its enthusiastic reception by Anglo-Catholics, the passing of time

has shown that the central thesis of the book is invalid. The apostles are not the prototypes of all future ministers nor do they institute 'the ministry' of the church. In the New Testament many forms of leadership emerged, most of them without apostolic direction

4   *WTM* pp. 55–58

5   ibid. pp. 29–41

6   Whereas the case against equality of opportunity in ministry for women does not

7   Jezebel is condemned as a false prophetess. She is not condemned because as a woman she prophesied

8   The teacher expounds apostolic teaching while the prophet proclaims the Word of the Lord as it has been personally revealed to him

9   When gifts of ministry are listed the order is normally apostle, prophet, teacher. See 1 Cor. 12:28, Eph. 4:11

10 Miriam (Ex. 15:20, Mic. 6:4); Deborah (Jud. 4:5)—a married woman; Huldah (2 Kings 22:8–20) also married; Isaiah's wife (Is. 8:3), Noadiah (Neh. 6:14); Anna (Luke 2:36:38). The rabbis, who usually had a very low view of women, held that 'Forty-eight prophets and seven prophetesses prophesied in Israel' (b. Meg. 14a Bar). It is interesting that Dr R.A. Cole (*Prophet Priest and Pastor*, Sydney, AIO, 1970) who argues that the office of prophet is the prototype of today's ordained full-time ministry does not, on this basis, go on to argue for the ordination of women

11 See *WTM* pp. 34–35 and especially B. Brooten 'Junia . . . Outstanding Among the Apostles Rom. 16:7' in L. and A. Swidler (eds) *Women Priests. A Catholic Commentary on the Vatican Declaration*, New York: Paulist Press, 1977, pp. 141–44. She notes that Chrysostom, Origen, Jerome, Theophylact and Peter Abelard, to mention a few, all accepted that Paul was here speaking of a woman apostle

12 It could even be that 1 Cor. 14:34–35 is a non-Pauline interpolation. Many New Testament scholars hold this view. See *WTM* pp. 59–60

13 See the whole discussion in *WTM* pp. 65–70. It is important to point out that there is no command here to women to maintain absolute silence in church. The word so often translated 'silent' in v. 11–12 means 'quiet' in the sense of tranquil or peaceful. This is how it is translated in v. 2 of this same chapter and in several other places in the NT. The interpretation given is not without its

problems, but some believe the passage so clearly contradicts Paul's stance seen elsewhere that the great apostle of liberty could not have written 1 and 2 Timothy and Titus (the so-called Pastoral Epistles). The Pauline authorship of these three letters, it is to be pointed out, has been frequently questioned in the last hundred years by scholars

14   John Stott *The Preacher's Portrait* London, 1961, pp. 9–28. Dr Stott cogently agrees that the preacher has no authority himself—all authority lies in God's work

15   But it can be understood in some ways, for while Paul would not condone authoritarian leadership among men or women he is like most men more upset by the latter. It was abhorrent to his mind that women should domineer over men in this way. His arguments to support this point are not very profound, as Calvin (see his comments on 1 Tim. 2:12, quoted in *WTM* p. 69) pointed out. That woman was created second or sinned first seems to have had little significance for Paul. Elsewhere Paul makes Adam the chief sinner. (In Gen. 1 Man is created last. Does this place him under the animals?)

16   Here we need to remember that 'minister' means servant or slave. 'Rector', which means ruler, is its antonym, not its synonym

17   See my study, 'The Order of creation and the Subordination of Women' *Interchange* 23, 1978, pp. 175–98

18   I take this point from Leon Morris 'The Ministry of Women' in *A Woman's Place* Sydney, AIO, 1976, p. 27

19   On this see especially V.R. Mollenkott *Women, Men and the Bible* Nashville: Abingdon, 1977, pp. 9–50

20   See *WTM*, pp. 79–83

21   See first of all the most authoritative Greek Lexicon, H.D. Liddle and R. Scott *A Greek-English Lexicon* Oxford: OUP, 1953, p. 945. Also S. Bedale 'The Meaning of *kephale* in the Pauline Epistles' *JTS* 5, 1954, pp. 211–15. In Greek and Hebrew thought decision-making took place in the heart

22   So C.K. Barrett *The First Epistle to the Corinthians*, London: A. & C. Black, 1968, pp. 248–50; F.F. Bruce *1 & 2 Corinthians* London: Oliphants, 1971, pp. 103–6. See also L. Morris 'The Ministry of Women' p. 25

23   One of the best discussions on this passage is R. and J. Boldrey *Chauvinist or Feminist: Paul's View of Women* Grand Rapids: Baker, 1976, pp. 33–40

24 The argument that all women or all wives should be excluded from ministry solely because of their supposed subordinate status is seen, apart from these biblical reasons, to be a piece of invalid logic simply because the idea is not universally applied. The Bible subordinates sons and daughters, no matter their age to their parents, citizens to their rulers and young men to older men (1 Pet. 5:5), while the Anglican Church subordinates deacons and priests to bishops, whom they must promise to obey. But we hear no one arguing that sons should not be ordained while their parents are alive or that no one should preach in the presence of a leader in society or someone older or a priest before a bishop

25 *WTM* pp. 93–96

5 The ordination of women: The position of the Catholic Church

1 'Declaration on the Question of the Admission of Women to the Ministerial Priesthood' in L. and A. Swidler *Women Priests: A Catholic Commentary on the Vatican Declaration* New York: Paulist Press, 1977, p. 38

2 K. Rahner *Theological Investigations* vol. 20, London: Darton, Longman & Todd, 1981, p. 37

3 ibid. pp. 38ff

4 John R. Donahue 'A Tale of Two Documents' in L. and A. Swidler (eds) *Women Priests* p. 30

5 K. Rahner *Theological Investigations* p. 40

6 Such as: 'In the Pauline Letters, exegetes of authority have noted a difference between two formulae used by the Apostle: he writes indiscriminately "my fellow workers" (*Rom* 16:3; Phil 4:2–3) when referring to men and women helping him in his apostolate in one way or another; but he reserves the title "God's fellow workers" (*1 Cor* 3:9; or *1 Thess* 3:2) to Apollos, Timothy and himself, thus designated because they are directly set apart for the apostolic ministry and the preaching of the Word of God', *Declaration*, 17. The 'exegetes of authority' are not named

7 Cf. L. and A. Swidler (eds) *Women Priests* p. 25

8 *Lumen Gentium* 12

9 *Declaration* 4

10 *Decree on Ecumenism* 4

11 Baptism, Eucharist and Ministry (BEM), World Council of Churches, Geneva, 1982, section 54, p. 32

12 ibid. Commentary, 18, p. 7
13 ibid. x
14 ibid. 54, p. 32
15 Quoted in *Pro Mundi Vita Bulletin* 83, October 1980, p. 8
16 Cf. L. Hay 'The Interrelation of Mysteries' (DS 3016) *Compass Theology Review* 11, 1977, pp. 35–37
17 *Pro Mundi Vita Bulletin* 83, October 1980, p. 8
18 *Declaration* 39
19 ibid. p. 40
20 Rahner *Theological Investigations* p. 47

6 The ordination of women: A psychological interpretation of the objections

1 Louis Bouyer 'Woman priests' *L'Osservatore Romano* 20 Jan 1977 pp. 5, 10; Louis Bouyer 'Christian priesthood and woman' in Peter Moore (ed.) *Man, Woman and Priesthood* London: SPCK, 1978

2 Hans Urs von Balthasar 'The uninterrupted tradition of the Church' *L'Osservatore Romano* 24 February 1977, pp. 6–7

3 Rose McDermott 'Internal ministry and legislation in the church today' *Review for Religious* 38, 2, 1979, p. 253

4 Robert L. Kinast 'The ordination of women: acceptable doctrinal development?' *Review for Religious* 37, 6, 1978

5 Sacred Congregation for the Doctrine of the Faith *Declaration on the Question of the Admission of Women to the Ministerial Priesthood* Rome, 1976, p. 13

6 Rosemary Ruether *New Woman/New Earth* Melbourne: Dove Communications, 1975

7 Quoted in Julia O'Faolain and Lauro Martines (eds) *Not in God's Image* New York: Harper & Row, 1973

8 Marie Neal 'Women in religious symbolism and organisation' *Sociological Inquiry* 49, 1979, pp. 2–3

9 Robert Terwilliger 'A fractured church' in Moore (ed.) *Man, Woman and Priesthood* p. 161

10 From a sermon reprinted in Elizabeth Clark and Herbert Richardson (eds) *Women and Religion: A Feminist Sourcebook of Christian Thought* New York: Harper & Row, 1977, p. 265

11 C.S. Lewis 'Priestesses in the Church' in C.S. Lewis *Undeceptions* (ed. Walter Hooper) London: Geoffrey Bles, 1971, p. 192

12 ibid. p. 194

13   ibid. p. 195
14   ibid. p. 196
15   Karl Barth 'The doctrine of creation' *Church Dogmatics* Edin-
     burgh: T. & T. Clark, 1961; Cyril Eastaugh 'Bishop sees woman
     priests as "unnatural"' (interview by Clifford Longley) *The
     Times* 14 May 1973, p. 14; Bouyer 'Women priests'; Terwilliger 'A
     fractured church'
16   von Balthasar 'The uninterrupted tradition of the Church';
     Bouyer *Women Priests*
17   Bouyer *Women Priests* p. 5
18   Barth *Church Dogmatics* vol. 3, sec. 4
19   Gerhard von Rad *Genesis* (trans. J. Marks) London: SCM Press,
     1961
20   John Morgan 'Survey on attitudes to the ministry of women' in
     John Gaden (convenor) Report of the Commission on the Ministry
     of Women *Synod Papers* Diocese of Melbourne (Church of
     England in Australia), 1980
21   Dorothy Dinnerstein *The Rocking of the Cradle: And the Ruling
     of the World* London: Souvenir Press, 1978
22   ibid. pp. 36–37
23   For example, *Beyond the Pleasure Principle* New York: Batman
     1959 (1928); *Civilization and its Discontents* London: Hogarth
     Press, 1930; *New Introductory Lectures* Harmondsworth: Pelican,
     1973 (1933)
24   Melanie Klein *The Psycho-Analysis of Children* London: Hogarth
     Press, 1932
25   Geoffrey Chaucer *Canterbury Tales* (ed. A.C. Cawley) London:
     J.M. Dent & Sons Ltd 1975, p. 176
26   Venetia Nelson *A Myrour to Lewde Men and Wymmen*, Middle
     English Texts No. 14, Heidelberg: Carl Winter, 1981, p. 129
27   Dinnerstein *The Rocking of the Cradle* p. 62
28   Marina Warner *Alone of all her Sex: The Myth and the Cult of the
     Virgin Mary* London: Weidenfeld & Nicholson, 1976
29   John Gaden 'Women and the Church' in Norma Grieve and
     Patricia Grimshaw (eds) *Australian Women: Feminist Perspec-
     tives* Melbourne: OUP, 1981
30   Michael Costigan 'The priest and the daughters of Eve' in
     Barbara Thiering (ed.) *Deliver Us From Eve* Sydney: Australian
     Council of Churches (NSW) Commission on the Status of Women,
     1977
31   Quoted in ibid. p. 8

32   Dinnerstein *The Rocking of the Cradle* pp. 211–12
33   ibid. p. 69
34   Mary Daly *Beyond God the Father* Boston: Beacon Press, 1973;
     Mary Daly *Gyn/Ecology: The Metaethics of Radical Feminism*
     Boston: Beacon Press, 1978; Ruether *New Woman/New Earth*
35   Sherry Ortner 'Is female to male as nature is to culture?' in
     Michelle Rosaldo and Louise Lamphere (eds) *Woman, Culture
     and Society* California: Stanford University Press, 1974
36   Bertil Gartner and Carl Strandberg 'The experience of the
     Church of Sweden' in Moore *Man, Woman and Priesthood*;
     Terwilliger 'A fractured church'
37   Lewis 'Priestesses in the Church?; E.L. Mascall 'Some basic
     considerations' in Moore *Man, Woman and Priesthood*
38   Dinnerstein *The Rocking of the Cradle* p. 93
39   ibid. p. 133
40   Gilbert Russell and Margaret Dewey 'Psychological aspects' in
     Moore *Man, Woman and Priesthood* p. 94
41   ibid. p. 93
42   Terwilliger 'A fractured church' p. 161
43   Audrey Oldfield 'No room for the real Mary' in Thiering *Deliver
     Us From Eve*; Jean Skuse 'Outside the sanctuary' in Thiering
     Deliver Us From Eve; Freda Whitlam 'The fathers and the
     brethren' in Thiering *Deliver Us From Eve*
44   Kevin Giles 'The ordination of women: a plea for a fair go' in
     Thiering *Deliver Us From Eve*; Ruth Teale 'Matron, maid and
     missionary: the work of Anglican women in Australia' in Sabine
     Willis (ed.) *Women, Faith and Fetes* Melbourne: Dove Publica-
     tions, 1977
45   J. Carpenter *The Inklings* London: George Allen & Unwin, 1978
46   Dinnerstein *The Rocking of the Cradle* pp. 28–29
47   Quoted in Carpenter *The Inklings* p. 164
48   Barth *Church Dogmatics* vol. 3, sec. 4, p. 171
49   Simone de Beauvoir *The Second Sex* (trans. H. Parshley) London:
     Jonathan Cape, 1960, p. 160

7   Institutional sexism and the Anglican Church

1   Ruth Teale 'Matron Maid and Missionary: The Work of Anglican
    Women' in Sabine Willis (ed.) *Women, Faith and Fetes*
    Melbourne: Dove Publications, 1977, pp. 119–20

2   Barbara Thiering *Created Second?* Sydney: Family Life Movement of Australia, 1973, p. 19

3   *Enquiry Into The Status of Women In The Church: Commission On The Status of Women,* Australian Council of Churches, NSW, 1974, pp. 11–17

4   Dixson *The Real Matilda.* 2nd ed see also Conway, 'Gender in Australia'

5   Personal correspondence

6   'Beatrice Pate. Is Ordination a Dead Issue?' *Movement For The Ordination of Women Newsletter* February 1984, p. 5

7   *Australian* 22 September 1983

8   Paul's authorship of the pastoral epistles (1 and 2, Timothy and Titus) has long been disputed by scholars. See R. Banks *Paul's Idea of Community* Exeter, 1980, pp. 192–98. Claims have also been made that 1 Corinthians 14, 33b–35 is a non-Pauline interpolation. For references to this material see Francis J. Moloney, *Woman: First Among the Faithful* Blackburn, Vic.: Dove Communications, 1984, p. 1, nn 37–40

9   Names in this chapter are fictitious

10 Mary Daly *Beyond God The Father* Boston: Beacon Press, 1974, p. 43

8   Ministers' wives: Continuity and change in relation to their husbands' work

1   Janet Finch *Married to the Job: Wives' Incorporation in Men's Work* London: George Allen & Unwin, 1983

2   As will be apparent from the references throughout this chapter I am indebted to Finch for several of the arguments advanced here and in particular for emphasising the inevitability of ministers' wives being incorporated in their husbands' work

3   Janet Finch 'Devising Conventional Performances: The Case of Clergy Men's Wives' *Sociological Review* 28, 4, 1980, pp. 851–70

4   Kenneth Dempsey *Conflict and Decline* Sydney: Methuen Australia, 1983

5   See ibid., also Kenneth Dempsey 'Country Town Religion' in A. Black and P. Glasner *Practice and Belief* Sydney: George Allen & Unwin, 1983, pp. 25–42

6   See also Finch *Married to the Job* ch. 13

7   Finch 'Devising Conventional Performances'

8   See ibid.

9   Dempsey 'Country Town Religion'

10 Finch *Married to the Job* p. 152

11 Feminism has of course been of unquestionable significance for many ministers' wives in other situations. The kind of impact the movement can have is well illustrated in a study made by Margaret Bottomley in 1976 of the attitudes, beliefs and behaviour of twenty wives of Victorian Uniting Church ministers. Her subjects spoke of a strong need for a high degree of independence from their husbands' work and for the opportunity to find personal fulfilment through pursuing their own careers and personal interests. These women did not define themselves primarily in terms of their relationship to their husbands' congregation or to his work; they 'rejected the description of themselves as ministers' wives because of the consciousness of their own identity apart from their vicarious role as ministers' wives and also because of the stigma attached to that label': Margaret Bottomley, 'And What Does Your Husband Do?', unpublished MA thesis, La Trobe University

12 E. Goffman *The Presentation of Self in Everyday Life* Monograph No. 2, University of Edinburgh Social Sciences Research Centre, Edinburgh, cited in Finch 'Devising Conventional Performances' p. 863

13 H. Becker *Sociological Work* Chicago: Aldine Publishing Co., 1970, cited in ibid. pp. 861–62

14 Despite the added pressure that this wife's behaviour placed on her husband's work the marriage has survived. The husband did, in fact, say that he understood his wife's position. At the same time he acknowledged that it would limit the number of invitations he received to new appointments. If he is right about its inhibiting effect then it corroborates the major argument of this chapter

15 See Finch *Married to the Job* ch. 13

16 ibid. p. 166

17 ibid.

18 ibid. p. 163

19 ibid. ch. 13

9 A clergy wife's story

1 Norman Grubb *C.T. Studd: Cricketer and Pioneer* Evangelical Press, 1935, p. 170

2 Mary Daly *Beyond God the Father* Boston: Beacon Press, 1973, p. 3

3   The word for Holy Spirit in Hebrew is a word of feminine gender,
    ruạch ('wind or breath') and is represented in Greek by *'pneuma'*,
    a neuter word. The Holy Spirit has been associated with inspira-
    tion, constant support, consolation, qualities traditionally associ-
    ated with women
4   Marlene's husband writes: Only in recent years have I even
    begun to understand some of the sadness my wife, and others in
    her situation, have suffered. I long for the day when her gifts, and
    theirs, are given opportunity for free expression, and when
    ecclesiastical sanctions catch up with the divine!

10   God and pronouns

1   Much of the Wisdom literature is in the Apocrypha (the Wisdom
    of Solomon, and Sirach or Ecclesiasticus), and is thus more
    authoritative for Catholics than for Protestants. However a
    central expression of the Wisdom doctrine is in Proverbs 8

11   Affirmative action in the Uniting Church 1977–83

1   Commission on the status of Women, Australian Council of
    Churches (NSW), Sabine Willis (ed.) *Enquiry into the Status of
    Women in the Church* Sydney, 1974, p. 5
2   This and all following quotations not otherwise specified are from
    letters in response to my advertisements, March–April, 1983

12   A quixotic approach: The women's movement
and the Church in Australia

1   Rosemary Reuther *Religion and Sexism* 1974; Mary Daly *Beyond
    God the Father: Towards a Philosophy of Women's Liberation*
    1973; Barbara Thiering *Created Second?* 1973; Jean Skuse, in
    Barbara Thiering *Deliver Us From Eve.* 1977
2   Jean Skuse's word
3   Quoted Catherine A. MacKinnon 'Feminism, Marxism,
    Methodology and the State: An Agenda for Theory' in Nannerle
    Keohane, Michelle Rosaldo and Barbara Gelpi (eds) *Feminist
    Theory: A Critique of Ideology* London: Harvester Press, 1982,
    p. 21
4   Julia Kristeva 'Women's Time' in Keohane et al. (eds) *Feminist
    Theory* p. 45

5   Barbara Thiering 'Up From Down Under?' in Queenie Fogarty (ed.) *Where Religion Places Women* Perth: WEL, 1983

6   Quoted M. Oliver *Mary Ward* London: Sheed & Ward, 1959, p. 87

7   Jean Beth Elshtain 'Feminist Discourse & Discontents: Language, Power and Meaning' in Keohane et al. (eds) *Feminist Theory* p. 140

8   ibid. p. 142

9   Susan Griffith 'The Way of All Ideology' in Keohane et al. (eds) *Feminist Theory* p. 292

10 ibid

11 I have argued this more extensively in my *Crucible of Prophets: Australians and the Question of God* Sydney: Theological Inquiries, 1982

12 Elizabeth Harrower *The Watch Tower* Melbourne: Macmillan, 1966

13 Glen Tomasetti *Thoroughly Decent People* Melbourne: McPhee Gribble, 1976

14 Adrienne Rich, quoted by N. Keohane and B. Gelpi in the foreward to *Feminist Theory*, p. viii

15 Karl Rahner 'Freedom in the Church' in his *Theological Investigations* vol. 2, London: Darton, Longman & Todd, 1963, p. 91

13   The feminisation of structures in religious orders

1   *The Origins and History of the Family* (1884) quoted in Rosemary Ruether *New Woman/New Earth: Sexist Ideologies and Human Liberation* Melbourne: Dove Communications, 1975, p. 3

2   Elisabeth Schüssler–Fiorenza *In Memory of Her: A Feminist Theological Reconstruction of Christian Origins* New York: Crossroad, 1982, chs 5, 6, 8

3   *Liberation Theology: Human Hope Confronts Christian History and American Power*, quoted in Judith Vaughan *Sociality, Ethics and Social Change* Landham, Md.: University Press of America, 1983, p. 105

4   Rosemary Haughton, Feminine Consciousness in the Church, lecture, Brisbane, January 1984; Eleanor McLaughlin 'Women, Power and the Pursuit of Holiness' in R. Ruether and E. McLaughlin (eds) *Women of Spirit: Female Leadership in the Jewish and Christian Traditions* New York: Simon & Schuster, 1979, ch. 3; Margaret Brennan 'Women and Men in Church Office' in V. Elizondo and N. Greinacher (eds) *Concilium: Women in a Men's Church* New York: Seabury, 1980

5   See the several published histories of Australian women's religious
    congregations, or Ronald Fogarty *Catholic Education in Australia,
    1806–1950* Melbourne: Melbourne University Press, 1959

6   *In the Beginning* Carysfort Park, 1967, printed facsimile of 1833
    written first copy and amendments

7   Y.M. McLay, Critical Appreciation of the Educational System of
    All Hallows' Congregation, unpubl. MEd thesis, University of
    Queensland, 1963; *James Quinn: First Catholic Bishop of Bris-
    bane* Armadale: Graphic, 1979, pp. 81–86

8   ibid. pp. 206–9

9   E.M. O'Donoghue *Mother Vincent Whitty* Melbourne: Melbourne
    University Press, 1972

10 Vaughan *Sociality, Ethics, and Social Change* ch. 5

11 Carol Gilligan 'In a Different Voice: Women's Conceptions of Self
    and of Morality' *Harvard Educational Review* 47, 4, 1977,
    pp. 482, 492

12 Rosemary Haughton, There is Hope for a Tree, unpubl. paper on
    the emerging Church; Rosemary Haughton *The Passionate God*
    London: Darton, Longman & Todd, 1981

13 See, for example, research cited in Paul E. Bumbar 'Notes on
    Wholeness' in Gloria Durka and Joanmarie Smith (eds) *Aesthetic
    Dimensions of Religious Education* New York: Paulist Press,
    1979

14 Cited Norma H. Thompson 'Art and the Religious Experience' in
    Durka and Smith (eds) *Aesthetic Dimensions* p. 44

15 *The Republic* Book 4, quoted in Bumbar 'Notes on Wholeness' p. 47

16 'Historical Background to the Relationship between Faith,
    Science and Technology' Australian Council of Churches Confer-
    ence, Melbourne, 1983

17 *Wellspring* Ramsey, New Jersey: Paulist Press, 1979, p. 89

18 John H. Westerhoff 'Contemporary Spirituality: Revelation,
    Myth and Ritual' in Durka and Smith (eds) *Aesthetic Dimensions*
    p. 24

19 Carla de Sola and Arthur Easton 'Awakening the Right Lobe
    through Dance' in Durka and Smith (eds) *Aesthetic Dimensions*
    ch. 5

20 ibid. p. 77

21 Marion Sawer and Marion Simms *A Woman's Place: Women and
    Politics in Australia*, reviewed *Courier-Mail* Brisbane, 31 May
    1984

22 John 15:9–17

14   Implications of the feminine and masculine in pastoral ministry

1   William A. Clebsch and Charles R. Jaekle *Pastoral Care in Historical Perspective* Englewood Cliffs, New Jersey: Prentice-Hall, 1964, p. 34
2   ibid. p. 36
3   Ann Belford Ulanov 'C.G. Jung on Male and Female' in Ruth Tiffany Barnhouse and Urban T. Holmes (eds) *Male and Female* vol. 3, New York: Seabury Press, 1976, p. 197
4   Ann Belford Ulanov *The Feminine in Jungian Psychology and in Christian Theology* Evanston, IL: Northwestern University Press, 1971, pp. 38, 42
5   Ulanov 'C.G. Jung on Male and Female p. 197
6   Ulanov *The Feminine in Jungian Psychology* p. 48
7   ibid. p. 37
8   Ulanov 'C.G. Jung on Male and Female' p. 198
9   Ulanov *The Feminine in Jungian Psychology* pp. 37, 45
10 Ulanov 'C.G. Jung on Male and Female' p. 199
11 Ulanov *The Feminine in Jungian Psychology* p. 229
12 ibid. p. 40
13 ibid. p. 200
14 Stephen Sapp *Sexuality, the Bible, and Science* Philadelphia: Fortress Press, 1977, p. 10
15 Dietrich Bonhoeffer *Creation and Fall* London: SCM Press, 1959, p. 62
16 Samuel Terrien 'Toward a Biblical Theology of Womanhood' in Barnhouse and Holmes (eds) *Male and Female* p. 19
17 ibid. p. 20
18 Bonhoeffer *Creation and Fall* p. 80

15   Christian conversion and the feminine

1   Elizabeth Schüssler-Fiorenza *In Memory of Her: A Feminist Theological Reconstruction of Christian Origins* London: SCM Press, 1983, p. 132
2   ibid. pp. 133ff
3   ibid. pp. 135ff
4   ibid. pp. 150ff
5   P. Lemonnyer as quoted by Y. Congar in his excellent chapter, 'Sur la Maternité en Dieu et la Fémininité du Saint-Esprit' in *Je crois en l'Esprit Saint* vol. 3, Paris: Cerf, 1980, pp. 206–218

6 'Male/Female Typology in the Church' *Theology Digest* 31, 1, 1984, pp. 23–26

7 For a good overview of European theological literature, see Karl Lehman 'The Place of Women' *Communio* Fall, 1983, pp. 219–39. For a more evocative English-language approach, see Sebastian Moore *The Inner Loneliness* London: Darton, Longman & Todd, 1982, esp. Section 2, pp. 45–76

8 See Schüssler-Fiorenza *In Memory of Her* pp. 160–99; also Frank Moloney SDB *Woman: First Among the Faithful* Blackburn, Vic.: Dove Communications, 1984

9 Moloney is especially good on this point.

Index

abortion, 34, 142, 143

Adam, 2, 4, 171, 173

affirmative action, x, 80, 120–40, 178

androgny, xii, 58, 117, 175–86

Anglican Church, vii, viii, x, 15, 16, 20, 22, 23, 24, 25, 29, 38, 52, 53, 65, 68, 69–75, 82, 106

Anglican schools, 23, 26

Anglo-Catholic, 36, 38

Anti-Discrimination Act (NSW), church exemption, 36

apostles, xi, 38–41, 49, 53, 55; *see also* Junia

Appellate Tribunal, x, xi, 73

Aquinas, Thomas, 3, 14, 15, 64, 109

Aristotle, 1, 2, 3, 5, 15, 56, 183

asceticism, xvi, 12, 13

Aspasia, 14, 25

Augustine of Canterbury, 12

Augustine of Hippo, 56, 64, 109

Australian Council of Churches Status of Women Commission, task forces 1978, ix, 1985, ix; *see also* Enquiry Into The Status of Women in the Church (NSW) 1973

authority-type leadership, forbidden, xii, 36, 44; *see also* bible as authority, man as head, ordination of women

Baptist Church, viii

Baptism, Eucharist and Ministry (BEM), 52

Barth, Karl, 58, 59, 66

Beale, Dorothea, 18, 21, 22

Benedictines, 155

Bennett, Joyce, 72

bible, authority of, xii, xiv, xv, x, 18, 28, 29, 30, 31, 38, 39; *see also* image of God, ministry

biblical interpretation, xiv–vii

Bouyer, Robert, 58

Brennan Patricia, x; *see also* Movement for the Ordination of Women

Buss, Frances, 18, 21, 22

Catherine of Siena, 144

Catholic Church, vii, viii, x, xi, xvii, 1, 5, 6, 7, 8, 9, 28, 36, 52, 53, 54, 70, 72, 141–48, 149; *see also* ordination of women, Catholic position; women, religious

Catholic schools, 11, 23, 26, 145, 146, 150

Charity School Movement, 19

Christian Brothers, 17, 150

Christian Science, viii

Christian Women Conference, vii, viii

Church of Christ, viii

Church of England *see* Anglican Church

church structures, 124, 127, 128, 129, 132, 133, 134, 135, 136, 138; hierarchial model, 3, 8, 9, 36; non hierarchial model, xvii, xviii, 9, 35, 36, 41; feminisation of, 152–63; *see also* ministry

Clark, Manning, 29

Clement of Alexandria, 13

Clough Anne, 22; *see also* Newnham College for Women

Coggan, Dr (Archbishop of Canterbury), 53

Commission of Doctrine of the (Australian) General Synod, x

Community of All Hallows, 23

Community of St Mary the Virgin, 23

Community of St Thomas the Martyr, 23

Community of the Holy Family, 23

Community of the Sisters of the Church, 23

Congregational Church, viii, 121, 123, 127, 128

contraception, 143, 154, 155

contrasexual self, vii, xii, xiii, xvi, xvii, xviii, 9, 154–55, 166, 167, 174

creation, two accounts of, 171, 172

creationism, 32

Cyran, 17

Daly, Mary, 57, 75, 142

Davies, Emily, 22

de Beauvoir, Simone, 62, 66, 146

de la Salle, Jean-Baptiste, 17

deacons, women, x, xi, xix, 72, 73

deaconesses, 12, 43, 70, 75, 76, 91, 150

Deborah, 118

Denison, Maurice Fredrick, 23

Dinnerstein, Dorothy, 55, 59, 60, 61, 62, 63, 64, 65, 67

disciples, women, 40

divorce, 34, 142, 143

Donaldson, James, 12

Eadburga, 13

Eastern Orthodox Church, viii

education of women, early christianity, 6–14; Medieval period, 14–6; post-industrial period, 25–7, 71, 145–46; Reformation, 20–5; Renaissance, 16–20

Einstein, Albert, 158

elders, women, 137

Elshtain, Mary Beth, 145

Engels, Friedrich, 149

Enquiry into the Status of Women in the Church (NSW 1974), viii, 70, 71, 74, 122, 123, 125, 131, 135

Episcopalian Church, 70

evangelical, 17, 30, 31, 32, 38, 74, 100

Eve, 2, 61, 109, 137, 173, 177

evil women, associated with, xvi, 2, 13, 60–1, 63; *see also* asceticism, Eve, women as unclean

exegesis of I Timothy, 45–6

Fall, xiii, 2, 40, 45, 100, 106, 107, 171, 173, 174

Falwell, Jerry, 28; *see also* Moral Majority

family, 34, 92, 184; *see also* head man as

feminine, vii, xii, xv, xvi, xvii, xviii, 9, 146, 148, 153, 157, 161; church as, 144; conversion and the, 176–86; in pastoral ministry, 164–74; *see also* Holy Spirit, Wisdom; *see also* androgyny, contrasexual self, image of God

feminist theology, viii, xii, 5, 122; *see also* women theologians

Finch, Janet, 81, 85, 89, 98, 99

Fletcher, Sheila, 22

Freud, 60, 185

Fry, Elizabeth, 18

fundamentalism, xvii, 28–37

gifts of ministry, women's, 39, 42, 45, 110, 111, *see also* feminine pastoral ministry

Goffman, 93

Greer, Germaine, 145

Grey, Lady Jane, 16

Griffin, Susan, 146

Guerin, Bella, 145

Harrower, Elizabeth, 147

head man as, xii, xvii, 12, 34, 35, 38, 40, 44–7, 70, 73, 107, 108, 137; covering, 43, 47

Hilda of Whitby, 24

Holland, A. C., 71
Holy Spirit, vii, xiii, xiv, xv, xvii, xviii, 9, 41, 42, 47, 51, 52, 102, 111, 119, 121, 161, 172, 182; as feminine, 199, Ch 9 fn 3
house churches, 150

ideology, 68, 69, 77, 113, 141, 143, 146; *see also* patriarchy
image of God, xvi, 4, 36, 56, 57, 64, 118, 182, 183
institutional sexism, 68, 69, 70, 71, 77, 142, 143, 144, 149, 151, 152, 153, 176, 177

Jesus and women, xi, xii, xv, xvi, 4, 5, 36, 40, 41, 118, 142, 149, 157, 186
Josephites, 145
Junia, 5, 43
Jung, xiii, 166, 167, 174, 185

Kelly, Tony, 3
Kephale, 46–7; *see also* head man as
Klein, Melanie, 60

Lang, David, 22
lay readers, 71, 74, 75–80, 83
Latter Day Saints, viii
Lawson, John, 13, 15
Leach, A. F., 13
Lewis, C. S., 57, 58, 64, 66, 69
Loyola, Ignatius, 17, 152
Lutheran Church, 19, 21, 25

marriage, 12, 34, 46, 70, 117; *see also* head man as, wives clergy
Martha, 40, 110
Mary Magdalene, 60
Mary the Virgin, 6, 15, 60, 61, 66, 144, 182
masculine in pastoral ministry, 164–174
Mason, Agnes, 23; *see also* Community of the Holy Family
McAuley, Catherine, 144, 150–51; *see also* Sisters of Mercy
McKillop, Mary, 145; *see also* Josephites
Methodist Church, viii, 19, 29, 82, 87, 91, 93, 121, 128, 129, 130; *see also* Wesley, Susannah

Ministry, gifts of, 39, 41, 42, 45, 52, 69; *see also* gifts, women's; ministers as servants, 35, 36, 44, 109; no formalised, xv, 26, 39, 47, 105, 106; of modern women, 8, 72, 73, 75–6, 78, 106, 110, 199; Ch 9 fn 4; *see also* women, religious; of women in early church, 5; *see also* deacons, deaconesses, prophets, preachers, teachers women; pastoral, 164–174; priesthood of all believers, xii
Mishnah, 109
Moloney, Frank, 186
Moore, Hannah, 19
Moral Majority, 33–4
Movement for the Ordination of Women, ix, 72, 73
Murray, Daniel, 150

National Society for Promoting the Education of the Poor, 20
Newnham College for Women; *see* Clough, Anne
Nietszche, 147

O'Farrell, Patrick and Deirdre, 5
O'Leary, 8, 9
ordination of women, vii, ix, x, xi, xii, xvii, 2, 6, 8, 9, 26, 36, 38, 39, 43, 45, 48, 55, 57, 58, 59, 63, 65, 71, 72, 73, 76, 91, 106, 142, 164, 165; Catholic position, 49–54, 56; *see also* Movement for the Ordination of Women
Orthodox Church, xiv, 37, 72

patriarchy, vii, ix, xv, xvi, xvii, 2, 3, 5, 55, 68, 80, 131, 139, 140, 152, 154, 180, 182; women's collusion in, 62–3, 177, *see also* ideology
Plato, 158, 183
Phoebe, 5
Pontifical Biblical Commission, 51
Pope Gregory I, 1, 13
Pope Paul VI, 53, 62, 110
Power, Eileen, 15
preaching by women, 5, 42, 44, 83
Presbyterian Church, viii, 82, 89, 91, 121, 123, 127, 128, 129

priesthood of all believers, xii
Prisca, 5, 42
prophets, women, 12, 42, 43, 44
Protestants, x, xvii, 6, 25, 28, 30, 31, 33, 82, 88

Quakers *see* Society of Friends
Quinn, James, 151

Rahner, Kahl, 50, 54
Raikes, Robert, 19
Rand, Ayn, 108
Reuther, Rosemary, 56, 142, 150, 154
Rich, Adrienne, 147
Ryan, Susan, 145

Sacred Congregation for the Doctrine of the Faith (SCDF), 49–54, 56
Salvation Army, viii
Samaritan woman, 40, 110
Sapp, Stephen, 171
Schopenhauer, 147
Schüssler–Fiorenza, Elizabeth, 180
Seddon, Priscilla, 23
sexist language, ix, xii, xvii, 57, 113–19, 135, 137
sexist theologians *see* Aquinas, Augustine of Hippo, Barth, Clement of Alexandria, Lewis C. S., Tertullian, Terwilliger
sexual stereotypes, 2, 3, 4, 7, 18, 23, 24, 25, 26, 27, 34, 37, 39, 64–5, 136, 142, 144, 145, 147, 178
sexuality and women, 62; *see also* Eve, women associated with evil, women as unclean
Sisters of Mercy, 23, 150–156
Skuse, Jean, 142
socialisation, 69, 77, 86, 92, 154
Society for Promotion of Christian Knowledge, 19
Society of the Most Holy Trinity, 23
Society of Friends, viii, 18
Socrates, 14
status of women, British women, Feudal Britain, 12, 13, Medieval, 14, 15, 16; Renaissance to industrialisation, 16, 18, nineteenth century, 2, 21, 22, 23, 25; in early church, 5, 9, 10, 12, 36,

42; French women, Feudal France, 14, Medieval, 14, 15, Renaissance to industrialisation, 17; Greek women, 2, 4, 5, 14; Jewish women, 2, 4, 11, 12, 34, 39, 68, 109, 110; Roman women, 4, 12; today, vii, ix, xi, 1, 4, 5, 6, 7, 8, 10, 26, 69, 70, 71, 76, 80, 87, 97, 98, 122, 127, 128, 142, 149, 164; *see also* Jesus and women
Stott, John, 30
symbols and ritual, 32, 135, 160, 161; *see also* sexist language, Mary the Virgin
Sunday School Movement, 19

teaching by women, 42, 43, 44, 197, Ch 7 fn 8
Terea of Avila, 144
Tertullian, 5, 12, 27, 109
Terwilliger, Robert, 58, 65
The Society of the Holy and Undivided Trinity, 23
theology, vii, viii, ix, x, xiii, xiv, 3, 4, 7, 32, 135, 165; *see also* feminist theology
theologians, women; *see* Daly, Reuther, Schüssler–Fiorenza, Thiering
Thiering, Barbara, 70, 142, 144
Thomasetti, Glen, 147
Tulip, Marie, viii
Tyndale, 21

Ulanov, Ann Belfour, 166
Uniting Church, vii, x, 82, 88, 91, 120–40
Ursulines, 23

Vatican, 7, 11, 50, 51, 52, 153, 155
Vaughan, Judith, 154
Veronese, 61

Ward, Mary, 144, 145
Wesley, Susannah, 19
Whitlam, G., 71
Whitty, Mother Vincent, 151
Ws, Wisdom of Solomon in *Apocrypha*
wisdom, 118, 156, 161, 177, 181

wives clergy, xvii, 69, 81–99, 100–12
women and uncleanness, 109, 110,
    142; *see also* evil associated with
    women
women deacons, xix
Women's Electoral Lobby, 71
women's liberation, 71, 110, 122, 123
women and nature, 63
women priests, offering hospitality
    to, 73

women, religious, 13, 15, 17, 18, 23,
    24, 26, 142, 144, 145, 149, 150, 151,
    152, 153, 155, 158, 159
women's movement, vii, 1, 8, 9, 71, 92,
    120, 141, 146, 147, 156
World Council of Churches Faith and
    Order Commission *see* Baptism,
    Eucharist and Ministry